Contents

AN ATHEIST IN THE FOXHOLE

JOE MUTO graduated from the University of Notre Dame with a degree in Film and Television, then landed a job at Fox News as a freelance production assistant. He remained at Fox for eight years. He was an associate producer for *The O'Reilly Factor* when he was fired after being outed as *Gawker*'s "Fox Mole." He lives with his wife in Brooklyn, New York.

Praise for *An Atheist in the FOXhole*

"Hilariously details the inner workings of the cable news network that has become perhaps the most consistent target of liberal ire since it launched nearly two decades ago." —*Newsweek*

"*An Atheist in the FOXhole* mixes work anecdotes with the story of the uncomfortable hours before [Muto] was led out of Fox's office. . . . His book isn't a diatribe, and is often funny." —Associated Press

"Well-written and structured in surprising ways . . . The material on O'Reilly is interesting . . . A compelling, detailed look at how cable's top anchor chooses stories and develops his onscreen image." —*Tampa Bay Times*

"*FOXhole* is a lot of fun. . . . Muto shines is in his vivid descriptions of day-to-day life at Fox." —*New Statesman* (London)

An
Atheist in the
FOXhole

A Liberal's Eight-Year Odyssey

Inside the Heart of the Right-Wing Media

Joe Muto

P

A PLUME BOOK

PLUME
Published by the Penguin Group
Penguin Group (USA) LLC
375 Hudson Street
New York, New York 10014

USA | Canada | UK | Ireland | Australia | New Zealand | India | South Africa | China
penguin.com
A Penguin Random House Company

First published in the United States of America by Dutton,
a member of Penguin Group (USA) Inc., 2013
First Plume Printing 2014

P REGISTERED TRADEMARK—MARCA REGISTRADA

ISBN 978-0-525-95395-1 (hc.)
ISBN 978-0-14-218101-0 (pbk.)

Printed in the United States of America
10 9 8 7 6 5 4 3 2 1

Original hardcover design by Nancy Resnick

For my parents, who certainly taught me better than this. . . .

And for Jenny: all the way.

There's tremendous power in television news. If you're calling the shots, you can help someone tremendously, or you can crush that person. With a well-positioned negative word, you can ruin a career or endeavor forever, virtually unchecked. You can make the most powerful people on earth tremble.

—Bill O'Reilly, *Those Who Trespass*

Television is not the truth. Television is a goddamned amusement park. Television is a circus, a carnival, a traveling troupe of acrobats, storytellers, dancers, singers, jugglers, side-show freaks, lion tamers, and football players. We're in the boredom-killing business.

—Paddy Chayefsky, *Network*

Great story. Compelling, and rich.

—*Anchorman: The Legend of Ron Burgundy*

The Beginning of the End for a Middling Cable News Career

My entire life, I'd always thought the phrase "my blood ran cold" was a cliché. Until Tim opened his mouth, that is.

"Oh, look, they caught him. They caught the Fox Mole."

Boom. Just like that. Cold blood as I felt the world start to cave in around my ears.

Suppressing a shiver, I swiveled in my chair to face Tim Wolfe sitting at the desk three feet away from mine. Both of us were tucked away into a corner of the seventeenth floor of the News Corporation building in midtown Manhattan.

Like me, Tim was an associate producer for *The O'Reilly Factor* at Fox News Channel in New York City.

Unlike me, he hadn't spent the past two days leaking video clips, pictures, and stories from inside Fox to the media and gossip blog *Gawker*.

"They caught him." The sentence lingered in my brain, bounced off the walls of my skull a bit, dropped into my stomach like a sandbag, sending it lurching toward my ankles.

They caught him.

They caught him?

They caught me?

So why was I still sitting at my desk, like it was a normal Wednesday? Why hadn't a corporate SWAT team at the disposal of my secrecy-obsessed, paranoid company president Roger Ailes thrown a bag over my head and dragged me to a gulag in the basement? I must have heard him wrong.

"What's that?" I asked, trying my best to keep my voice calm and casual.

"Check out *Mediaite*," Tim said, pointing to the website he had up on his screen. "Fox says they've got him."

I typed the address into my browser. Mediaite.com was a popular site for industry news, and it had been all over the Mole story since my first post had gone up on *Gawker* the day before. The site loaded and there it was in a screamingly large font: the headline FOX NEWS SPOKES-PERSON TELLS MEDIAITE: WE FOUND THE MOLE.

I clicked through to find a short, disturbingly ominous statement from a network spokesman:

"We found the person and we're exploring legal options at this time."

Shit.

"Wow, I guess they got him," I said to Tim, chuckling, all innocence. "Ha-ha. That was quick." I fake laughed.

Tim laughed, too. "I'd hate to be that guy right now."

"Oh, yeah," I said. "That guy is fucked."

Thirty seconds later, I was in the bathroom. I noticed that my hands were shaking as I turned on the faucet. I looked in the mirror and saw that my face had gone totally white, while my neck was flushing a deep red. I felt light-headed. At some point during the brief walk between my desk and the commode, I'd apparently morphed into a heroine from a Victorian novel. *Did I have the vapors? Would Keira Knightley play me in the movie version? If I fainted in the bathroom, would it gain me any sympathy from the company goons who were no doubt on their way to apprehend me?*

I splashed water on my face.

Pull it together, Joe. They're bluffing. They don't know it's you. You were very careful. You took every precaution. There's nothing they have tying you to *Gawker*. They can search your work computer, your phone, even your personal e-mail, and there's absolutely nothing. No proof. They're just saying they caught you to buy themselves time, or to make you panic and expose your identity. If they really knew it was you, do you think you'd still be in the building right now? Of course not. You'd have ten security guards at your desk, waiting to haul you away. Don't do anything stupid. Just act normal.

My little mental pep talk had the desired effect. After a minute or two more of water splashing and deep breathing, my color returned to more-or-less normal and my hands stopped shaking.

Leaving the bathroom, I passed Tim, who was conferring with another producer at her desk. He looked at me with narrowed eyes as I walked by, a concerned look on his face. *Maybe I haven't recovered as much as I thought. Maybe he's on to me.* I shot him a reassuring smile.

All is well, I hoped my grin said. *I'm mere minutes away from having a total nervous breakdown* is what it probably broadcast, in retrospect.

Back at my desk I tried to concentrate on my duties. If, as I hoped, management was bluffing about having found me, I needed to act normal and do my job. Shirking my duties in panic was a surefire way to draw attention to myself.

Calm and casual, I told myself, and leaned back in my chair, my foot kicking the duffel bag under my desk, which had slipped my mind until that very moment. I had spent the previous night at my girlfriend Jenny's apartment and headed straight into the office from her place, carrying my soiled clothes with me to the office.

That brought two things to mind immediately. One: I hadn't told Jenny a thing about any of this. She'd flown to Pittsburgh that morning to visit her family, and arguably would not react well to an over-the-phone revelation that I'd decided to make a career transition from cable news producer to potentially criminal corporate espionage agent without consulting her first. (You know how women are. They hate when you do that.)

Two: More pressing, I had something else in the bag, something nestled up against my dirty undies—an iPad filled with the *Gawker* posts I'd written and copies of the behind-the-scenes videos I'd leaked. I'd been so busy congratulating myself for my cloak-and-dagger tactics that I'd completely forgotten I had brought into the building all the proof they'd ever need to nail me, sitting in a bag under my desk, marinating in my day-old crotch sweat.

Okay, maybe now *is the proper time to shirk my duties in panic.*

I grabbed the duffel and popped out of my chair. I knew I needed to get the evidence out of the building. The prospect of getting fired was scary enough, and something that I (wrongly, as it turns out) thought I had mentally prepared myself for, but it occurred to me that my company *did not fuck around.* While I didn't actually *believe* Fox News had a hidden subterranean dungeon that they'd stash me in while a crack antiespionage team went through all of my personal possessions, I didn't completely dismiss it as a possibility, either.

Tim and I were a little bit separated from the other members of the O'Reilly staff, a seating arrangement left over from the days when O'Reilly was still doing a radio show, on which I had originally been a staffer before transitioning to the TV side. We had the unique experience of having desks immediately outside O'Reilly's office, yielding hours of fascination and entertainment; but the separation from my peers *could* feel a bit isolating at times. That day, however, I was thankful that the dozen or so other producers were located fifty feet down the hall and couldn't see me indecisively pacing holding a duffel bag.

My floor was arranged into three concentric rings. Anchors, reporters, and a few high-powered producers occupied the coveted window offices on the outer ring. The middle ring, where I was, consisted of lower-level producers scattered among desks separated by chest-high cubicle walls. The inner ring was a few windowless offices, video editing suites, break rooms, janitor closets . . . and the elevator bank.

It was that elevator bank I needed to get to, walking along the middle ring straight past the other O'Reilly producers—a potentially risky move, since, with the realization that I was in possession of the incriminating iPad, I was guessing that my briefly absent Victorian lady complexion had returned; and if my appearance didn't give me away, the fact that I was leaving the building with a bag a good seven hours before quitting time was bound to raise a few eyebrows.

There was another way, though. If I followed the ring in the opposite direction, I wouldn't have to pass my colleagues; I wouldn't even have to use the seventeenth-floor elevators. It's true that was a longer route, weaving through the base camps of several of the other shows that were stationed on the seventeenth floor; but it also led to a little-used, virtually unknown stairway that would allow me to climb to the much less populated eighteenth floor, where I could use the elevators to escape to the ground floor. The longer route would potentially bring me in contact with more people, but, hopefully, they wouldn't think a sweaty, pale-faced O'Reilly producer making a beeline for the exits was anything out of the ordinary.

As I started down the long way out, I passed O'Reilly's office. The door was open, but he wasn't inside; in fact, he wouldn't be there for a few more hours. Though the man was intimately involved in every aspect of his show's production and started his workday at seven A.M., he spent roughly four hours a day actually *present* in the office.

It's good to be the boss.

And for the time being, it was good to be me. Or lucky to be me, anyway. Because my path was blessedly devoid of people. It was early lunchtime, and most of the desks along my route were empty. A few bored staffers munched salads at their desks, heads dipped as they grazed; others inhaled sandwiches, eyes glued to their screens, checking Facebook or Twitter or, alarmingly, Mediaite. I breezed past them one by one with no incident, calmly walking down the nearly abandoned hallways, past desks and cubicles and offices, until finally I was so close I could see the source of my freedom: the door that would bring me to the out-of-the-way staircase that led to the floor above.

Twenty feet to the doorway. Ten feet. Five feet.

Then a voice from behind.

"Hey, Muto!"

So close.

I turned to face the speaker. It was Nick De Angelo, a producer I'd worked with on another show a few years back.

"Where you goin' in such a rush?" he asked, peering at me over the top of his computer monitor.

"Oh, just to get some lunch," I lied, uncomfortably shifting on my shoulder the duffel bag that suddenly felt like it weighed seventy-five pounds.

"I have something to ask you," Nick said, a deadly serious look on his face.

He took a deep breath, then said: "Are you the Mole?"

My heart flip-flopped. *How did he know?*

And then I saw that he was laughing, his shoulders shaking, a goofy smile plastered on his face.

He was just giving me shit.

"Yup!" I replied, matching his laughter, pretending to enjoy the ball busting. "You got me!"

But I must not have gotten the tone right. Or my frantic, nervous eyes gave me away. Or maybe he already suspected, and was testing me to see how I reacted. Either way, the laughter faded from his face, replaced with a wry, curious look.

He studied me. When he spoke again, his voice was quieter, more tentative. "No, seriously, though. Is it you?" he asked.

I kept up my fake dumb grin. "I told you, man. You got me!"

As he furrowed his brow, watching me thoughtfully, I turned on my heel and walked as calmly as I could through the doorway.

And it was only at this moment—long past the point when the thought could have done me any good—that the little voice in my head stated what should have been obvious to anyone who wasn't a moron.

This might have been a terrible idea.

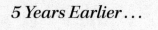

5 Years Earlier . . .

CHAPTER 1

Slacking Your Way to Success and Shame

The Old Man was angry that day.

We all knew it, too, though if you had asked us, we wouldn't have been able to explain how we knew. No one had told us. There had been none of the usual signs—no shouting heard from behind the closed office door; no hushed, panicked *what-do-we-do-now* phone calls between the senior producers; no unlucky associate producer getting screamed at for a minor infraction. An outsider would think he or she was witnessing a calm, normal meeting.

But we knew better. It was some mysterious sixth sense that we'd all developed to pick up on his moods, something that science couldn't explain. Maybe it was telepathy, or pheromones, or something with magnetic fields, like how a flock of birds knows to shift direction simultaneously. It doesn't matter how we knew, but we did.

And though we would never admit it to each other, we were scared.

Bill O'Reilly was sitting on a chair in the middle of the *Factor* "pod," the collection of low-walled cubicles where his staff was headquartered. The other producers and I were standing in a loose semicircle around him, clutching our pitches—computer printouts, articles clipped from newspapers, books from authors who were dying to get on the show—in our trembling fists.

Looming over the proceedings was The Board, a massive eight-foot-tall expanse of cork with a wooden bezel, covered from top to bottom with a calendar grid fashioned from electrical tape and studded with index cards held up with pushpins. The ragged, torn edges of the electrical tape and the sometimes illegible scrawl on the cards gave The Board a makeshift feel, one that belied its strict mathematical precision. Designed by our head guest booker, Eugene Flarmben, it was divided into rectangles: four rows, each denoting a week's worth of shows, with the current week perched at the top and the following weeks underneath; five rectangles per row marking Monday through Friday; space for six index cards per rectangle, the proper number of segments to fill a single show. The index cards were color-coded: blue cards for firm-booked guests, pink cards for guests or topics that were tentative, green cards for segments that had been pretaped, and ominous blank spaces where there were no segments planned.

Our job was to fill the holes.

We weren't particularly good at it.

The pitch meetings took place on Mondays and Thursdays. At two thirty in the afternoon on those days, the troops would all line up, reluctantly, for what usually amounted to a twice-weekly exercise in futility, a half-hour parade of failure: Bill shot down 95 percent of ideas, usually peppering his rejections with ridicule. Mockery was his standard response to a pitch he didn't like: *How can you be stupid enough to present me with this dumb idea?*

But sometimes mockery simply wasn't enough for him to display the contempt he felt for an idea, and that's when he turned to anger, which could manifest itself explosively, without warning, especially on days when his mood was already sour, which we sensed it was that day. So we were all on edge. Me especially.

It was the spring of 2007. I'd been on the show just a few months, having previously worked for some of Fox's smaller, less prestigious programs. Now that I was in the big leagues, I was frustrated to find myself striking out more often than not, the boss rejecting pitch after pitch, week after week.

To be fair, the rejections that came my way in those early months were much gentler than those that came later in my career, or those that my more seasoned coworkers received. O'Reilly seemed to have an unofficial policy of going easy on the new hires, at least until they got their feet under them a little bit. (Very sporting of him, actually, like a hunter refusing to shoot a baby deer. Though after some of the more brutal pitch meetings, a quick merciful bullet between the antlers would have been a relief.)

It wasn't 100 percent failure on my part. I'd managed to sneak a few minor pitches past the goalkeeper, but nothing to write home about—they were mostly B or C stories, small items that got thrown into the hopper to be discussed by the panel at the end of a longer segment, maybe getting only a minute total of screen time. I still hadn't scored with a headlining pitch, something that would lead the show or, at the very least, get its own segment. That was the Holy Grail. Every producer in that semicircle was praying to Jesus, or Yahweh (or in my case, no one), that the big pitch would land in their lap, that they would not get mocked or yelled at but praised, held up to the other producers as a golden child, an example to which the others should all aspire.

My marquee story that day, the pitch I was going to lead with, was something I'd stumbled upon mere minutes before the meeting. An errant blog link had led me to an article in the *Navy Times*, a military newspaper. The piece pointed out a major error in a recent *New York Times Magazine* story about women who experienced PTSD after getting deployed to war zones. It turned out that one of the women profiled in the *Times* piece had never been in combat—and had in fact never even set foot in Iraq.

I printed out the article, then double-checked the *Drudge Report*—a conservative news-aggregating website that we all checked religiously—to see if it had picked up on the scoop yet. If *Drudge* had it, chances are that one of my colleagues had also seen it and would beat me to it, mentioning it in the pitch meeting before it was my turn to go, and stealing my thunder. But there was no mention of it on Drudge, and it looked like no other blogs—aside from the obscure one I had been reading—had posted it yet.

I was pretty confident that I was sitting on a winner—mostly because it involved *The New York Times*. Fox News has always had a bizarre institutional animosity toward the *Times*. The newspaper was routinely caricatured by O'Reilly and the rest of the network as a liberal rag, a monolithic left-wing institution full of reporters and editors crawling all over themselves to destroy the Republican Party and promote a grab bag of progressive causes—atheism, homosexuality, Hollywood depravity, big government, and so on. In a way, Fox's depiction of the *Times* was an exact mirror image of the left's depiction of Fox, but that irony was lost on O'Reilly, who took delight in skewering the *Times* at every available opportunity. (With the exception of the admittedly frequent occasions that one of his books charted on their Best Sellers list, in which case he was happy to tout their wisdom and authority.) I was heading into the pitch meeting with a potential blockbuster.

But as the gathering got under way, I began to lose confidence. Our fears about the boss's ill mood had been well founded. He was impatient, snarling at pitches that didn't get to the point fast enough. The mockery was even more vicious than usual. Producer after producer came up empty. Pitch after pitch went down in flames.

One producer suggested that we do a segment on the trial of Scooter Libby, a former Dick Cheney aide accused of outing a covert CIA agent.

Bill was not interested.

"I don't care about that story. Not one bit," he said. "Our audience doesn't care about that story. I'm not even sure Scooter Libby cares about it at this point."

Another producer suggested a segment on the flat tax, offering up a guest who wanted to advocate for it.

O'Reilly scoffed: "What makes you think we would *ever* do a story like that on this show?" he demanded. "That might be the most boring thing anyone has ever pitched at one of these meetings. I think I fell asleep while you were talking."

The producers all laughed, and not entirely sycophantically. Bill's rejections were often funny, especially when they weren't happening to you. Those of us who still were waiting our turn couldn't bring ourselves to laugh as hard, though. This was shaping up to be an epically bad pitch meeting. No one had gotten too severely burned just yet, but we all knew that, on a day like this, we were all just one dumb pitch away from triggering a spectacular explosion.

And then it was my turn.

"All right, Muto," Bill said, turning his attention to me. "Whattaya got?"

"Bill, the Pentagon is very angry," I started, "because *The New York Times* got a *major* detail wrong in a story this weekend."

I saw him perk up immediately. As I'd suspected, the *Times* angle grabbed his attention.

I laid out the rest of the pitch and watched O'Reilly's mood change almost instantly, with him getting more and more excited until he could no longer contain himself.

"Yes!" he yelled triumphantly, interrupting me mid-sentence and karate chopping the air in celebration. His eyes swept the rest of the group as he pointed to me: "Everyone, *that* is how you pitch. That is a *great* story."

I was stunned. I gazed around the semicircle at my fellow producers, soaking up the looks of envy on their faces.

"Flarmben," Bill said, swiveling his chair to Eugene, "get a card up there. It's the lead segment tomorrow. I'll do a Talking Points Memo on it, too."

I watched, suddenly overwhelmed by a feeling of thrill that surprised me, as Eugene wrote out a blue card and rose from his chair, pinning it to The Board for the next day's show.

"Muto," O'Reilly said, returning his attention to me, "that was *perfect*. More of that, please."

I was on a high the rest of the day. Compliments from Papa Bear were incredibly hard to come by, and I'd just been given a huge one. It was my first experience basking in the warm-by-comparison light of his praise.

And to my absolute horror, I found myself enjoying it.

The fact that I even had the opportunity to be ambivalent about getting kudos from the most prominent conservative cable news host in America was something of a minor miracle.

In the spring of 2004, in the course of about six weeks, I'd gone from a jobless, left-wing film student to a cog in the machine at the New York City headquarters of what I had always assumed was a cartoonishly evil, far-right, conservative media cabal.

It all started when I was a few months shy of graduation at the University of Notre Dame. The university—a Midwestern Catholic school that proudly celebrates its Irish heritage by deploying as a mascot an angry-faced, presumably drunk leprechaun with raised fists—was relatively hard to get into, which I liked because it was impressive on a résumé. But like all top-tier liberal arts schools, it was secretly easy on the academic side, allowing me to breeze through four years with minimal effort and maximal mind-altering substances.

Helping me in minimizing my effort was the school's Department of Film, Television, and Theatre, which was a perfect refuge for those of us who wanted a somewhat artistic field of study but couldn't figure out how to tell our parents with a straight face that we'd decided to become ceramics majors.

"You know, there's a lot of money to be made in film and TV," I told my father at the end of my freshman year, right after informing him that I'd be dropping all of my business classes.

"There better be," said my father, "because if you think we're supporting you financially for the rest of your life, you've got another thing coming."[1]

My parents, Joan and Tony, were both New Yorkers who had met as members of the class of '72 at the University of Dayton. They'd bonded over their shared working-class Italian backgrounds; both were the first

---

[1] Now would probably be a good time to thank him profusely for the loan he gave me to stave off eviction when I very publicly destroyed my career at the young, impressionable age of thirty.

in their families to go to college. After a postgraduation wedding, a move fifty miles south to the relatively-sleepy-but-still-better-than-godforsaken-Dayton city of Cincinnati, and ten years of married bliss, I came along in 1982, followed soon by a brother, Stephen, and then a sister, Theresa. (She was given the nickname Teddy shortly after birth, a play on the way my fresh-off-the-boat great-granny with her thick Italian accent pronounced the name Terry.)

Neither of my parents was overtly political. I don't remember having any political conversations as a child—unless you count the time I was six years old and I told my mom I was sad that Ronald Reagan was leaving office because he had been the president the whole time I was alive—but if you asked him, my dad would readily cop to being a conservative. He was fond of quoting the maxim "If a young man isn't a liberal, he has no heart; if an old man isn't a conservative, he has no brain," a quote that is often attributed to Winston Churchill (and should, by the transitive property, be attributed to gin).

My mother was more a moderate; she'd voted for Clinton, twice, a fact she enjoyed needling my father with. But she also voted for George W. Bush twice, a fact she enjoyed needling *me* with. She was an equal-opportunity needler.

I had political opinions at a very young age—conservative ones, oddly enough. I remember being ten years old and lying in bed, listening to conservative talk radio. A local talk show host named Bill Cunningham lulled me to sleep most nights with complaints about Slick Willie Clinton and his shrewish wife. The political conversion for me came in high school, when I noticed that a wonderfully crusty history teacher whom I loved had the odd habit of giving himself the sign of the cross every time he mentioned FDR's name.[2] When I looked into this Roosevelt fellow, it was like a gateway drug into Democratic politics.

---

2 It was a Catholic high school, so this was totally copacetic. It was all boys, too, which was probably advantageous academically, minimizing distractions in class, but was undoubtedly damaging socially. I spent my entire first year of college dealing with the culture shock, having trouble getting acclimated to an environment where students no longer received spontaneous applause from the rest of the class after farting audibly.

With my newfound knowledge (and the help of a few *real* gateway drugs), I completely changed my ideology over the course of a semester. By the time the Lewinsky scandal rolled around, I was totally on Slick Willie's side.

The relative ease of my first two decades of life lulled me into a false sense of complacency: My idyllic Midwest upbringing had been marred only by an unfortunate bed-wetting stint that lasted well into middle school, and an equally unfortunate obsession with Star Wars that peaked a few years before that series' late-'90s resurgence in popularity.[3] I coasted on autopilot through college, earning mediocre grades in an easy major and paying very little attention to what I considered bourgeois concerns like "my future" and "a career" and "making a living."

I'm an artiste, I reasoned, mistaking the mild notoriety that my twice-monthly column in the student paper had garnered me for something resembling a career plan. *The job opportunities will come to me,* I delusionally told myself, assuming that the article I wrote complaining about how the members of the football team were the only ones on campus getting laid would *obviously* grab some big-timey magazine editor's attention. Job seeking just didn't appeal to me; I was much more interested in my humanitarian work, spending my senior year heroically attempting to rid South Bend, Indiana, of drugs *by doing them all myself.* (I later listed this on my résumé as "Community Anti-Drug Initiative.")

In retrospect, I was probably a pretty typical college senior, but for someone like me, whose life had always had an inexorable forward motion, I found myself terrifyingly unsure about my next step as I approached graduation. The expected job opportunity had not, as I'd naively assumed, materialized out of the ether. And none of the employment listings I browsed online seemed to be seeking pot-addled, would-be campus radicals who were good at writing eight-hundred-word, dick-joke-filled newspaper columns every two weeks.

---

3 I still maintain that I was truly ahead of my time when I dressed as Luke Skywalker for Halloween in 1995; but the knowledge of my ultimate vindication still doesn't erase the sting of shame that lingers when I picture the cringing looks of homeowners who greeted me, a thirteen-year-old with acne and a lightsaber, shouting, "Trick or Treat!"

I started sending out résumés frantically. I had a vague idea that I wanted to be in New York City, doing something with writing, film, television, or journalism, so I hit up all the big media companies that I thought I might want to work for: CNN, MSNBC, NBC, CBS, ABC, *Time* magazine, the *New York Times*, Comedy Central, MTV, VH1, and, just for good measure, *Martha Stewart Living*. I even e-mailed a résumé to Lorne Michaels's production company, offering to clean toilets and empty wastebaskets if it would get me onto the set of *Saturday Night Live*.[4]

It was not my finest hour.

After a few months of dispatches, I had gotten zero responses, and my résumés and cover letters were getting increasingly desperate.

Finally, the answer came to me in the unlikeliest of places—a tropical-themed, northern Indiana dueling-piano bar called Rum Runners.

It was graduation week, and the Notre Dame senior class was celebrating our entry into adulthood and maturity by guzzling cheap margaritas straight from the pitcher and heckling two middle-aged guys with ponytails as they pounded out classic rock songs on grand pianos.

It was there, under an indoor tiki hut, that I bumped into the man who would change my life: Rufus Banks.

Rufus and I were friendly, but we mostly ran with different crowds. I had first noticed him freshman year, when we had a genetics class together. The survey class was easy, and the teacher was a notorious grade inflator, making it a magnet for athletes, slackers, and arts and letters students trying to check off a science requirement, and earning the course the accurate (if predictable) nickname Genes for Jocks. Rufus didn't stand out in the massive lecture hall until Halloween, when he showed up in class dressed as a mime: face paint, white gloves, black turtleneck, and beret. Out of two hundred kids in the room, he was the only one in costume. Immediately realizing this fact upon entering the room, he shrugged, walked down the middle aisle of the stadium-style

---

4 Lorne, that offer still stands, by the way. Though now that I have eight years in television under my belt, I'm going to have to insist that you provide me with gloves for the toilet cleaning.

seating, and sat directly in the front row, calmly ignoring the stares and snickers from much of the class, as well as some light sassing and "Oh, shit, look at that dude" style commentary coming from the football player contingent in the back of the room.

I instantly admired how fearless he was about drawing attention to himself, a unique quality for a freshman at a school where conformity was expected. It was a quality that had apparently stuck with him over the four years of college, considering that he was proudly wearing a loud Hawaiian shirt at the piano bar that night.

We were making the typical "I can't believe this is all over/what are you doing after graduation" small talk when I had to ask him to repeat himself.

"You're trying to get a job with who?" I yelled in his ear, struggling to be heard as the piano men banged away on a raucous duet of "Bennie and the Jets."

"Fox News Channel!" he yelled back in my ear. "The website. I interned for them last summer. I'm waiting to hear back to see if they'll take me full-time."

"What about their politics?" I asked. "Don't they bother you? They're pretty right-wing."

He shrugged. "Nah. It's mostly a bunch of computer nerds, like you'd expect to be working at any website. Why don't you apply, too? You can do it for a few months just to get established in New York, then find something else."

The next afternoon, I sat at my computer, the smell of the previous night's booze still sour on my breath. My fingers hovered over the keyboard as I struggled with some pretty severely mixed feelings. On one hand, I was reassured that Rufus had suggested the company was not—as I, and most other liberals assumed—a top-to-bottom den of slavering right-wingers. To hear him describe it, Fox was a few powerful ideologues surrounded by professionals who just wanted to do their jobs. On the other hand, that sounded suspiciously close to the rationale offered by everyone throughout history who'd ever worked for organizations with questionable goals. ("I'm just keeping my head down and doing my job! I can't control what my bosses do" is something I'm sure multiple Nazi storm troopers said after the fact.)

In the end, I erred on the side of potential gainful employment. While I was fairly turned off by the idea of working for an organization as conservative as Fox, I was even more turned off by the prospect of kicking off my adult life by moving into my parents' basement. I decided to bite the bullet and apply.

Anyway, what were the odds I'd even get a response? No one else had responded to my increasingly desperate entreaties. And the Fox application process was relatively low-tech and not exactly confidence-inspiring: While other media organizations had required complicated online forms and usernames and passwords, Fox just wanted me to toss an e-mail to resumes@foxnews.com. Chances were I'd just be casting my information into the electronic equivalent of a black pit.

With that in mind, I did something a bit different with the cover letter. I don't know if it was desperation, or if I had stopped giving a shit, or even if I was subconsciously trying to sabotage my application, but I decided to throw out the rote, generic form letter I'd been sending that had gotten me zero responses so far.

Here's what I sent instead:

Subject: Award-winning[5] writer seeks entry-level NEWS-WRITING POSITION; willing to work crappy hours for peanuts . . .

Dear Hiring Manager,
  Okay, so imagine that you've gone through four years of college and have mercifully graduated. You're blessed . . .

---

5 I couldn't tell you what specific award I was referring to, since I can't recall, and my original résumé that listed the alleged "award" is lost to history. (I apologize in advance to my future biographer.) I know I trumped up something and made it sound important, but I can't remember exactly what. I suspect it was not something I actually received for my writing ability, but was, rather, related to my recent participation in an off-campus Beer Olympics event.

nay . . . cursed, really, with this amazing writing ability, but you've given little thought to what you actually want to do with your worthless life once you leave the comforting, womblike bubble that is existence at an American university.

Basically, you are me.

So here's my proposition. Read this article from the University of Notre Dame's alumni magazine: [link] If you read it and don't like it, I give you full permission to print this e-mail out, post it to the office bulletin board, and subject me to the ridicule of your coworkers.

If, however, you do like it, and you do think that I can write for FoxNews.com,[6] then I'd be eternally grateful if you'd peruse my résumé below. I've spent a lot of time on it and have used every ounce of my skill to overhype nearly every position I've ever held. I'm sure that if you've been a hiring manager for anything more than a month, then you are truly a connoisseur of the overblown résumé; I assure you, my friend, you'll find my résumé most agreeable in this regard.

In closing, I'd like to apologize for the unconventional cover letter. I felt compelled to write it, mostly because I have a conscience and I refuse to subject you to the antiseptic tripe that Monster.com suggested I send you.

Hope to hear from you soon.

Yours,

Joseph R. Muto

I spent all day writing it, polishing it, perfecting it, then I closed my eyes, crossed my fingers, and hit SEND.

I heard back a week later.

---

6 Ironically, if they had just done what I asked and given me a website job instead of a TV one, you almost certainly would not be reading this book.

I was home in Ohio, having uneventfully survived my graduation ceremony. I was riding in a friend's car on my way to a party, enjoying a pleasant beer buzz, when I noticed a voice mail on my cell phone. "Joseph, this is Jessica [Italian Name]. We really loved your résumé and would like you to come to New York to interview for a job. Please call me back when you can at the number . . ."

Two weeks later, I was standing outside of Fox News's midtown Manhattan headquarters.

And I was sweating my balls off.

My four years as a slovenly liberal arts student in the frozen tundra of northern Indiana had left me spectacularly ill-equipped to dress for both business situations and warm-weather situations. I was wearing a blue blazer that was too big in the shoulders, gray flannel pants that were too tight in the butt, and a tie—borrowed from my father—that had probably been produced the same year as the *M*A*S*H* finale.

It wasn't even ten A.M. and the temperature had climbed past 75, according to the conveniently located time-and-temperature display mounted on a tall pole across the street. Sweat was forming on my temples and running in little rivulets down to my neck. I could feel an unpleasantly swampy sensation brewing in my flannel-clad under-carriage. Trying to ignore my leaky body, I took in the sight of the building in front of me.

It was at the corner of Forty-Eighth Street and Sixth Avenue, or Avenue of the Americas, as the street signs, guidebooks, tourists—and no one else—called it. The official address was 1211 Avenue of the Americas, a rather unassuming one for the building that was the U.S. head-quarters of News Corporation, the giant media conglomerate that was the parent company of Fox News, the Fox TV network, 20th Century Fox movie studios, the *New York Post*, *TV Guide*, and countless other media properties. The company had been founded by Rupert Murdoch, a wizened, Bond-villain-esque Australian zillionaire who had made his fortune in the UK buying newspapers and transforming them into screaming right-wing tabloids.

To be fair, that might actually be selling him a little short; he also invented a feature so brilliant and wildly popular and disgusting that I'm surprised it hasn't shown up in the United States yet: pictures of bare titties in newspapers.[7]

Though he wasn't a quirky, cuddly, charismatic billionaire in the Richard Branson mold, I'd later find out that Rupert still garnered a surprising amount of respect and even affection from the News Corp. rank and file—a sentiment that the company's internal PR team attempted to foment with cult-of-personality building exercises. For example, the theme of the News Corp. holiday party one year was international travel, and the invitations whimsically invited attendees to take a trip with "KRM Airlines"—as in Keith Rupert Murdoch. The man himself even appeared at the party that year, a massive affair that consumed two entire banquet floors of the Hilton Hotel a few blocks away from HQ. Rupert was spotted in the crowd throughout the evening, mingling with the commoners, at one point watching tipsy employees belt out karaoke tunes on a stage, much to the delight of the singers.

I think the secret of Murdoch's appeal among the grunts is that we always felt we knew where he stood. We were aware that he was an ideologue, but as far as ideologues went, he was a particularly pragmatic, money-grubbing one. Profit always trumped politics for Rupert. If he could make money on a conservative-boosting endeavor like Fox News, great. But if he could *also* make money on a routinely conservative-bashing show like *The Simpsons*, that was also fine with him.

His pragmatism was apparent in the architecture of his chosen corporate headquarters. Unlike NBC, with its grand Rockefeller Center base of operations, or ABC, which had a flashy Times Square studio, the News Corp. building was relatively modest. I say "relatively"

---

7   True story! In the early 1970s, Murdoch started the tradition of featuring a new topless model each day on the third page of his paper *The Sun*. The so-called Page Three girls were much beloved by readers, and the feature was eventually copied by other British newspapers in a mammarian arms race that I'm deeply disappointed I didn't have the opportunity to live through.

because, if you plunked down the forty-five-story tower in the middle of downtown Cincinnati, it would actually be quite impressive—the tallest skyscraper by more than a few stories. However, in midtown Manhattan, it was nothing, just another face in the crowd. A dozen buildings within a ten-block radius were taller. The two towers on the next two blocks up the avenue were built at the same time as the News Corp. building and had virtually identical exteriors, except for being—yes—taller.

So there was nothing terribly distinctive about the building, except one thing: the Fox News "ticker," an LED banner that wrapped around the side of the building, scrolling pithy news headlines in three-foot-tall glowing red letters, day and night.

Inside the building, the news channel took up the entire basement with a large newsroom and several studios and control rooms. More control rooms and studios were on the ground floor. Corporate offices were on the second floor. Most of the on-air personalities were given offices on the seventeenth floor, and additional spillover was located on three or four other floors.

Fox News vied for space with other News Corp. properties, like the *New York Post* and *TV Guide*, each of which had a sizable presence in the building. Even the Fox Network, 20th Century Fox movie studios, and Fox Searchlight—which had their main operations in Los Angeles—still had their own space in New York. And though they weren't yet there when I started in 2004, *The Wall Street Journal* and Fox Business eventually set up camp in the building, too. Finally, a large law firm, unrelated to News Corp., occupied the upper floors of the building.

The mixture made for an eclectic crowd in the lobby, with buttoned-up lawyer types and corporate suits from the parent company mingling with the schlubby journos from the *Post* and Fox News, as well as the occasional celebrity. It wasn't unusual to step off the elevators and run into, say, the entire cast of *Glee*, or Gene Simmons from KISS.

I was twenty-five minutes early for my interview, so I plopped down on a bench in the stark concrete plaza in front of the building (five or six sad trees and a couple of wooden benches, mostly frequented by a rotating cast of vagrants and cigarette-breaking burger flippers from a nearby Wendy's) and attempted to gather my nerves. I watched the bright red news scroll for a few minutes, catching a half dozen typos and misspellings. The headlines mostly related to the day's[8] top story, the resignation of CIA chief George Tenet, who, in my liberal opinion, was largely responsible for slam-dunking America into the disastrous Iraq War, which was at that point just over a year old. *Good riddance,* I thought, the campus radical in me still rising up, despite the fact I was mere minutes away from begging for a job with a right-wing news organization and I was dressed like I was going to a Halloween party wearing an Alex P. Keaton costume.

I checked my bag, a handsome blue canvas messenger with my school's logo monogrammed on it. Inside, only the essentials: pack of cigarettes, pack of gum, tourist map of the city, and a faux-leather portfolio filled with multiple copies of my résumé and printouts of some of the less offensive and inflammatory columns that I had written for my college newspaper.

And I waited, watching employees file in and out of the revolving doors, wondering what it would be like to be one of them. They looked generally happy. I don't know what I imagined crazed wing-nut Republican hacks would look like, but it didn't look like these people. (I didn't see anyone goose-stepping, anyway, which probably would have been a dead giveaway.)

Fifteen minutes before my interview, I decided I'd crossed the threshold from "annoying-suck-up early" to "business punctual," so I headed inside the building. The air in the huge cathedral-like lobby was chilled to roughly the same temperature as a zoo's penguin habitat. I felt the beads of sweat that had been accumulating on my brow begin

---

8 An odd side note—my interview was Friday, June 4, 2004, the day before Ronald Reagan died. The news reports all gave pneumonia as the cause of death, but I'm like 30 percent certain he ended his own life because he'd sensed that Fox was on the verge of hiring a goddamn commie/hippie like me.

to crystallize, and a single drop of icy cold perspiration began an arduous Lewis and Clark–style journey from the small of my back down toward the crack of my ass.

I told the bored-looking security guard sitting behind the substantial, thirty-foot-long wooden kiosk that I was there for an interview with Fox, and he made a phone call while I looked around. The lobby was marginally impressive, if generic: soaring thirty-foot ceilings, walls and columns clad in marble panels with wooden accents, a massive abstract painting on a canvas—blotches of color with squiggly lines, clearly calculated for maximum boring corporate inoffensiveness—hanging above the guard station.

After a few minutes, a fresh-faced assistant came to fetch me and brought me up to the second floor, where all of the Fox News executive and administrative offices are located. She deposited me in a waiting area, and told me to grab a seat. Eyeing my forehead, still covered with now frozen sweat, she said, "Um, can I get you a towel or something?"

"Maybe a Kleenex, if you have it?" I managed to get out. She gestured to a box on a table and I greedily mopped my brow with a handful of tissues.

After a few minutes in the holding pen, I was rescued by my interviewer, the same Jessica with the Italian last name who had left me the voice mail. She was attractive, with a friendly smile, and surprisingly young for someone who had earned her large office with windows looking out onto Forty-Eighth Street.

Jessica Italian-Name launched right into it, telling me how much the people around the office had enjoyed the cover letter that I'd sent with my résumé, and how funny they all thought it was.

"Oh, I don't know if it was all *that* funny," I said with all the false modesty I could muster. "I just dashed it off in a few minutes one day."

This job interview is no big deal! I have dozens of them! I hoped the lightness in my voice said. (*This is my one and only shot! I'm very, very desperate!* I'm pretty sure the haunted look in my eyes said.)

With the initial pleasantries out of the way, the interview began in earnest, and it was going swimmingly. I was expecting a grilling, but this was really more a breezy conversation. Jess (as I'd mentally nick-named my new best friend) asked me about school, my extracurriculars, how I liked my major, and growing up in the Midwest.

In turn, she told me about Fox, the culture, how it was different from the other networks: "We are totally viewer driven. The reason people who watch the network love us is that we give them the stories they want to watch. And in return, our viewers are *very* loyal."

She wasn't lying. I hadn't realized how successful Fox News was until I started researching it in anticipation of my interview. It had been around only since 1996, yet the ratings routinely beat those of the main competitors, CNN and MSNBC. It wasn't even close. Fox often had more viewers than the other two networks *combined*.

Jessica pointed to the TV mounted on the wall behind her desk. "You see that little logo in the corner of the screen?" Sure enough, the square Fox News logo was prominent on the lower left of the frame. "We call that the 'bug.' Watch how it rotates every few seconds," Jessica said.

I waited obediently, and sure enough, a few seconds later, the square revealed itself to be a cube, and spun a quarter turn to reveal a new face. FAIR & BALANCED, it now read.

"The reason they did that," she explained, "is because our viewers kept the channel on so many hours in a row, every single day, that the logo would actually get burned into their screens and ruin their TVs." She laughed. "Isn't that hilarious?"

This was not, as it turns out, the last time that I heard this anecdote. It was relayed to me at least a half dozen times over my first few months on the job. People seemed unusually proud that our viewers were so loyal that they were ruining their TVs. But the only thing it ever called to mind for me was that our audience was either so elderly that they hadn't figured out the remote control and/or so infirm that they were literally unable to change the channel.

But obviously the interview was no time to voice that sentiment, so I smiled broadly as Jessica laughed heartily at her own anecdote. *I'm really nailing this*, I thought.

I thought too soon.

We had come to the end of the interview, the part where the interviewer asks if you have any questions. Feeling cocky from the smoothness of the proceedings up to that point, I decided to open my dumb mouth.

I had noticed on her TV at that moment that a reporter was doing a piece on *the* tabloid story of the moment: the Scott Peterson trial.

Scott was a smug-looking guy in his early thirties whose eight-months-pregnant wife, Laci, had disappeared on Christmas Eve. Cops became suspicious of him when it turned out he was having multiple affairs behind his wife's back. His laughable alibi for the day his wife disappeared was that he had been alone in his boat, out on the San Francisco Bay, fishing. When Laci's body washed up on a nearby shore several months later, cops arrested Scott, who appeared to be in the midst of preparing to flee to Mexico.

Almost a year after his arrest, his trial was huge news and was getting wall-to-wall, breathless coverage on Fox, coverage that I'd noticed while watching the channel the week before, studying up for the interview.

It was, understandably, an irresistible story for a certain segment of the population—there would always be an audience for salacious murder trials involving attractive, well-off white people. But it struck me as a little odd that the sordid details were being covered so extensively by a "news" channel while the country was in the middle of an increasingly bloody war in Iraq and was also about five months away from a presidential election.

So when Jessica asked me if I had any questions, it turns out I did—a really unwise one, in fact: "Do any of the journalists here complain about having to cover stories like the Peterson trial instead of, you know, *real news*?" I asked.

The atmosphere in the room changed instantly. The smile dropped off her face. The laughter went out of her eyes. And I don't know how she did it without touching them, but I swear the blinds lowered a little, darkening the room.

Realizing my mistake, I instantly felt like throwing up.

"No," she said in a voice that was suddenly quiet and pinched. "Our viewers love that story. It gets great ratings. We cover stories that our viewers want to watch. And we wouldn't want to hire anybody who would second-guess our viewers like that."

I wish I could tell you what the rest of the interview was like, but I have zero recollection of it. I've totally blocked it out of my mind—a defense mechanism, no doubt, against the trauma of that moment. All I remember was that she ended it very quickly after my question. I was out on the plaza, already starting to sweat again, in what felt like ninety seconds later.

I'd blown it. My only job interview. My one chance to get to New York, to escape the infamy of being a college graduate with parents for roommates. Loads of potential, squandered, because I couldn't keep my stupid mouth shut.

Oh, well, I thought, *at least I have the rest of the weekend in the city to enjoy myself before I have to go back to the Midwest to start the rest of my sad life.*

Six days later, they called and offered me the job.

"This is Jim Siegendorf, an executive producer at Fox News Channel," the voice on the phone said. "We want to hire you as a production assistant."

I cradled the phone against my ear in my childhood bedroom in Cincinnati, rendered momentarily speechless. I had been rushed out of the interview so quickly after I dared to question the journalistic soundness of a salacious murder trial, that I was absolutely certain I'd blown it.

In my despair I'd gone full Bridget Jones and immediately started depression eating. I bought and devoured a giant lamb pita sandwich from a food cart advertising itself as halal[9] parked outside the Fox

---

9 I didn't find out until a few weeks after moving to New York that halal was not a guy's name but was basically the Muslim version of kosher. Halal carts dot almost every side street in midtown, serving chicken and lamb topped with hot sauce and a mysterious

building. The food helped, but it still felt like a long nine-block walk of shame back to my hotel to peel off my interview clothes, which were now drenched with flop sweat in addition to heat sweat, and speckled with lamb grease.

So, yeah, I was a bit surprised to be offered a job. But I managed to hold it together and not betray my utter shock.

"Production assistant? What's that?" I asked.

"You'll be helping out with the TV shows we produce," Jim said. "I don't know yet what show we'll put you on. It depends on what slots we have to fill."

TV? I had only applied for a website job, but this was actually even better. *I'm going to be a rich television producer!*

"The job pays twelve dollars an hour," Jim said.

I'm going to be a frugal-living television producer!

"I have to tell you, it starts out freelance, so there aren't any health or dental benefits right away."

I'm going to be a frugal-living, disease-ridden, toothless television producer!

The salary was a bit of a disappointment, but since it represented a 50-percent raise from the eight dollars an hour I'd been making at my landscaping job the previous summer, it didn't sound too bad.

But now I was again confronted with the same moral quandary I had been wrestling with when I sent the application in the first place. It's true that I was desperate for a job, any job, to prove to my parents that their faith in me, their indulgence of my frivolous-in-retrospect film and television studies, hadn't been a huge mistake. And I was eager to move to New York City, a place that I'd fallen in love with at a very young age and, to paraphrase Woody Allen, a town I idolized all out of proportion.

But it was also true that I'd essentially be working for the enemy. Could I swallow my distaste for Fox News's conservative leanings? If I

"white sauce." You can get it served over rice or in a pita. The cleanliness of said carts is suspect. You often see the vendor flipping raw chicken parts with a spatula, then immediately using the same spatula to dish out rice to a customer. New Yorkers refer to it derisively as "street meat." It's goddamn delicious.

took the job, I realized with a queasy feeling, I'd be selling out at age twenty-two—and not even for a lot of money.

"So what do you think?" Jim's voice on the phone snapped me out of my mental Hamletting. He sounded like a nice guy, polite, soft-spoken, and eager to recruit me. And he hadn't asked for any sort of ideological purity test. Neither had Jessica, for that matter. No one seemed to notice, or care, that I was a bleeding-heart liberal. Maybe I could handle this.

"We'd *really* love to have you," Jim's voice urged.

My eyes swept across a map that I'd pinned to the wall just the day before. I'd bought it at a souvenir stand near Times Square shortly after my blown interview. The island of Manhattan stretched from the top to the bottom, filling the space, rendered in yellows and reds, and vaguely phallic. When I'd tacked it up, I'd been certain that staring at it every day would be the closest I would ever get to actually living there. But now the opportunity had re-presented itself, unexpectedly.

I sighed. It might be my only chance.

"I'm in."

April 11, 2012—11:45 A.M.

I had made it past the suspicious Nick De Angelo, though the encounter had left me rattled. Rather than risk being spotted getting on the elevators on my own seventeenth floor, I'd decided to take a little-used staircase up to the eighteenth-floor elevator bank, where I was less likely to bump into someone who would find it odd that I was fleeing the building with a duffel bag at eleven thirty in the morning.

I climbed the stairs and emerged into the long narrow space that was currently being uneasily shared by the staffs of Sean Hannity's and Greta Van Susteren's shows.[10] The two crews, despite airing back-to-back on the same network, were, in a very real sense, competitors, with each staff independently pursuing the same scoops and the same hard-to-get guests. It was an awkward arrangement, to say the least, to have a rival producer ten feet away and able to hear your every word when you were trying to work the phones; but the two staffs had somehow made do for a few years. The room was mercifully mostly empty, with most of the late-working staffers not yet in for the day; the few people who *were* there seemed to pay me no mind.

The space was divided equally, with each show getting its own side, but the décor was pure Hannity, the walls plastered with various

---

10 Along with the O'Reilly staffers, Greta's and Sean's people had been unceremoniously booted from the newsroom during a 2008 remodeling that turned the three former prime-time pods into the new hub of the digital video system.

campaign signs for Republican candidates, and one very large fan-donated piece of art.

Now, it wasn't unusual at Fox for some of the more zealous viewers to mail artwork and other mementos to their favorite hosts. The O'Reilly pod a floor below was studded with some of the more memorable examples—most of them of dubious artistic merit, but all of them glorifying the host: a wooden, hand-painted Bill O'Reilly bobblehead doll; a watercolor painting of Bill's famous on-air confrontation with congressman Barney Frank; a nightmare-inducing papier-mâché depiction of O'Reilly dressed as a lumberjack, for some reason, complete with an ominous, shiny-bladed ax.

The point is, for a show to display viewer-made art wasn't unusual in and of itself, but the piece mounted next to the door in the Sean/Greta headquarters stood out; it was enormous, and clearly done by someone who knew how to wield a paintbrush. The giant oil-on-canvas showed Sean Hannity's massive grinning head on a TV screen with a Fox News logo, with confetti flying through the air behind him. The artist, in an inspired bit of wishful thinking, had added an on-screen graphic that read OBAMA DEFEATED IN HISTORIC LANDSLIDE.

At least if they fire my ass, I thought as I passed the thing, *I'll never have to see that fucking asinine painting again.*

CHAPTER 2

I Coulda Been a Contender...

S o is this fat fuck dead or what?"

Kurt Karos, a producer in his late twenties, was barking into the phone, raising his voice to be heard over the din of the control room. We had just received a report that Marlon Brando, legendary actor, star of classic films like *On the Waterfront*, *Apocalypse Now*, and *The Godfather*, noted recluse—and alleged fat fuck—was, in fact, dead. But the report had come from just one source, Fox's affiliate in Los Angeles, and Karos was on the phone with the assignment desk, trying to get a second source to confirm the news so we could go to air with it.

"Don't fuck with me on this, Steve," Kurt was shouting. "I *know* it's still early on the West Coast. . . . Wake them the hell up, then! . . . Look, if CNN gets this first, they might as well stay in bed because I swear to Christ I'll make it my business that they no longer have jobs to wake up to!"

I was taking this all in from my perch in the back corner of the cramped, chaotic control room, itching to do something, to help in any way I could; but I was by far the lowest-ranked person in the room, and the producers and technicians seemed to have forgotten that I was even there. So I watched, and waited, as the number one cable news network in America struggled to be the first to inform a blissfully unaware public that a Hollywood icon had dropped dead.

It was July 1, 2004, my very first day at Fox News.

I was about three hours into it.

Four days earlier, I had arrived in New York City with my entire life packed into three suitcases, only six weeks removed from the comforting bosom of college. My diploma was still at the framer's in my hometown of Cincinnati, Ohio—which was just as well, because I wasn't going have an office wall to hang it on anyway.

I took a cab straight from LaGuardia Airport to my friend Sloane Coupland's Manhattan apartment. Sloane was a delightfully manic brunette I'd known since freshman year. The first time I met her, she'd brought me back to her dorm room and nonchalantly changed her clothes in front of me. For any other girl, that would have been a brazen come-on, but for Sloane, it was simply a practical matter: She needed to change, and it was rude to ask a new friend to wait outside while she did so. Of course I didn't know that at the time, and diligently waited for a sexual entanglement that never materialized. By the time I realized that the bra and panties she'd flashed at our first meeting was the nakedest I would ever see her, it was too late: We were friends. Most recently, as seniors, we'd collaborated on a truly overwrought pro-choice student film that she'd written, I'd photographed, and we'd both directed. It didn't win any awards in the student film festival, but it did give Sloane and me a lot of time to talk about our future plans, with both of us having aspirations to head to New York.

Sloane had arrived in the city three weeks prior. She was living in a luxury high-rise overlooking the East River, in a spacious one-bedroom that no twenty-two-year-old had any business having all to herself. Sloane was one of those lucky cases that seemed to crop up occasionally in New York: Her parents had agreed to support her for a year while she made a go of it in the film industry.

When the taxi dropped me off at Sloane's building, one doorman helped me with my luggage while another held the door for me and a third greeted me at the front desk of the lobby, a soaring marble-clad space with a curtain of water running down one wall and gathering in a little pool. I was still taking it all in, slack-jawed like a moron, when Sloane stepped off the elevators and wrapped me in a hug.

"You're here!" she shouted, squeezing the air out of my lungs with her surprisingly powerful embrace. "Finally!"

"You really expect me to stay in this fleabag?" I wheezed. "The doormen didn't even offer me champagne on the way in."

"Ha-ha, very funny, asshole. Let's go upstairs."

A quick ride in the elevators and we were at her nineteenth-floor apartment.

"Welcome to New York!" Sloane said with a grand flourish of her arms as we crossed the threshold. "Let me give you the tour!"

My first impression was actually that the place was small—maybe about six hundred square feet. I would soon come to realize that it was a *fucking palace* by regular Manhattan standards. But I had been tricked by years of watching New York–based sitcoms, and all I could think was that Sloane's apartment was even smaller than Joey and Chandler's.

The place was decorated and furnished almost entirely with IKEA, but Sloane and her mother had arranged it into what I had to admit amounted to a very chic, put-together setup. It still felt a bit like a dorm room, but it was at least a *very grown-up* dorm room. Not to mention it was way nicer than anywhere I envisioned myself living anytime soon.

The tour ended with a big reveal from Sloane, who clearly had been waiting for this moment. We stopped in front of a door adjacent to the small galley kitchen.

"So this was supposed to be my pantry . . ." she started. "But I decided to turn it into"—she flung open the doors, flourishing her arms like a model at a car show—"my shoe closet!"

Sure enough, the floor-to-ceiling shelves were filled with three dozen pairs of shoes.

"Wow, you're really living the dream, Slo," I said, wondering if *Sex and the City* had claimed yet another victim.

Later that night, we were on the roof of Sloane's building sharing a bottle of wine—the very cheapest white that a grumbling wine store clerk had in his small refrigerator—and toasting to our mutual future success, which in our youthful exuberance we both agreed was virtually guaranteed, merely on the basis of our both showing up in the right place.

As I looked out over the city, the lights from thousands of windows piercing the humid early-summer evening, the majestic stainless-steel-clad Chrysler Building looming nearby, all I could think was *Forget shoe closets—I'm the one who's really living the dream.*

The next morning, I woke up on Sloane's couch. My head was pounding, the result of our not only finishing the cheap wine but later attacking with gusto the equally cheap bottle of vodka that—aside from an empty ice cube tray—was the lone inhabitant of Sloane's freezer. She was already gone, having left for her unpaid "internship" at an independent film company that was all too willing to take advantage of eager young college grads trying to break into the industry. I was still three days away from starting work, so I decided to explore the city a little bit.

I set out on foot for my future office, thinking it might be prudent to time the walk so I wouldn't be late on my first day. I passed through Sloane's neighborhood, which my pocket tourist map told me was Murray Hill. I found out later that the area had a reputation for being an ersatz college campus, despised by most locals for the proliferation of bars and high-rise apartments overrun by annoying twenty-two-year-olds fresh from graduation. (Fair enough, considering our circumstances.) But walking through it that day, I was struck by how quiet and orderly it seemed, especially compared to the other parts of the city I'd seen up to that point.

Soon enough the calm of Murray Hill gave way to the traffic and mayhem of midtown. The News Corp. building was just a shade under a thirty-minute walk from Sloane's apartment. Not a terrible commute for the few weeks that I'd be living with her.

My new office was smack-dab in the middle of the part of town you'd probably take your parents to first if they came to visit. A couple of blocks north up the avenue was the familiar sight of Radio City Music Hall, its neon-lit façade stretching skyward. Just to the east of that was Rockefeller Center, the masterful Art Deco complex of buildings, home to NBC, the

Today show, the famous Christmas tree, and the skating rink that, I was delighted later to find out, turns into a bar in the summer months.

To the southwest of my new office was the flashing video-screen over-loaded, tourist-crammed clusterfuck of Times Square, filled with street artists hawking caricatures, food vendors generating an ungodly amount of smoke from their grills, and dazed tour groups of old ladies from New Jersey shoving their way through the crowd, hustling to make curtain time for *Mamma Mia!*

Farther north up Sixth Avenue, past Radio City, you could just make out a massive expanse of green: Central Park, which is where I headed. Rather than enter the park itself—despite rumors of a recent revitalization, I still knew the park only from the movie *Home Alone 2* and the TV show *Night Court* as a haven for crackheads, prostitutes, and terrifying old ladies who breed armies of pigeons to do their bidding—I hooked a right turn onto Central Park South. It's the street where all the hansom cabs line up, waiting to give tourists horse-drawn rides.

New York City visitors have a very romantic vision of the horse-and-carriage ride, but the reality is a disappointing letdown. Instead of a proud, beautiful steed pulling your cart, you have a sad, plodding creature with its head stooped in misery. Instead of a merry driver dressed like a Victorian caroler pointing out landmarks, you have a surly guy in jeans who ignores you and won't stop texting on his cell phone.

Also, the entire length of the street smells like horse shit.

I was walking past the depressing queue of horses, idly wondering whose job it was to empty those little poop-catcher aprons strapped underneath each animal, when I almost ran over a guy about my age standing in the middle of the sidewalk.

"Excuse me, sir. Would you like to donate to help us defeat George Bush this November?" He was carrying a clipboard and wearing a shirt identifying him as an employee of the Democratic National Committee. He had a JOHN KERRY FOR PRESIDENT button pinned to his chest.

"Sure, I'd love to," I replied, digging into my back pocket for my wallet. "How does five bucks sound?"

The kid, obviously too blown away by my generous offer to speak, scribbled something on the clipboard and handed it to me.

"I just need your information there. Name, address, employer, and so on."

"You know, it's funny that I'm making this donation," I said as I filled out the form. "I'm actually starting work in three days for Fox News Channel."

"Oh, my God! Why?" He looked at me, horrified. "Why are you going to work for *them*?"

"Ummm . . . that's a great question," I said. "I guess . . ."

I was completely taken aback by the anger I heard in his voice. I was still coming to grips myself with the fact that I was in the city to take a job with Fox News, so I wasn't yet completely prepared to have to justify it to a stranger a full three days before I even started.

My immediate impulse was to tell the guy that this was just a *temporary* job, a way to get my foot in the door, to establish a life in New York while I searched for something that I *really* wanted to do. That I didn't buy into Fox's philosophy, and in fact believed the *exact opposite*. That while I was there I was going to do my best to keep them honest, and to maybe even *change* them from the inside, to bend the entire organization to my way of thinking through sheer force of will, using my dazzling powers of persuasion. I was going to be a force for *good*. I would not let the questionable values of my employer change my values, or who I was as a person.

But I didn't say any of that.

What I did say was: "I guess you gotta make a living, right?"

The volunteer frowned at me but said nothing as I handed him back his clipboard and a five-dollar bill.

I could still feel his disapproving gaze on my back as I slunk away, the smell of horse shit lingering in my nostrils.

———

True story: I showed up for my first day of work with bloody socks.

All my shoes were brand-new, bought during a spending binge at a Cincinnati department store. In those heady pre-financial-crisis days, the fine people at Macy's had foolishly decided that I was trustworthy enough for a three-thousand-dollar line of credit. This was good, because I desperately needed some big-boy clothes. I wasn't 100 percent sure what I was supposed to wear to a Manhattan office job, but I was fairly certain that my standard college uniform of orange athletic warm-up pants paired with an ironic thrift store T-shirt wasn't going to cut it. ("Mr. Ailes, don't you find my SOUTH BEND GIRLS' CHOIR T-shirt hilarious? I picked it up for three bucks at the Salvation Army.")

The problem was that three days of walking around the city wearing cheap shoes that hadn't been broken in yet had taken a toll, and opened enormous blisters on the heels of both feet. It was just my luck that one of them had started bleeding during the half-hour walk from Sloane's place to the Fox building.

I could only hope that my new coworkers wouldn't notice the red stain blooming on the Achilles tendon on one of my tan dress socks. I didn't want to be known around the office as "Joe the Bloody Sock Guy." (It would seriously undermine my plan to get known as "Joe the Large-Penised Genius.")

I limped into the lobby a little bit before eight A.M. and checked in again at the security desk. The guard checked my ID and made a phone call, and after a few minutes, a dark-skinned—Indian, I guessed—pretty woman in her late twenties appeared.

"Hi, I'm Nina. You must be Joseph Mutt-Oh?" she said, mispronouncing my surname.

"Nice to meet you," I said, shaking her hand. "It's Moo-Toe, actually. And I go by Joe."

She nodded. "Okay. Follow me."

I obediently trailed after her toward a set of security gates. She pressed her ID badge—suspended from a lanyard around her neck—against a sensor, and two clear glass partitions parted with a satisfying mechanical *whoosh* noise, letting her pass through. I did the same with the temporary paper ID that the security guard had printed for me.

"Cool," I muttered. "Just like Star Trek."

Nina looked back over her shoulder.

"I mean, high-tech and stuff . . ." I said, trailing off awkwardly.

"There used to be a lot less security in the building," Nina said. "They'd let anyone come and go. But then, you know. Nine-eleven, I guess."

"Oh, sure," I said, nodding. "You can't be too careful with terrorists. After all, the *TV Guide* offices are in this building, right?"

Nina looked at me through narrowed eyes.

I followed her onto an escalator that took us down to the basement of the building, into a long, barren, fluorescent-lit hallway. Straight ahead was an entrance to the subway and a subterranean Wendy's restaurant. The smell of hash-brown-flavored frying oil filled the space.

"Whoa, it's way too early for a burger," I cracked.

"Oh, they actually don't have burgers this early," Nina said, ignoring my joke. "And their breakfast kinda sucks."

We rounded a corner, passed two workers in Wendy's uniforms unloading a pallet stacked with forty-pound bags of frozen French fries, and approached two security guards standing sentry in the middle of the hallway. I couldn't imagine what exactly they were guarding, because there didn't appear to be anything else in the corridor except exposed ductwork overhead and a stack of beat-up folding chairs piled against a wall.

"Be honest," I said to Nina. "Are you taking me somewhere to murder me?"

This time she laughed. I'd finally cracked the Ice Queen!

"No," she said. "I'm taking you to the newsroom."

As we got closer to the security guards, I saw that they were actually posted outside a set of thick, heavy glass doors. One of them pulled a door open as we approached, grunting a little with the effort.

As we stepped through the doorway, Nina smiled at me and said, "Welcome to your new home."

I have to admit—I was impressed.

The Fox newsroom was built in a space formerly occupied by a Sam Goody record store. It was a massive room, about the size of two end-to-end football fields. It was packed with people—about 250 of them—sitting elbow to elbow at workstations, each equipped with a computer and a small television set with a cable hookup. Most sets were tuned to Fox, though I noticed that some were showing CNN or MSNBC. The volume was up on most of the televisions, and the din from the clashing audio was constant and relentless. I noticed a lot of people eating breakfast at their desks, and the smell of coffee and eggs and fried potatoes and toasted bagels hung thick in the air.

At the near end of the room was a glassed-in area with a half dozen people staring at a wall of forty tiny monitors, each screen no bigger than a postcard. There was a bank of ten VCRs, each about the size of a large microwave oven, arranged on shelves underneath the monitors. The technicians were jamming tapes into some machines, and snatching them out of others; hitting RECORD on the machines with new tapes and boxing the old ones, labeling them with Sharpies.

"That's intake," Nina said. "The satellite feeds come in from all over—updates from our reporters in the field, international footage from AP and Reuters, local news packages from our affiliates. They get recorded onto tapes, logged into the system, and filed away in the library."

"Why are those VCRs so big?" I asked.

Nina shrugged. "They're just old, I guess. They've had the same equipment here since the network started in ninety-six."

Near intake were two large oval tables, each with about a dozen people sitting at them, most of them talking on the phone. I heard a smattering of foreign languages coming from several workers at one of the desks.

"Those are the two assignment desks—foreign and domestic," Nina continued. "They keep in touch with all of our sources, gather the information, and spread it to everyone else at the network."

We started walking toward the back of the room. The seating arrangement changed to squared-off areas of six desks apiece, bordered on all sides by waist-high cubicle walls.

"Each show has its own little seating area—we call them pods." Nina started pointing as we walked past each pod, naming each show in turn. "Here's the *Fox Report*. Here's *Studio B*. That's Greta. Then O'Reilly, Hannity and Colmes, and Cavuto." Each pod had a large sign on the wall behind it identifying the show.

About halfway down the length of the room was a glassed-in studio with lights suspended from the ceiling, a bulky camera on a tripod, and a shiny, metallic anchor's desk.

"Most of the studios are in other parts of the building, but we have one here. This is Studio N," Nina said as we walked past. "*N* as in *newsroom*, as you probably figured out."

"Oh, yeah, I definitely figured that out on my own," I lied.

At the very back of the newsroom was another glassed-in area with monitors and VCRs.

"Is this another intake?" I asked. It looked very similar to the room we'd already seen.

"This is playback," Nina said. "The videos that you see on air are all played from here." A woman behind the glass was sitting in a chair, loading tapes into each machine. There was an intercom in front of her, with a disembodied voice barking commands. The door was propped open, so I could hear what was being said.

"Playback, ready number three," the voice said.

I watched as the woman's hand moved to the VCR marked *#3*, her index finger hovering over the PLAY button.

The intercom crackled again: "Ready, aaaannd . . . roll three!"

The woman's finger shot forward and stabbed the PLAY button, and on the tiny monitor above the VCR, the video sprang into motion. It was footage of American troops marching through the desert. I looked over to a TV on a nearby desk and, sure enough, the same footage was playing on the air, with a slight lag of a second or two.

"Whose voice is that?" I asked Nina.

"That's the director. He's in the control room on the ground floor." She pointed toward the ceiling.

"Wait, so they have to have someone whose job it is to just put the tape in the deck and press PLAY? Can't they do that remotely?"

Nina shrugged. "Probably. But this is the way they do it."

She led me away from playback toward an area where the activity seemed more frantic than the rest of the newsroom. Employees who looked about my age scurried among twenty shelves filled with tapes from floor to ceiling, darting from shelf to shelf, lingering briefly until they found the tape they were looking for, then moving on to the next shelf. They reminded me of honeybees flying from flower to flower. They all carried white plastic bins marked UNITED STATES POSTAL SERVICE, into which they tossed tapes with abandon.

"Did they steal those from the post pffice?" I asked.

"I dunno," Nina said. "I guess at some point. But we just get them from the mailroom here in the building." She pointed to a corner where the empty bins were piled into three tall stacks, each of them at almost my chin level.[11]

"The tapes you saw them recording in intake come back here to the tape library," Nina said. "The production assistants take the tapes they need and bring them to edit rooms, where editors cut them."

Sure enough, the PAs—some of them carrying bins filled to overflowing with tapes—would periodically break away from the shelving area and haul their stash to one of several closet-size rooms that lined the wall. Inside each room, I could see an editor sitting in front of dual monitors, working the control wheels of a tape-to-tape editing rig.

Nina led me to an area that seemed to be the center of all the activity, with PAs hovering over computer screens, taking notes, then darting toward the library. "This is the PA pod," Nina said. "And this is Jim Siegendorf, the executive producer in charge of all the production assistants." She gestured to a plump, baby-faced man in his early forties sitting at a desk amid the busy production assistants. He was the oldest person in the pod by about fifteen years, and the only one wearing a suit and tie. (Everyone else was in nothing fancier than khakis and a button-down shirt, though jeans and a polo were more common.)

Executive producer struck me as an impressive title then, and I later found out that it was actually the highest position you could obtain within the company without being named a vice president. The duties of an EP at Fox varied widely, depending on the specific position. Some

---

11 I found out much later that it's apparently illegal to keep these bins, and that the post office loses millions of dollars a year because of unauthorized hoarding. Fox had literally hundreds of these bins stacked all over the newsroom. So remember that the next time you're watching the network and a host complains about government waste.

EPs were running prime-time shows, or even entire blocks of shows—there was an EP for the overnights, responsible for everything that aired between eleven P.M. and six A.M., for example. Another EP was in charge of all the weekend programming. Jim had arguably the least enviable EP job: managing the unruly lot of irresponsible sub-twenty-five-year-olds who made up the production assistant pool.

Jim spotted Nina and me, and stood to greet us.

"You must be Joe Muto," he said. "We spoke on the phone a few weeks ago. Good to meet you in person, finally." I took his outstretched hand and shook it. Jim raised his voice for the benefit of the people standing around us. "Everyone! This is Joe, our newest PA!"

A few of the PAs looked my way and vaguely nodded in my direction, or gave little half waves, before darting off to pull more tapes. Most of them ignored Jim entirely and went about their business. Jim seemed not to notice.

"Are you enjoying the big city so far?" Jim asked. "Must be a real change from all the farms in Ohio."

"Actually," I started, "Cincinnati is a pretty decent-size metropolitan area—"

"Anyway," he interrupted, checking his watch, "let's get you your ID badge, and then let's get you to a control room. We're putting you on script duty."

———

Nina dropped me off at the control room less than half an hour later. My ID badge hung on a lanyard around my neck, still warm from the laminator. I wasn't thrilled with the picture—the photographer had caught me in sort of a half smile, and due to the early hour, my eyes were barely open, so I looked completely stoned. My hair was still wet from my morning shower, and the collar of my shirt hung open at a weird angle. *Oh, well, I can always take a better picture when I get this one replaced eventually.*[12]

---

12 Eight years later, that picture was still on the ID badge that two Fox security guards confiscated before physically removing me from the building.

The control room was smaller than I expected. It was on the ground floor of the building and had a large window looking out onto Forty-Eighth Street. Tourists would amble by, press their faces against the dark tinted glass, and wave as if the room held Matt Lauer and Katie Couric instead of a bunch of grumpy, stressed producers and tech guys. There was an odd dank, moldy smell in the room, supposedly the result of an ongoing drainage problem on that side of the building. A large air purifier sat in the corner and ran continuously to no apparent effect.

Even worse, as I learned later, the room smelled strongly of dead animals for a day or two after any heavy rain. Exterminators came in at one point and searched the crawl spaces for rat and raccoon carcasses, but no source for the smell was ever discovered. (A popular joke around the office was that it was the corpse of the last person to cross Roger Ailes.)

The control room was laid out like mission control for a space launch. The front of the room was a solid wall of monitors, with the biggest screen in the middle showing what was on air at that moment, and dozens of smaller screens around it showing the various camera feeds, satellite hookups, and video playback machines. Even more monitors were suspended from the ceiling, tuned to our competitors: CNN, MSNBC, Headline News, and CNBC. (We were supposed to monitor at all times what they were doing, in case they picked up on a story that was more exciting than whatever we had on air. If we saw they had a good car chase, or live pictures from a fire or tornado or something exciting like that, we were expected to jump on it as well.)

The room was jammed with about a dozen people arranged into two rows. The front row was tech: three guys who controlled the on-screen graphics, the video feeds, and the satellite connections, respectively; and the director, who bossed those three around. The second row was editorial: a senior producer, one or two producers, and a copy editor. A glassed-in booth in the back of the room had Metallica posters on the walls, giant speakers, and a mixing board that was manned by a long-haired rocker type who was apparently day-jobbing it as an audio technician.

And jammed into one corner was a rickety card table topped with an ancient-looking computer hooked up to a pair of brand-new laser printers. There were two rolling desk chairs, one of which was occupied by a girl my age. She was cute, with a sweet smile and chin-length light blond hair that framed a pleasantly round face and bee-stung lips. She was probably the best-dressed person in the room, wearing a preppy ensemble of a sleeveless dress with a pearl necklace and high heels. She looked like a sexpot version of a GOP politician's wife, or a sorority girl on her way to her first mixer. She eyed Nina and me coolly as we approached.

Nina introduced us. "Joe Muto, this is Camie Strong."

I held out my hand. "Nice to meet you."

She reached to complete the handshake. "Nice to meet y—"

"Back from commercial in one minute!" the director called out from the front row. "One minute!"

Camie's eyes went wide. "Ohhh!" she exclaimed, and jumped out of her chair, grabbing a stack of papers off the printer and bolting from the room, almost knocking me over in the process.

I looked at Nina with surprise. "What was that all about?"

Nina chuckled, shaking her head. "She's got to drop off those scripts for the anchor before they come back from commercial break. Watch the monitor." The big screen in the middle of the video wall showed the square-jawed anchorman on the set, looking down and shuffling through papers on his desk, frowning as if he couldn't find what he was looking for.

"Thirty seconds!" the director called out.

Suddenly, Camie burst onto the screen. She said something to the anchor and thrust the sheaf of papers at him. The anchor's mic was turned off during the commercial breaks, so I couldn't hear what she said to him, but the look on her face was apologetic. The anchor said something back, then waved her away. Camie turned and darted out of the camera frame.

"Fifteen seconds . . . ten . . . five, four, three, two . . ."

Music started playing and an animated Fox logo whooshed across the screen.

"Welcome back to *Fox News Live*," the anchor began. "Continuing now with our top story: Saddam Hussein appeared in court today for the first time since his capture. . . ." I turned to Nina. "I don't get it.

They're reading off the teleprompter, right? Why do they need the script printed for them?"

"The prompter goes down sometimes. They need backups."

"But why does she wait until the last minute like that to drop them off?"

"Most of these scripts don't get written until about five minutes before the anchor reads them. Then the senior editor has to go through them, and the copy editor. You have to wait until they both give their approval to print them for the anchor."

Camie came back into the room, out of breath, with her hair a bit disheveled. "That was close." She plopped back down in her seat, finger-combed her hair, and straightened her pearls.

"Have you ever missed a delivery?" I asked.

"Not yet," she said, crossing her fingers. "But I've only been on the job a week and a half."

"Wow," I said. "That's not a lot of time to get the hang of it."

"Let's hope it is," Nina said. "Because she's going to be training you."

Camie spent the next hour showing me the ropes. There was only one computer for us to share, so I watched over her shoulder while her fingers skipped across the keyboard. The entire show—scripts, names of guests, videos, etc.—was laid out like a spreadsheet in a software program called Avstar. Each show was divided into blocks, broken up by commercial breaks. The blocks were identified by letters—A-block, B-block, and so on.

Each hour was produced by a totally new staff, Camie explained. The senior producer and producer picked all the stories a few hours before showtime, then the producer assigned each story to one of the three or four writers, who were toiling away at their desks in the newsroom. After the writers finished with the script, they put their initials next to it. Then the copy editor gave it a once-over and put *her* initials next to it. Finally, the senior producer checked and initialed it. It was then, and only then, that we were allowed to print it and run it to the studio.

Ostensibly, the purpose of all those layers of approval was to cut down on typos, misinformation, and so on. But the end result was that, as Nina had said, sometimes the scripts weren't ready for us to print until mere minutes before the anchors read them. This complicated matters for Camie and me, since the studio wasn't anywhere near the control room. To get to the studio, you had to exit the control room, go down the hall, through a set of magnetically locked security doors into the lobby, travel forty yards through the lobby past three elevator banks, go through another set of security doors that a guard had to open for you, into another hallway, and finally through one more set of doors into the backstage area of the studio. It was about two minutes just to *walk* the route that we sometimes had less than thirty seconds to complete, which meant that more often than not, we had to make the journey at a full sprint. It was bad enough for me and my bleeding feet, but it must have been even worse for Camie, who clacked down the corridors like a madwoman, hauling ass in high heels, pearls chattering.

"Doesn't it bother you to run in those things?" I asked after witnessing her third sprint of the hour.

She rolled her eyes at me. "What am I going to do, wear *sneakers* with this dress?"

Camie and I, as script PAs, were stuck in the control room all day. But everybody else in the room changed out every hour, on the hour. As the previous show wrapped up, a whole new group of producers flooded the room, standing anxiously in the back while their predecessors logged off their computers. This awkward baton handoff had only a very small window in which to happen, basically the span of a commercial break.

After two or three of these changeovers, I began to get lulled into complacency. I'd never actually watched the news for so long at one stretch. It was shockingly repetitive. Each hour had the same set of stories (Saddam, Iraq, Bush campaign update, Kerry campaign update, rinse, repeat), the same reporters in the field, the same video clips. Only the anchors and the pundits changed. And even they started to blur together after a while, just a steady stream of bleached teeth and pouffy hair and precise diction, all repeating the same conservative-leaning analysis (Saddam's trial will help President Bush by reminding voters that he's a strong commander in chief, the Kerry campaign is in disarray because it hasn't yet figured out how to counter Bush's strength, etc.)

And then all hell broke loose.

The Avstar program had a folder marked URGENT, a place to post memos so the assignment desks could keep the entire network informed of breaking news without spamming everyone with e-mails. Every time a new message was posted in the folder, the program made an obnoxious metallic buzzing noise, an electronic scream for attention. Most of the messages were useless—incremental updates about some international story that no shows on the network had been following in the first place (something like URGENT: PERU ELECTS NEW FINANCE MINISTER or BREAKING: ZANZIBAR POLICE CLASH WITH PROTESTERS; 2 INJURED). So ninety-nine times out of a hundred, the software would buzz, everyone in the room would immediately click over and glance at the update, then close it with a disdainfully muttered *"Who gives a shit?"* That had happened multiple times in the few hours I'd been in the room. So Camie didn't even bother to click over when it buzzed again. *Probably just another false alarm from the assignment desk.*

"HOLY FUCK!"

Camie and I both jumped as Kurt Karos, the producer for the hour, yelled and smacked his work surface with the palms of his hands, rattling his keyboard.

"Our LA affiliate is reporting that a source at UCLA Medical Center says that Marlon Brando's dead," Karos read off his screen.

The control room went silent as we all absorbed the information.

"I guess Sollozzo's people finally got to him," one of the front-row tech guys cracked, breaking the silence.

"He sleeps with the fishes," the director said, laughing.

Carrie Lipton, the senior producer, was also studying the alert on her screen, her lips pursed as her eyes darted across the text. "Just one source for now, Kurt," she said. "It's still a rumor at this point. We can't go with it yet."

Kurt turned in his chair to face her. "I say we do it now, as soon as

we come back from commercial, or one of those assholes"—he gestured toward the ceiling-mounted bank of monitors displaying our
competition—"is going to beat us to it."

Carrie held firm. "No, we wait. What if the report is wrong? Do you
want to explain to Roger why we ran with a bullshit rumor about a
major celebrity?"

Kurt didn't like it, but he was outranked. "Fine. I'll light a fire under
the desk's ass and see if they can confirm it." He picked up the phone
receiver and dialed. "But if CNN beats us on this, I'm going to anger-
shit my pants. I'm literally going to shit."

"No one is going to shit themselves," Carrie said.

"I bet Brando did," a tech guy chimed from the front row. Carrie
ignored him.

"So is this fat fuck dead or what?" Kurt was barking into his phone
as Carrie flipped the switch on the console in front of her that allowed
her to speak to the anchor Jon Scott.

"Jon, we've got word that Marlon Brando may be dead. I'm just giving you a heads-up. We're going to alert it as soon as we can."

I could see Jon on the main monitor, listening to Carrie through the
tiny earpiece on the right side of his head. He nodded and began pecking at the laptop in front of him. When he answered, his voice boomed
from the two large, clear-sounding speakers at the front of the control
room. "Are we going to go into the alert straight out of the break?"

Carrie flipped the switch again. "Negative. We're back in less than
a minute, and we're still waiting on confirmation. But I'll get in your
ear if we get it confirmed while you're on air."

Next, Carrie picked up the phone and dialed. "Jim," she said—
Siegendorf, I realized—"tell whatever PA we have working on this hour
to drop everything and pull footage of Brando in *The Godfather*. Also,
see if we have any good b-roll of him handy. Red carpet stuff, interviews, whatever you got." She listened to the receiver, nodding her head
as Siegendorf spoke, then replied: "Well, I'd prefer young and handsome if you can dig any up, *quickly*. But we'll take old and chubby if
you've got it." She listened for a moment more, this time shaking her

head. "No, I don't think we'll need the full obit package just yet. Get it ready to go, though. We may run it later in the hour." She clicked the receiver back into place.

That was my first brush with a not-so-well-kept dirty little secret of the news industry: Fox had hundreds of slick, preproduced four-minute obituary videos filed away and ready to go at a moment's notice for almost every prominent celebrity and politician over the age of sixty. Every once in a while if a shift was particularly slow, I'd give myself a morbid thrill pulling the obit compilation from the tape library and watching a few of the pieces. Fox was hardly alone in this practice—my understanding is that all the networks and cable channels have similar compilations. But Fox stood out with the unique spin it gave certain figures. My favorite was Bill Clinton's, whose obit is hilariously Foxified, spending almost half the running time on Lewinsky and other bimbo eruptions. Meanwhile, the Dick Cheney obit makes him out to be a heroic freedom fighter, practically Abraham Lincoln and Winston Churchill rolled into one.

While Carrie was ordering up Brando's obit package, Kurt Karos was finishing his call with the assignment desk, throwing in a few more *fat fuck*s for good measure before hanging up.

"All right, they're working on it," he announced to the room. "They think that the Associated Press might move something on it shortly. If that's the case, we'll have to work fast, because then the other guys will have it, too."

"We have an alert ready to go," the director said. "And we're back in thirty."

We came back from commercial with the anchor throwing to a reporter for an update on the Iraq War. Midway through the reporter hit, Kurt's phone rang. He picked it up, listened for a second, then yelled out in excitement.

"We've got it! We got confirmation!"

Carrie nodded. "Dave, are you ready with the alert?" she asked the director. He grunted in assent.

"Good," Carrie said. "I want you to hit it straight out of this report."

The Baghdad reporter was wrapping up on-screen. Carrie flipped the intercom switch to talk to the anchor.

"Jon, we've got confirmation on Brando. We're going to hit it with an alert as soon as Baghdad is clear." I could see him on the camera feed, nodding.

Kurt glanced up at the rivals on the overheads. "Let's do this, people," he said, drumming his fingers on the desk in excitement. "CNN and MS still don't have it. We're going to be first with this."

The Baghdad update ended with the reporter saying, "Back to you, Jon."

"Hit that gong!" Dave the director yelled, and the tech at the console next to him punched a button. A red animated graphic swept across the screen with a whooshing noise, followed by a loud *ba-bong*, as if someone had struck a giant bell.

FOX NEWS ALERT, the graphic read.

The screen dissolved back to the anchor, his face somber, his voice even deeper than normal, his delivery slow: "This is a Fox News Alert. We've just received word that Marlon Brando, legendary actor, has died at age eighty."

The control room exploded into applause and whoops.

Carrie was jubilant. "Nice work, everybody. Nice hustle."

Kurt had stood up and was extending both middle fingers at the overhead monitors. "Fuck off, CNN! Fuck off, MSNBC! Yeah! We beat you fuckers!"

Less than thirty seconds later, CNN flashed its own alert, and about ten seconds after that, MSNBC had one up, but the celebration in the control room continued.

We were first.

The celebration would have been silly to me, except for one thing: It was one of the most oddly exhilarating experiences of my entire life.

I looked at Camie. She met my eyes and just nodded. *I know, right?*

April 11, 2012—11:49 A.M.

Is it just my imagination, or are there more security guards than normal stationed in the lobby?

I'd made it past the painting of Hannity's bloated, mid-celebration head, down the hall to the eighteenth-floor elevators without anyone stopping me, and caught an empty car down to the lobby.

And now I was staring at three building security guards, standing about twenty feet away from my elevator bank, where normally there would be none.

Take it easy. They could just be on a lunch break. It *was* almost noon. The lobby was swarming with lunchers, some of them on their way out, others returning with plastic bags from nearby take-out places swinging at their sides.

One of the guards looked straight at me, pondering for a second, then slowly turned his head and said something to his two companions. And then all three turned to look at me. One of them went for the walkie-talkie at his belt.

And that's my cue, folks!

It was all I could do to stop myself from running through the lengthy lobby toward the building's back exit. I walked as briskly as I could while still appearing normal, willing myself to not look over my shoulder to see if they were following. I assumed that once I got outside,

I'd be fine. This is America, after all. Sure, corporations are powerful, but they can't just seize people on the street, right? Right?

I powered through the revolving doors and emerged into the midtown Manhattan air, which for once smelled sweet to me. It smelled like freedom, and relief—not at all like the usual scent of curbside garbage and hobo pee.

Once I was outside, I felt it was safe to check behind me. I turned and looked.

No one.

No one was following me. Gazing through the glass doors into the lobby, I couldn't even spot the three guards who had spooked me. They had disappeared from the spot they were standing. Maybe I was right, and they were just meeting up to go to lunch together. Was I being too paranoid? Was I losing my mind?

I had to call *Gawker*.

CHAPTER 3

When Rupert Met Roger

Fox News was, by the time I joined it in July 2004 as a lowly production assistant, pretty obvious in its rightward lean, even as it staunchly clung to the ass-covering catchphrases "Fair and Balanced" and "We Report, You Decide." The truth was, Fox had been conceived from the very beginning as a venue for TV news with a deliberate slant.

Liberal alarm bells went off in early 1996, when Rupert Murdoch announced that he was going to start his own cable news network to compete with CNN and the still-in-the-works MSNBC. The suspicion on the left only increased when it was announced that the head of the network was going to be Roger Ailes, a jowly, fire-hydrant-shaped former GOP operative and media consultant who had made his bones during the 1968 Richard Nixon campaign. Under Ailes's sharp tutelage, Nixon was able to skillfully leverage television to trick the American public into believing he was a halfway reasonable human being instead of the sweat-soaked paranoid head case that he actually was. His reputation as a TV genius solidified, Ailes went on to advise more GOP presidents, most notably Bush the elder.

With Ailes's skill set joining forces with Murdoch's fire hose of endless money, it seemed like a plot hatched in the bowels of the Republican National Committee headquarters.

"Will FNC be a vehicle for expressing Mr. Murdoch's conservative political opinions?" *The New York Times* asked in an article shortly before Fox News Channel went live. The *Times*'s question seems hilariously naive in retrospect, but the truth is that in those early years, the answer was initially unclear. Instead of the partisan firebrand it later became, the young network's content was mostly of the anodyne "news you can use" variety. The daytime programming featured lengthy segments on travel, culture, and religion, topics to which the Fox News of later years would give screen-time only in passing. On weekends, there was a two-hour animal-themed call-in show called *Pet News*. If Murdoch and Ailes were aiming for right-wing indoctrination straight off the bat, they sure had a funny way of going about it.

But some of the seeds for the future rightward lunge were already there. *Hannity & Colmes*, for one, was in place in the nine P.M. slot the day the network launched. *H&C* was a debate show featuring the robust, square-jawed, thick-haired, all-American-looking conservative Sean Hannity squaring off against the thin-haired, sickly looking, bespectacled liberal Alan Colmes. It was an article of faith around the office that the visual mismatch had been a *deliberate* choice by Ailes, a transparent but effective attempt to make the conservative host—and by extension his ideas—more appealing. The show had in fact been conceived from the start as a vehicle for Hannity, with the addition of a liberal foil as an afterthought. (The working title for the show was *Hannity & LTBD*, meaning "Liberal To Be Determined," Colmes revealed in an interview once.) Ostensibly, it was supposed to be a fair fight, but as the show progressed, a lopsided dynamic emerged—one in which Colmes got clobbered on a nightly basis, as the aggressive Hannity held him personally responsible for every single transgression of the Clinton administration.

My future boss, Bill O'Reilly, was also present at the launch, though his six P.M. *O'Reilly Report* was still clearly a work in progress; it had yet to get its eight P.M. prime-time slot and catchier name, *The O'Reilly Factor*. Content-wise, it wasn't as overtly political as its later iteration—politics generally took a backseat to zeitgeisty cultural issues: drugs, gangster rap, teens gone wild, and so on. These topics jibed with his past work as the host of *Inside Edition*, a tabloidy syndicated news magazine show that he had brought to prominence in the late 1980s and early 1990s. With his show on Fox, O'Reilly—who had gotten his start as a straight news reporter—had editorial independence for the first time in his career, and he took the opportunity to develop the persona that eventually became his signature, the populist everyman who is protecting the average people (or "the folks," as he loved to say) from the forces trying to harm or corrupt them: liberals, atheists, college professors, the mainstream media, and Hollywood celebrities. Bill's brand of cranky populism was groundbreaking, and was eventually adopted as the editorial persona for the entire network.

Essential to O'Reilly's narrative was the pretense that he was an independent; the claim was that he wasn't partial to the Republicans or the Democrats, the right or the left—he went after both sides, doling out scorn to whomever deserved it more. It *just so happened* that those on the left were the ones who deserved rebuke 95 percent of the time. The remaining 5 percent of the time when he went after the conservatives—on certain carefully chosen issues like the death penalty and climate change—gave him plausible deniability. *I'm fair, I'm balanced. I call it like I see it.*

Fox launched just a few months after MSNBC, which—due to the backing of Microsoft and NBC News—was deemed by media critics as a more credible competitor to CNN. But Murdoch had given Ailes a mandate: Do whatever you can to beat CNN. And Ailes thought he had a solid strategy to do so, reasoning that the conservative hordes who flocked to talk radio were being underserved by CNN, which had a perceived liberal bias. *Give those conservatives a home on cable TV,* Ailes's reasoning went, *one that serves up both openly conservative opinion and conservative-slanted reporting that is thinly veiled as "straight" news, and they'll become habitual watchers.*

The first turning point for the network came during the Monica Lewinsky scandal. Fox News had started broadcasting only about a month before the '96 elections, too late in the game to make much of an impact. Having missed a chance to beat up on Bill Clinton then, Fox made up for lost time, hammering Bubba for his illicit blowjobs. O'Reilly and Hannity were especially tenacious, and their spirited denunciations of Clinton juiced the ratings to the point where Fox's prime time was nipping at the heels of CNN.

Ailes's strategy was working. He was proving that a fiercely loyal niche audience, one that watched so fervently that they literally ruined their TV screens (as I was reminded repeatedly), could bring in higher ratings than the wishy-washy broad audience that CNN was pursuing. As if to punctuate the point, in 2000, O'Reilly for the first time topped Larry King in the monthly ratings, becoming the most-watched show on cable news.

He's never been beaten in a monthly rating since.

If the Lewinsky scandal was good for Fox's ratings, the 9/11 attacks were nothing short of great. With the whole country traumatized, viewers had little patience for middle-of-the-road nuance, and even the staunchest liberals found themselves drifting a little bit rightward.

All the news networks went the full patriotic route following the terrorist attacks—plastering their screens with flags and red, white, and blue graphics—but Fox did it with the most relish and conviction, and the ratings soared. In January 2002, the 9/11 bump led to another ratings milestone—Fox's network-wide numbers passed CNN's for the first time.

Again, the network has not been beaten since.

Another benefit of 9/11 for Fox—it helped the network ratchet up support for the Bush agenda while maintaining plausible deniability. *We're not being partisan—we're simply being patriotic!* Consequently, Fox ended up being one of the biggest cheerleaders for the Iraq War, with, in the words of *The New York Times*, "anchors and commentators who skewer the mainstream media, disparage the French and flay anybody else who questions President Bush's war effort."

And this was the place I found myself working.

When I started in summer 2004, the Iraq War had just started to go bad but was still at the *Hmmm, this could be a problem* stage (as opposed to the later *Holy shit, what in Christ's name were we thinking?* stage).

Meanwhile, the election was heating up, and the Democrats, apparently not having learned their lesson with Michael Dukakis, were serving up yet another aloof, effete Bay Stater to be shredded by the Republican attack machine. The difference is that in 1988, Roger Ailes was skewering Dukakis from within the Bush campaign—where he was alleged to be the mastermind behind the infamous Willie Horton TV ads that portrayed Dukakis as soft on crime[13]—while in 2004 he found himself as the head of the highest-rated cable news network in the country, able to push whatever narrative he wanted for free.

I suppose that, as a godless liberal, I should have been more concerned about this, but on that first day of work, watching my new colleagues spring into action, frantically leveraging the full resources of a multimillion-dollar global news-gathering operation in order to break news of a celebrity death to the world a full half minute before the competition, I was too fascinated by the spectacle of it all to register any qualms I had with the tone of the political coverage.

"Well, that was intense," I said to Camie once the Marlon Brando fuss had tailed off. "Is it always like that in here?"

She nodded. "Oh, yeah. It gets real wild when there's breaking news."

"But I mean with, like, all the cursing and whatnot. Is that normal?"

She nodded again. "Sure is. It's like a frat house. You'd think they'd tone it down a bit with me around, but no." She paused for a second, a thoughtful look on her face. "Of course, the women are just as bad as the men. Maybe worse, in some cases."

---

13 Ailes denies to this day that he was directly responsible for the ads, which were produced by an outside group that was run by a former employee of his media consulting firm. The Federal Election Commission started an inquiry to discover if Ailes had illegally colluded with his former employee. The FEC commissioners, divided between Republicans and Democrats, voted on whether to launch a full investigation. They deadlocked, splitting evenly down party lines, and ended up dropping the matter entirely when neither side would budge. Ailes, though he has always denied having a hand in the ads, certainly relished the effect they had on the election, and was quoted at one point saying, "The only question is whether we depict Willie Horton with a knife in his hand or without it."

That was true, I found out soon enough. Most of the female producers were tough as nails, and just as profane as the guys. They had to be, really, or they'd get eaten alive because they were vastly outnumbered; while the ranks of producers were fairly evenly split between male and female, the tech guys—who filled half the slots in the control room— were almost exclusively men.

So, much to my delight, the control room was filled with constant shit-talking. They talked shit about everyone.

They talked shit about the bosses:

"When are they going to fix that fucking smell in here?"

"Those cheap asses would probably have to pay a contractor to put in more drainage . . . so my guess is never."

They talked shit about the guests on the air:

"Mike, this guest we have on right now is not exactly a looker. Can you throw up some b-roll to cover her face? I don't want to scare away viewers."

"Want me to get on the headset with the stage manager and see if she can scrounge up a paper bag real quick?"

They talked shit about the anchors:

"They told me Brit isn't sitting for the six o'clock tonight. What gives?"

"I heard he had an appointment to get the bolts in his neck tightened."

I'd listen and laugh so hard that I'd get distracted from doing my actual job, and then they'd talk shit about me:

"Hey, kid, I'm glad you're finding all this so amusing, but why don't you get off your ass and bring Rick his scripts so he isn't just sitting there with his dick twisting in the wind?"

On a typical weekday, Fox News is live from six A.M. to eleven P.M. Seventeen hours a day. For seven of those hours, Camie and I huddled at our tiny workstation in the back of the control room, printing scripts for anchors and taking turns running them into the studio. Here's the lineup as of 2004, when I first started running scripts:

6:00 A.M.–9:00 A.M.

Fox & Friends, the morning show, featured three grinning jackasses sitting on a couch, bantering about the news. The format called for one of the anchors to introduce the story, often getting the basic facts wrong, then for the other two to join in and chat about it for a few minutes, making opinionated pronouncements that were as emphatic as they were ill-informed. They didn't need me to deliver scripts for this show, as they had their own production assistants who worked exclusively for them. In any case, the anchors (smug blond former weather guy Steve Doocy, not-too-bright sports guy Brian Kilmeade, and uptight conservative-but-still-sexy housewife E. D. Hill) veered away from the prepared text so often that any written words were rendered essentially meaningless, lost in the verbal diarrhea of stupidity.

9:00 A.M.–1:00 P.M.

These were four interchangeable hours that, in theory, each had their own names. (*Fox News Live*? *Fox Newsroom*? *World of Fox*? Something like that, I think.) They were generic by design, the closest thing that Fox had to "straight" news—meaning news delivered without a strong POV. Each hour had its own staff and own anchor, and each was free to pick its own stories; but all of them still somehow ended up with an almost identical lineup of stories and guests. This was probably a testament to herd mentality more than anything. Because of their generic nature, it was considered less prestigious to be a producer on one of these shows. All the producers wanted to get off these shows and land one of the higher-profile assignments, and they figured the best way to do this was to toe the company line and do the same stories that every other show was doing. The repetitive nature of these hours led to the unflattering moniker "newswheel." I had to run scripts for all the shows, one of which broke the Brando news.

1:00 P.M.–2:00 P.M.

DaySide with Linda Vester was a program with a live studio audience, sort of a low-rent, slightly newsier version of an afternoon talk show. This was a good idea in theory—the host was supposed to periodically let audience members speak, surveying them about their opinions on the day's events. Nothing like a live audience to add energy to a broadcast, right? In practice, however, the audience was filled with bored tourists who had been reluctantly wrangled from Times Square mere minutes before the broadcast, enticed into the studio by fast-talking audience coordinators who stood on street corners promising a "REAL DEAL NEW YORK CITY LIVE TV SHOW EXPERIENCE." This disinterested, gullible posse of onlookers was then subjected to Linda Vester, a woman who could have been a great host if only her face didn't chronically appear to register utter contempt for the warm bodies assembled to watch her show. The end result was a tense-looking Vester stalking the aisles of the stadium seating with a handheld microphone, barking questions at obviously uncomfortable audience members and nodding impatiently, trying to maintain an appearance of interest as they stuttered out their incoherent responses. It was a glorious train wreck, but mostly I loved it because they didn't need me to do anything, and it gave me a full hour to get lunch.

2:00 P.M.–3:00 P.M.

Another hour of the newswheel! For Camie and me, another hour of running scripts up and down the hall!

3:00 P.M.–4:00 P.M.

Studio B with Shepard Smith would have been yet another hour of the newswheel except it had a secret weapon: the anchor. Shep was whip-smart, funny, and irreverent, and his presence made for a fast-paced, witty, and endlessly watchable newscast. It wasn't an opinion show, and was tightly scripted, but the host still managed to add his interjections between stories. It's as though somebody figured out a way to clean up the control room banter and put it on the air. I liked delivering scripts to him.

Shep was dogged by rumors—both in the building and in the rest of the media—that he was both secretly liberal and secretly gay. It's not clear which of those two things, if confirmed, would hurt his career at Fox more.

4:00 P.M.–5:00 P.M.

Your World with Neil Cavuto was Fox's daily business show, timed to coincide with the market closing. The show was mostly notable for finding gratuitous ways to shoehorn tits and ass into a financial broadcast. For example, interviewing the CEO of Hooters while he was flanked by three of his waitresses—in uniform, of course—during a segment about the restaurant industry. Or doing a piece on the "economics of spring break," and using it as an excuse to run nonstop b-roll of co-eds bouncing around Cancun in bikinis. Cavuto was utterly shameless, and quite possibly a genius, but we did not have to deliver scripts to him. He had his own minions who did it for him, while we gathered our strength for the final push of the day.

5:00 P.M.–6:00 P.M.

The Big Story with John Gibson was my last script-running hour of the day. The show was sort of an O'Reilly Lite, with the white-haired Gibson offering a more low energy version of Bill O'Reilly's cranky right-wing populism. The outrage was the same, but the wattage was lower, the shouting muted to a dull rumble, as if a dimmer switch had been slid down ever so slightly.

At this point, my day was done. But the network kept going. Let's run through the rest of the shows, just so we're all on the same page.

6:00 P.M.–7:00 P.M.

Special Report with Brit Hume was the political roundup, which was handled entirely by Fox's DC bureau. Hume (he of the aforementioned neck bolts), a crusty veteran newsman and former ABC correspondent, had a chip on his shoulder after twenty years of being forced to sublimate his conservative impulses, and the anger sometimes seeped into his broadcasts. That being said, the DC bureau took journalism a lot more seriously than the ratings-obsessed New York crew. As a result, the six P.M. hour was probably the most credible, serious show on our air, and was the closest thing to "straight" news we had with the exception of any time Shep was on the air. Speaking of which . . .

7:00 P.M.–8:00 P.M.

The Fox Report with Shepard Smith was basically an evening version of *Studio B*. But where *Studio* was laid-back, *Report* was frantic, cramming almost twice as many stories into an hour. Shep sometimes seemed out of breath as he went from story to story, the camera constantly swirling around him and attacking him from different angles as if possessed.

8:00 P.M.–9:00 P.M.

The O'Reilly Factor with Bill O'Reilly kicked off the network's primetime lineup. Bill, as the most powerful, controversial, and highest-rated host on Fox, was also the network's most well-known personality, a mascot of sorts. He was who most people thought of when they thought of Fox News. As someone who didn't watch the channel that much before I took the job, he was most recognizable to me as the guy who picked a fight with George Clooney over the funds raised by the 9/11 celebrity telethon (Bill was mad because he thought the cash wasn't being disbursed fast enough); the guy who cut off the microphone of a guest, Jeremy Glick, the son of a 9/11 victim (Bill was mad that Glick was opposing the invasion of Iraq); and the guy who got rapper Ludacris fired from a Pepsi endorsement deal (Bill was—wait for it—mad because Ludacris used dirty words in his songs).

9:00 P.M.–10:00 P.M.

Hannity & Colmes was the second-highest-rated show on the network, and don't think that Hannity or O'Reilly ever forgot the pecking order, a source of constant tension between the two.

Alan Colmes was largely an observer from the sidelines for the eternal dick-measuring contest that the network's two superstars were locked into. Presumably Colmes, who was a fairly smart, pragmatic guy, realized that despite the decent chemistry he exhibited with his conservative cohost, he was completely expendable—easily replaced with another liberal to be determined. Consequently, he didn't waste any time playing ratings-based, power-trippy mind games with O'Reilly. He was just happy to be allowed in the building.

As the most openly partisan Republican show on the network, *H&C* attracted a fair amount of scorn and derision from the rank and file: "Goddamn, Hannity is completely unwatchable lately," I heard one daytime producer say in the control room during one of my first few weeks. "You're acting like it was ever watchable in the first place," one of the techs responded. (And these were two conservatives I'd heard casually trashing John Kerry a week earlier. Even they were bored with the constant repetition of Republican talking points that the show had devolved into.)

10:00 P.M.–11:00 P.M.

On the Record with Greta Van Susteren was the final live show of the day. Greta, a lawyer/pundit who ascended to fame in the 1990s based on her analysis of the O. J. Simpson trial, had been a CNN host until Ailes poached her in 2002. She was an odd fit for Fox. She ran in conspicuously Democratic circles—her husband was a big Clinton donor and supporter. And even worse, she was plain-looking, a poor fit for a network teeming with sparkly blond prom queens in the anchor chair. But Greta's focus was not political; she was much more interested in legal and crime stories, and rarely let her own political opinions slip into the show. And in the months before her new show started, she opted for a mind-boggling amount of plastic surgery, which, to her credit, she openly admitted to, appearing on the cover of *People* magazine in before and after photos.

After Greta signed off at eleven P.M. every night, the schedule went into repeats, re-airing the prime-time shows until the morning, when *Fox & Friends* picked things up again.

Aside from all the first-day excitement surrounding the death of Don Corleone, my time running scripts had flown by with little incident. Even though I got the hang of it after a day or two, Camie stayed on as my "trainer" for a full two weeks. We'd spend all day shoulder to shoulder at our cramped little workstation, taking turns sprinting the printed pages down the hall to the studio. We fell into an easy rhythm, keeping conversation to a minimum while the shows were on air, communicating in glances, gestures, flicks of the head, or arches of the eyebrows. She had a habit of fiddling with her jewelry while staring at the screen—absentmindedly twisting her strand of pearls until I thought they might break, or fingering the silver charms dangling from the bracelet on her wrist—as if the fidgeting itself might cause the senior producer's initials to pop up next to the script's slug line, allowing us to print. And then her sigh of relief, the sharp exhalation of breath when she saw initials finally appear in the rundown, followed by a flurry of hitting CTRL-P on the keyboard, the laser printer spitting out pages, the brief, mutually deferential tug-of-war over whose turn it was to run ("I'll go." "No, you went the last two times. I'll go this time."), then the hustling through the convoluted route that brought us to the studio, and finally depositing the bundle of paper onto the desk in front of the anchor, who was usually only half paying attention, waiting for the commercial break to end.

In our downtime we'd chat—about what school had been like for each of us (she'd gone to a small, genteel Southern college, one where the girls wore big floppy-brimmed hats and sundresses to the football games, which went a long way toward explaining her current wardrobe), about moving to New York (she felt it was a big transition, even though her hometown was only two hours away, somewhere in Connecticut), and once, briefly, about politics. I was the one who broached the topic, actually, after hearing her scoff quietly to herself while a John Kerry sound bite was playing.

"So I take it you're pretty into the, you know, politics of this place?" I said.

"Oh, sure," she said, nodding. "I think everyone is, right?"

I shrugged. "I dunno. I'm not really that political of a guy, I guess." I felt bad fibbing to her so soon after meeting, but I wasn't ready to blow my cover just yet—at least not until I'd figured the lay of the land a little better.

After two weeks, it was time to split up the band. Camie had told Siegendorf that I was more than fully trained, ready to go it alone, and he'd pulled her to start on other duties.

"You sure you're ready?" she'd asked me on our last day together.

"Piece of cake," I said, cockily flashing her my winningest grin. "I can do this shit blindfolded by this point."

My first screwup came two days later.

It was during the taping of *Studio B* with Shepard Smith. I was waiting backstage for Shep to finish a segment so I could drop off his scripts. I heard him deliver the tease that meant the show was going into the break, something like "we'll be back in two minutes." Taking his cue, I stepped from behind the wall and began to stride toward his anchor desk. I'd barely taken two paces when I heard a voice behind me hiss quietly but insistently: "Wait!"

I glanced over my shoulder at the stage manager, a look of panic on her face, frantically beckoning me to rejoin her backstage.

I froze in my tracks, suddenly noticing that one of the jib cameras—which was on the end of a pivoting fifteen-foot-long arm, allowing it to perform swooping vertical movements—had a red light glowing on the front and was pointing straight at me.

Red light meant on-air.

The director had apparently decided to show one last wide shot of Shep as the program cut to commercial. *Studio B* did this move a lot; it was a flashy little outro to show off the gleaming high-tech set. A set that currently had a twenty-two-year-old production assistant standing in the middle of it, mouth agape, frozen in place with a wide-eyed stare directly into the camera lens.

The on-air light blinked off as I was looking at it.

"And, *now* we're clear," the stage manager said, stepping out from behind the wall and marching toward me angrily.

"What the fuck was that?" she said.

"Uhhh . . . I thought we were in a commercial break," I answered.

"Well, we are *now*."

"Was I in the shot?"

"Oh, yeah, you were in the shot."

"I'm really sorry," I said, horrified to have screwed up so early. "I'm kinda new here."

"No shit," she said, before turning and storming back to her post.

I sheepishly walked up to Shep at his desk and slid the stack of scripts in front of him.

He grinned at me. "If you're trying to start an on-air career, you're going about it the wrong way, pal," he said, laughing.

Thankfully, word of my fuck-up didn't get back to Jim Siegendorf, and two weeks later, I had my own scripts trainee, along with the promise that as soon as he was ready to go it alone, they'd move me along to other duties.

My trainee was a guy fresh off the bus from South Carolina with the unlikely name Red Robertshaw. Red was a natural script PA, and took it very, very seriously, sprinting through the halls even when he wasn't pressed for time, sweating every single missed page, to the point where I was almost shamed by my own lack of effort.

Red also wore a tie to work, which I found excessive. I wore khakis and a button-down, which actually put me in the upper echelons of PA formal wear; this was mostly a jeans, polo shirt, and sneakers crowd. But Red's tie elevated him another level above me, and I started to resent him for it. *Hardworking AND well dressed? Who the fuck was this kid trying to impress?*

Once I had Red trained to my satisfaction,[14] I went to Siegendorf and told him that the new guy was ready to go.

"All right," Jim said. "Camie says you're a fast learner, so we're going to put you on videotape."

Thank fucking Christ. I made a mental note to thank Camie for sparing me the indignity of the graphics department.

While she was still training me, Camie had explained that there were three types of PA duty at Fox: scripts, graphics, and videotape. Scripts was the easiest, and the first job for all new employees, stage one of a weeding-out process. Unless you were supremely stupid, or the victim of unfortunate timing (i.e., you're the last new employee right before a hiring drought), you'd be off scripts in less than two months.

Graphics was a bit more complex. Fox had a large graphics department that churned out on-air visuals. The small pictures with the headlines underneath that appeared next to an anchor's head as he was reading a news item were called over-the-shoulders—OTS for short. Larger graphics—anything from maps to poll results to bullet-pointed lists to photos—were called fullscreens, usually abbreviated as FS.

The job of the graphics production assistant was to act as go-between for show producers (the ones ordering the graphics) and the artists (the ones producing them). The graphics department was separated from the newsroom both physically (they were based in an airy second-floor workspace with giant windows) and temperamentally (the pace in the graphics department was leisurely compared to the frantic rush that often gripped the newsroom).

What Camie was too polite to tell me but I soon picked up from

---

14 He was probably ready to go well before I realized. I found out later he was sharp as a tack, but before I got to know him better, his thick Southern accent caused me to unfairly dock him a couple dozen IQ points.

other PAs, was that graphics was not considered a choice assignment. The department was regarded as something of a joke, known for turning in work that was late and often riddled with errors. If a PA was assigned there, it was generally assumed it was because Siegendorf had determined that he or she couldn't hack it at a more important job.

That left videotape. Video was obviously incredibly important for a TV news organization, and the vast majority of it at Fox was handled almost exclusively by PAs.

There were some feeble attempts at quality control and oversight, but most of the time the requirement for a quick turnaround and deliberate understaffing meant that roughly 90 percent of video that went on the air at Fox was seen exactly once before being broadcast to millions of Americans. These gatekeepers were, by and large, production assistants fresh out of college who were barely trained, laxly supervised, and paid dog shit.

And now I was joining their ranks.

April 11, 2012—11:51 A.M.

I waited until I was two blocks away, in the thick of Times Square, to pull out my phone. I had never before been so thankful for thick throngs of camera-toting tourists. Normally unbearable, today they were my shield, allowing me to blend in—a relief to me, just in case my paranoia was well founded and there was in fact someone tailing me.

I dialed my phone.

"This is John," the voice said.

John Cook was a writer and editor for *Gawker*, and my main contact. Speaking in espionage terms, if I was indeed a mole, that would make him my case officer.

"Hey, it's Joe."

"Okay, fill me in. I assume you saw Mediaite. Is it true? Did they catch you?"

I looked around. Still no sign of any company stooges.

"If they found me, it's news to me. I just walked unfettered out of the News Corp. building. No one tried to stop me. None of my bosses have asked to talk to me today."

"So why is Fox saying they have you?" John asked.

"My best guess is that they're bluffing. They're just trying to smoke me out, hoping that I'll panic or do something to give myself away."

"So they don't know it's you?"

"I can't imagine them letting me sit in that building even one second longer if they actually thought it was me."

"Okay." John paused, thinking. "I'm going to put up a post saying that they haven't gotten you. In the meantime, can you find a way to take a picture of something from inside or near the building, something with a clock or something like that, that proves that you're still roaming free?"

I immediately thought of the time-and-temperature sign across the street from 1211, the one I had noticed when I was sweatily awaiting my job interview.

"I might have something," I said. But then it hit me. "On second thought, they know I'm outside right now. Anyone can see that I'm not sitting at my desk. If *Gawker* puts up a picture, it won't be too big a leap for them to make that connection. Assuming they don't know already."

"Yeah, I guess so," John agreed. "Okay, maybe you'll think of something else. In the meantime, I'll get this post up saying you're still a free man. Is there anything else tying you to us?"

I patted the bag slung over one shoulder, containing my iPad with its reams of incriminating text.

"There's still one thing. But I'm taking care of it right now."

CHAPTER 4

Paradise by the On-Air Light

Y ou've been here, what—a month?" Marybeth asked, looking back over her shoulder at me. I nodded, and she turned back to her computer screen, shaking her head with a smile.

"One month, and you're already training to cut tape?" she said. "You know what you'd be doing at CNN after a month? Coffee runs. And not even on your own. They'd still be *training* you on coffee runs."

It was my first day in the videotape department, and Marybeth, the slim, pretty brunette PA that Siegendorf had tapped to get me up to speed, was attempting to *lay down some truth*. She sounded like a grizzled veteran, despite having less than six months on the job under her belt.

As near as I could tell, her knowledge of conditions at CNN was based entirely on rumor and hearsay, both of which were rampant in the PA pod, the small area in the back of the newsroom where all the tape production assistants sat. For example, it was *common knowledge* that MSNBC paid production assistants much better than Fox; the downside was that working for them, you'd be forced to commute to their headquarters in Secaucus, New Jersey.[15] CNN was also *known* to

---

15 It was only three miles as the crow flies from midtown Manhattan, but thanks to the vagaries of New York/New Jersey public transit, it would have added an extra forty-five minutes of travel time for most of us. Also, the psychological effect of being banished to a relative backwater when most of us had come to conquer the media capital of the world

offer higher compensation, but allegedly didn't trust their production assistants with anything aside from menial tasks.

Marybeth kept up a monologue about how lucky I was to be in the position I was in as other PAs swarmed around us, going about their business. The others were cutting for the hours; the nine A.M. news-wheel had two production assistants assigned, the ten A.M. had a differ-ent two, the eleven A.M. had yet another pair, and so on, all day long. The pairs of PAs were picked out from the pool and scheduled by Jim Siegendorf and his deputy, Nina. But Marybeth and I weren't in that pool; our job was to produce tape for the daytime cut-ins, short two-minute news updates that hit in the middle of other shows (*cutting into their programming*).[16] I was watching over her shoulder as she looked at the rundown for the cut-in, a short list of five or six stories and their corresponding videotapes.

"One of the upsides of working here," Marybeth was saying, "is that they give you a lot of responsibility right away."

"What are some of the downsides?" I asked.

She pursed her lips, thinking. "I'll show you." She stood and grabbed a tape off her desk, some footage of President Bush that we needed for the next cut-in. "Follow me."

She led me over to a row of edit rooms that lined one of the news-room walls. We paused outside one of the rooms. The door was closed, but through the glass partition, I could see a backward-baseball-cap-wearing video editor hunched over a sandwich, watching the small TV next to his editing rig, which he'd switched from Fox News to ESPN. (Editors generally flouted the rule that our televisions, which received

---

was enough to keep any of us from seriously considering a move, extra money or no. This is probably why MSNBC eventually moved out of Secaucus and into 30 Rock with their bigger siblings at NBC News proper.

16   If it seems redundant, putting a two-minute news update in the middle of an hour of news, it's because *it is* redundant. But the rationale is that the cut-in team stays on top of some of the ongoing stories that the hour-show teams are either ignoring or giving short shrift; this allows the hours to focus their attention on longer, more in-depth reports and interview segments, and not have to worry about updating viewers constantly on what the stock market is doing, or what's going on in Europe, or whatever other foreign place that Fox viewers don't care about is having a crisis at the moment.

most of the basic cable channels, had to be tuned to Fox—or at least one of our competitors—at all times.)

"They *love* to understaff here," Marybeth said. "So that means we don't get an editor assigned to us. We either have to interrupt a PA who's cutting for one of the other shows and ask to borrow their editor, or scrounge up an editor on his lunch break and convince him to do it for us."

"How do you do that?"

She smiled. "Just watch."

She rapped on the door lightly with her knuckles, then turned the knob, easing the door open a crack and poking her head in.

"Go away," the editor said, without even looking up from his sandwich to see who was intruding. "I'm on lunch."

"Chris . . ." Marybeth cooed. "That's no way to talk to your favorite PA *in the world*." He sat up and swiveled around in his chair as she pushed the door open all the way and glided into the room. His face lit up when he saw her.

"MB! How's it going, girl?"

She laid a hand on his arm. "Oh, you know me. Can't complain." She made a pouty face. "But I can't find any editors to cut this tape. And it hits in *ten minutes*. Could you cut it for me? *Please please please?*"

Chris wiped his hands on a napkin and sighed. "What is it? *I guess* I could probably do it for you."

Marybeth beamed. "Oh, could you? Thank you, thank you! It's just Bush talking. It'll be *so quick*."

"Sure. Give me the tape."

She handed it to him. "You're the best."

He slid the source tape into the deck, twisting dials and punching buttons. As President Bush's face popped up on-screen, Chris seemed to notice for the first time that I was in the room.

"Who's this kid?" he asked Marybeth.

"This is Joe. He's a new PA. I'm training him this week."

"Hey, Joe," Chris said. "Where you from, man?"

"Hi," I said. "Cincinnati."

"Ohio!" he barked with a laugh. "How big is your family's farm?"

I frowned. "Why does everyone keep asking me that?"

A few minutes later, we were back at Marybeth's desk, freshly cut tape in hand. I watched as she labeled the cassette and the box with a numbered label, and typed the corresponding digits into the rundown on the computer.

"So that's your method?" I asked. "You just flirt with the editor until he does what you want?"

She grinned. "Yup. It gets the job done, right?"

"That's fine for you, but what the hell am I supposed to do?"

"I dunno," she said, shrugging. "Just go to the girl editors?" She yawned and stretched in her chair. "That, or grow a pair of tits."

The Fox News hierarchy was dead simple: Roger was in charge.

The man who a startling number of employees referred to only as "Mr. Ailes" was something of a mythic figure in the company, especially among those who had been there in the early days. To listen to some of them, Roger had single-handedly built the network from the ground up through sheer force of will.

It all seemed a little much to me. There's no doubt that Fox News's rise was impressive, meteoric, and unprecedented; in less than eight years, it had gone from a bare-bones operation with minuscule viewership to a just-slightly-more-than-bare-bones operation with more viewers than CNN and MSNBC combined. But the worship of Ailes as some sort of renegade television genius was maybe giving him too much credit. Yes, he had come up with a good concept, bringing the talk radio model to cable news to attract conservatives who were underserved by the market; and yes, he had a good eye for talent, picking O'Reilly, Hannity, and Shep Smith when they were still essentially unknowns and molding them into stars. But the success of Fox News owed just as much to luck, timing, and Uncle Rupert's dump trucks of money as it did to anything Roger Ailes had done. With Fox News he had hit on a serendipitous combination that was not easily repeatable, TV genius or no. (And even money can't put you over the top sometimes, as evidenced by the still-anemic ratings of Fox Business Network, launched in 2008 to much fanfare.)

But I kept those treasonous thoughts to myself, wary of becoming an office apostate early in my career. Also, the PA pod was rife with rumors—only half joking—that Roger had bugged the whole building with hidden microphones and some CIA-developed software that listened for mentions of his name to weed out disloyal employees. (Another popular theory: The hidden microphones were there to snag any secret liberals. Either way, I kept my mouth shut.)

This widespread institutional paranoia was probably symptomatic of the very paranoid man at the top of the institution. A fascinating 2011 profile in *Rolling Stone* magazine[17] plumbed the depths of Roger's apparently disturbed psyche:

> Ailes is also deeply paranoid. Convinced that he has personally been targeted by Al Qaeda for assassination, he surrounds himself with an aggressive security detail and is licensed to carry a concealed handgun. . . . Murdoch installed Ailes in the corner office on Fox's second floor at 1211 Avenue of the Americas in Manhattan. The location made Ailes queasy: It was close to the street, and he lived in fear that gay activists would try to attack him in retaliation over his hostility to gay rights. . . . Barricading himself behind a massive mahogany desk, Ailes insisted on having "bomb-proof glass" installed in the windows—even going so far as to personally inspect samples of high-tech plexiglass, as though he were picking out new carpet. Looking down on the street below, he expressed his fears to Cooper, the editor he had tasked with up-armoring his office. "They'll be down there protesting," Ailes said. "Those gays."

---

17 There was much consternation and confusion within the building when the *Rolling Stone* article came out. *Why would Roger give so much access to a reporter from that liberal rag?* Everyone had a theory, but to my eyes, it seemed to be an ill-conceived attempt at image-burnishing that had gone awry.

Ailes made no mention of "those gays" during any of the biannual
State of the Business speeches he'd give in the middle of the newsroom,
my earliest contact with him. Some flunky would set up a little microphone and underpowered speaker, and producers, editors, and PAs
would wander over and arrange themselves, awkwardly standing among
the cubicles, some of which were occupied by annoyed people in the
midst of doing their actual jobs. (At a twenty-four-hour cable news network, you were never able to schedule an event when everyone was off
duty at the same time. There was always someone, or several someones,
who were getting screwed by a loud, distracting corporate pep rally
taking place in their laps.) Roger would speak for about half an hour,
revving up the troops with stats about ratings victories, how many
households and cable systems we were available on, how well the network had covered various recent events, and so on. At the end he'd open
the floor to questions from the crowd, which tended to be either extremely technical ("What's the timeline on our conversion to a digital
tapeless system?") or sycophantic ("To what factors do you attribute our
continued ratings dominance?"). He'd invariably toss out an anecdote or
two about his past work in television, one of his favorites being the time
he worked for *The Mike Douglas Show* and had overseen the construction
of a fully operational bowling alley in the studio in a matter of hours.
(The moral of the story: Hard work? Ingenuity? I can't quite remember.
He told it many times, and each time it had a different point.) The
funny, affable Uncle Roger who showed up at these meetings was nothing like the sharp-elbowed, cutthroat Mr. Ailes who had built the company in his own image.

The ideology at Fox was strictly a top-down affair. Roger was a conservative. All of his deputies were conservatives. Most of the hosts were
conservatives, or at least were good at pretending to be while on television, if they knew what was good for them. But under that, it was a
more mixed bag. The ideology varied job by job, and show by show. For
example: While Hannity's staff was mostly simpatico with him,
O'Reilly plainly didn't care one bit about the ideology of his employees.

He never once in five years asked me my personal opinion. His staff's political views were totally irrelevant to him, in fact, because the only viewpoints that ever made it onto the show were his own.

Directly under Roger were several vice presidents. Each VP had a different and somewhat vague title—VP of programming, VP of development, VP of news editorial—but in practice their roles were often quite similar: They were Roger's hatchet-men (and at least one woman, as of this writing). The VPs, as near as I could tell, were all staunch conservatives, too. Whether by coincidence or design, Roger had effectively surrounded himself with fellow travelers.

One level below the VPs were executive producers. As I said earlier, the purview of an EP could vary. Some were in charge of a single show, some were in charge of multiple shows or entire chunks of programming, and some, like Siegendorf, were managers. This was the level where the ideological firewall started to go wobbly. There's no doubt that most of the EPs were true believers, but a few of them seemed to be moderate, and at least one whom I knew, when he got a few drinks in him, gave several distinct hints that he was a frustrated liberal trapped in a nightmare of his own making.

The next level down was senior producer. An SP on one of the smaller shows (a newswheel, or a weekend show) was generally the boss; on one of the more important shows (a prime-time show or *Fox & Friends*), an SP was high-level but not in charge. The senior producers tended to be the most openly right-wing people in the whole building. I was confused for a while as to how SPs ended up to the right of EPs, but someone eventually pointed out to me that most of the seniors had come up through the ranks at Fox, earning their promotions by slavishly toeing the company line, while a lot of the execs had been imported from other networks.

Under senior producers were producers, the utility players of the newsroom. Producers could book guests or select stories or time out the shows, ensuring that the commercial breaks hit at the right times (this was also known as "line producing"). Producers were generally too busy and harried to be ideological, but the smart, ambitious ones who wanted to eventually be promoted to seniors knew to occasionally let their conserva-flags fly.

It was in the scrum of the bottom two levels where the ideological diversity really started to ramp up. People outside of Fox tended to assume that the whole building was filled with lockstep conservatives, but at a certain point, it was simply impossible to staff a business based in New York City, and consisting of people who were attracted to the field of journalism, without letting at least a few pinkos in.

So the ranks of the associate producers—the title generally given to guest bookers, writers, and segment producers—and the production assistants were actually quite mixed. The conservatives, who made up at least 50 percent, as near as I could tell, were naturally not afraid to speak their minds at the office—like Camie, the pearl-wearing ingenue who had trained me on scripts. Another 30 percent were professed moderates, or at least agnostics who claimed they didn't care about politics either way. And the remaining 20 percent, the ones who tended to keep their mouths shut and roll their eyes whenever the discussion turned political? Well, those people didn't tend to last very long at the company. To borrow Mitt Romney's parlance, they'd eventually self-deport.

Except for the one idiot who wrote this book. He decided to stick around.

For the entire month of August, I shadowed Marybeth, taking notes. Tape was a simple process in theory:

- The producer picks a video by writing a slug line in the rundown with clear, concise, and specific instructions.
- You find a source tape for the video, cue it up to the right spot, and bring it to an editor in one of the tiny edit rooms lining the walls of the newsroom.

- The editor operates the machinery, copying shots from the source tape to a blank tape while you watch and offer guidance.
- The finished product will be a tape that's ready for air, about forty seconds in length, with ten extra seconds of "pad," footage that ensures the screen won't go to black if the director accidentally runs the tape too long.
- You slap a numbered sticker on the tape, type the number into the rundown, and give the tape to the tape coordinator, who will insert it into the deck in the playback room and play it at the designated time.

That's in theory. In practice, what happens is this:

- The producer asks you for a tape with a vague line in the rundown like "VO—TROOPS."
- You instant-message the producer, asking for clarification. "Do you want American troops or Iraqi troops? Do you want them training, or on patrol, or in combat? Do you want the newest stuff? Or can I use older stuff that's better-looking?"
- The producer responds: "i don't give a shit just pick something."
- You guess the producer would probably want the newest stuff, and decide to pull something from the latest Reuters tape feed.
- The Reuters tape is missing from the shelf in the tape library—it's been checked out. In its place is an index card with a person's last name, and a phone number scrawled in an illegible hand that you can't decipher.
- After dialing what you think is the right phone number, and getting someone who works in the mailroom and has no idea what you're talking about, you decide to use the

newsroom's overhead paging system[18] to track down whomever is using the tape you need. You despise the sound of
your own voice as it's broadcast across the entire newsroom by speakers embedded in the ceiling: "If you have
the Reuters tape from the last hour, please call me . . ."

- You immediately get a call from the offending PA: "Oh,
you need this tape? Sorry about that. It's just been sitting
on my desk for, like, an hour. I'm not even sure I need it
anymore. You can come get it if you want."

- Tape finally in hand, you bring it to a screening machine,
a hulking VCR that's inexplicably the size of a large microwave oven. It's in real bad shape, held together by chewing
gum and duct tape, buttons coming off, control wheel
barely responsive.[19] You search for the right portion of the
video, a ninety-second snippet of a two-hour tape. You
pray to the God of Production Assistants that the decrepit
machine doesn't go haywire and eat the tape, as it tended
to do every third or fourth time you used it.

- Tape in hand and cued up to the right spot, you find an
edit room, which is occupied by a PA from the extremely
video-heavy *Fox Report*. She has a stack of twenty-eight
tapes waiting to be cut, and a frantic, hunted look in her
eyes. "Can I get in here?" you ask, giving a meek, hopeful

---

18 The overhead page was an amazing feature, allowing you to use your phone to dial
into an intercom system that broadcast your voice throughout the entire newsroom. Ostensibly, it was there to reach people who had stepped away from their desks and were
needed urgently. In practice it was used to prank the entire newsroom. For example, a
writer for the *Fox Report*, during a slow news day right before Christmas, dialed up an
overhead page, then simply placed his phone receiver next to his computer speakers, which
were playing a novelty version of "Silent Night" featuring the Star Wars character Chew-
bacca warbling the tune. He walked away from his desk and let the strangely beautiful
melody play for five minutes.

19 "They bought like two hundred of these decks when the network started," Marybeth
told me in 2004. "But they're having trouble fixing them now because the manufacturer
doesn't even make them anymore. Our engineering department is buying old decks off
eBay for spare parts. Apparently, we're the only company in the world that still uses this
format. Everyone else has gone digital."

smile. "I just have one tape to cut." The *Fox Report* PA show-ily glances at her massive stack of tapes, then to you, raising her eyebrows and giving you a dramatic *are-you-fucking-kidding-me* look. She shakes her head, saying, "I'm really crashing here. Can you find someone else?"

- You go to the edit room next door, which is empty even though, according to the paper schedule posted on the door, it's supposed to be occupied by an editor. You find the editor in question at an empty desk nearby, using a computer to rearrange the lineup of his fantasy football team. "Can you cut something for me?" you ask. "It's for a cut-in. It hits in, like, fifteen minutes." The editor sighs and looks up at you wearily. "Isn't there anyone else on right now?" You don't answer. He sighs again, gets up slowly, and makes his way to the edit room.

- Once he's seated at the machine, you hand him the tape and he pops it in. "I need forty seconds," you say, watching over his shoulder. "Just troops marching around. Whatever shots are there." The editor scans through the tape. "You've only got twenty-two seconds of troops," he says. "The rest of it is just talking heads of Iraqi officials. In Arabic." Cursing yourself for not screening the footage in its entirety, you look at the clock and decide that now is not the time to be choosy: "Just do it. I'll call it twenty seconds even. Freeze the last shot."[20]

- You deliver the cut tape to playback, go back to your desk, and plug the ID number into the rundown, and mark it *:20*, indicating twenty seconds running time. And you still have five minutes to spare until your cut-in! Job well done.

---

20 This was a common trick if you didn't have enough footage to spare. It certainly wasn't ideal for the picture to freeze on air, but it was even worse if the tape went to a black screen.

- Three minutes later, your phone rings. It's your producer. He's in the control room and is absolutely losing his shit. "WHAT THE FUCK? Why is that troops tape only twenty seconds? The script times out to more than thirty! We're up after this commercial. Find a new fucking tape, stat!"

- You jump up from your desk, fly to the shelf with all the tapes that had been cut for previous shows, and grab the first one you see that's labeled TROOPS and has a running time of :40. You catch a glimpse of the closest TV, which shows they're back from commercial, which means that the tape currently in your hands is supposed to be on the air in about fifteen seconds.

- It's time for a Death Run. You sprint, full speed, toward playback. Other PAs see or hear you coming and step out of the way. "TAPE'S COMING!" you scream to the playback operator as you run.

- You burst into the playback room, hand the operator the tape, and watch as she feeds it into the deck, barely three seconds before the director's voice on the intercom tells her to play it.

- You watch as the tape plays, troops patrolling on-screen for a full nine seconds before the anchor finishes reading and the shot cuts back to his face.

- When you get back to your desk, there's an instant message from the producer: "Guess we didn't need the full forty seconds after all. Thanks anyway. [winking smiley face]"

Of course none of that needed to happen. There was no reason why Fox, which, by the time I joined, had been in business for nearly a decade and had been number one in the ratings for more than two years, should still have been running such a rinky-dink operation, with broken-down tape machines, control rooms that smelled like a sewer whenever it rained more than half an inch, chronic intentional understaffing, and a workforce composed of barely trained, underpaid children like myself. But that was the business model, and the ratings were good enough—and the on-air product was just this side of mistake-free enough—that there was no incentive for the bosses to change it.

───

I never did find out if the Meat Loaf Story was true or not.

Oh, sure, everyone *said* it was true. There were even a few people—some of the video editors, a few of the older PAs—who swore they had seen it go down. They had been on duty that day and had seen the whole thing play out while watching one of the always-on TVs in the newsroom. Or they had pulled the tape after the fact, going to the vault where all the air checks were kept, bringing it back to the newsroom, huddling around a screener, five or six of them at a time, laughing their asses off.

The story went like this:

The PA was new, but not *that* new. Anyway, everyone agreed that he had been around at least long enough to have known better. He's covering the eleven A.M. hour. The news item is a brief one, just a twenty-second read by the anchor. It's about Meat Loaf, the singer. You know—fat guy, long hair, gothic clothes, *Rocky Horror*—that dude. He's in the hospital, the bulletin says—he'd fallen off a stage, or gotten dehydrated or food poisoning or something like that. Either way, he's in the hospital, so the producer sticks a quick item about it into the rundown. No more than a twenty-second read, sandwiched between other short trivial entertainment updates. It should go real quick, bing-bang-boom: weekend box-office grosses, latest celebrity wedding, Meat Loaf hospitalized, *American Idol* results, then straight into commercial break.

The producer, naturally, wants video of Meat Loaf to go with the story. He could have asked for a fullscreen, just a photo with the guy's name under it, but moving video is always better. If it's going to be up on-screen for twenty seconds, that's an eternity to have a still picture with no motion. This is supposed to be a dynamic broadcast, right? So, yeah, video is better. The producer checks the wires, and there's no new video, nothing good like Meat Loaf collapsing on stage, or paparazzi swarming as he's wheeled into the hospital on a gurney (that would have been *so* perfect, right?). But you work with what you have, so file footage it is. He makes a slug line in the rundown:

VO—Meat Loaf—File

The PA, by most accounts a go-getter, is actually running ahead of schedule. He's paired with a partner for the hour, and together they divide up the rundown, putting their initials in the rundown next to the tapes that they're going to be responsible for. His initials go in next to the Meat Loaf tape. He heads to the edit room, an editor cuts the tape, the PA slaps a numbered sticker on it, a corresponding sticker on the box, and plugs the digits into the rundown. The tape coordinator comes to get the cassette, sticks it on her little cart in the playback room where it sits, waiting to get played in the next hour. Everything is going just fine.

Cut to an hour later. The show is under way. The entertainment update segment starts. They get to the Meat Loaf story. The anchor starts reading: "Singer Meat Loaf was hospitalized today. The legendary rocker . . ."

The director in the control room yells, "ROLL TAPE!"

The tape starts rolling, and what plays on the big screen in the control room, what plays on the hundreds of tiny TVs in the newsroom, what plays in the millions of living rooms across America, is file footage . . .

Of meat loaf.

The food.

It's absolute pandemonium in the control room. The senior producer is fucking flipping out: "Kill the b-roll! Back to the anchor! Now! Do it! Do it! Do it!"

But the director is on the fucking floor, laughing, just howling, and he refuses to drop the video! "No fuckin' way," he says. "This is too goddamn good."

So the anchor, consummate professional that he is—even though he can clearly see in the monitor facing him, the tiny screen hanging right under the camera lens, that someone completely fucked up the video—keeps reading, giving details about Meat Loaf being dehydrated or breaking his leg or whatever; and all the while, America is looking at generic video of a smiling housewife slicing up a scrumptious-looking loaf of beef and serving it to her family.

Finally, after what seems like an eternity, the script ends. The director grudgingly gives the order to switch back to the anchor.

"That, um, obviously was not the right video," the anchor says. "Our apologies to Mr. Loaf."

The PA actually doesn't catch as much hell as he should have, because everyone, with the exception of the senior producer, thought it was so fucking funny. It turns out the poor dumb kid didn't even realize there was a singer named Meat Loaf—an embarrassing lapse in pop culture knowledge, sure, but maybe not an unforgivable mistake for someone who wasn't even a glimmer in his dad's eye when *Bat Out of Hell* was released.

What *was* unforgivable was that he hadn't bothered to read the script. He just saw the slug line that said MEAT LOAF and immediately started searching for dinner footage. If he had even so much as *glanced* at the script, it would have been immediately obvious that the producer wasn't looking for food.

That story was repeated to me so many times by so many different people while I was training, that as contrived and sit-commy as it sounded, I couldn't help but believe it was true. At the very least, I took the message to heart: Keep your head out of your ass.

Of course there were plenty of on-air mistakes. Luckily, the viewers at home never noticed the vast majority of them. For every single blatantly obvious Meat Loaf incident, there were fifty subtle errors that made air, with the audience none the wiser.

My favorite of these was the story of an unfortunate video editor named Kevin, tasked with producing a video to illustrate a segment on the business of Internet pornography for the pervy four P.M. financial show. The job was simple—take X-rated images off the Internet, blur the naughty parts, and string them together with nice, slow dissolves between the pictures. Kevin dutifully went through the images that one of the show's producers had assembled for him—he actually thought they were relatively tame—and covered up all the bare breasts and butts he came across, using a special editing rig that created video effects like blurs, pixelations, and shapes of all colors, effects that were mostly used to obscure the faces of the innocent and the genitals of the guilty.

The completed tape aired during the segment, and no one thought anything more of it.

A few days later, Kevin's boss, the head of all the video editors, called Kevin into his office. Another editor had been going through the old footage and noticed something on the tape that Kevin had cut. Kevin's boss played the tape for him, and paused it on a picture of two women posing seductively, their naked breasts pixelated.

"Do you notice anything, Kevin?"

"Looks fine to me," Kevin said. "What's the problem?"

"This," the boss said, pointing to the very much un-blurred, very much erect penis in the background of the shot. By some fluke, no one had noticed it—not the producer who'd picked out the picture, not Kevin while he was editing it, and, miraculously, not anyone in the control room when it played live to a million viewers.

"Let's just keep this one between us," the boss said. "I don't think we need to stir up the Cavuto people by telling them you put a boner on their air." None of the higher-ups ever found out.

An image hiding in the background of a shot was the culprit another time when I got into a heated argument with a *Fox Report* PA. She claimed that the video she'd cut of the aftermath of a suicide bombing[21] in Israel showed nothing but crime scene technicians cleaning up debris and placing it into garbage bags. I begged to differ, and grabbed an

---

21   On air, Fox anchors were supposed to refer to these as "homicide bombings," a term that supposedly avoided glorifying the perpetrators but, I suspected, just ended up confusing our viewers.

editor to zoom into one of the shots, which very clearly showed an Israel Defense soldier picking up the severed leg of the bomber.

Clearly, the displaying of aroused members or dismembered limbs was generally frowned upon for a basic cable channel. But Fox had some other less obvious rules about what we couldn't show on air.

"You can't use tape of the Twin Towers going down," Marybeth told me. "The bosses think it upsets people."

"Fair enough," I said. "So what do we use when the producer wants nine-eleven footage?"

"They like that shot of the people running down the street with the dust cloud behind them."

"That makes sense," I said. "There's nothing *too* upsetting about terrified people fleeing for their lives."

Another rule: If we were producing tape of same-sex weddings to illustrate a gay marriage segment, we had to cut away before the couple kissed.

"We showed two guys kissing once, and people at home completely freaked out," Marybeth explained. "Hundreds of calls to the switchboard, thousands of angry e-mails."

Yet another rule—and this one was by no means unique to Fox—if the segment was a discussion about something negative or controversial, we had to be extra careful with the generic b-roll we used to illustrate it. Specifically, we couldn't show any faces, on the off-chance that someone featured in the footage was sitting at home watching and somehow objected to being associated with whatever the topic was.

This most often cropped up in relation to health stories. You'd see producers request videos like "PEOPLE SMOKING—NO FACES" or "EATING FAST FOOD—NO FACES" or "KIDS PLAYING—NO FACES" or, my personal favorite, "FAT PEOPLE—NO FACES" (and its spin-off, "FAT KIDS—NO FACES").

Every so often, Siegendorf would send a camera crew out to expand our no-face footage library. The tapes would come back filled with hours of nothing but obese people walking the streets of Manhattan, secretly shot at a distance, from behind or from the neck down. We'd study those tapes, searching for the perfect shots to use, hypnotized by the jiggling guts spilling out from under too-tight T-shirts, the lumpy asses inexplicably shoved into stretch pants, the unfortunate hefty victims completely unaware that their bulk was condemned to be anonymously ambling across a cable news screen in perpetuity.

The Fox News business model is as follows: Hire gullible twenty-two-year-olds straight out of college, pay them next to nothing, give them minimal training, and set them loose with little to no adult supervision. You'll have high turnover, and many, many on-air mistakes, but you're saving enough money that it's probably worth your while.

I was a direct beneficiary of this business model.

In the fall of 2004, when I was just a few months removed from senior year of college keg stands, there was no rational reason why I should have been given absolute control over videotape for the two-minute news cut-ins that aired during our most important prime-time shows. Yet there I was.

Luckily, I was *very* good at it—my film and television major, the one my father had worried would leave me completely unemployable, had actually left me overly prepared for the field I was in. I worked fast, I picked video that was visually interesting, and—most important—I was unflappable under pressure. I was the anti-Siegendorf. My boss tended to lose his head when the heat was on; I was the exact opposite—in times of extreme stress, I was able to achieve maximum focus, becoming incredibly calm and tuning out all distractions until the emergency was over.

At the end of a month of training, Marybeth had taught me everything there was to know about videotape. I was moved full-time to the evening cut-in unit, which was a small team consisting of two PAs, a writer, a producer, and an anchor. We'd start work at three P.M., when the newsroom was still bustling with activity, and finish at eleven P.M., when it was mostly empty.

My producer in those first few months was a wry, blond twenty-eight-year-old name Angie. She'd started with Fox straight out of New York University as a production assistant, and had climbed her way up the ladder from there.

The writer was a crusty old-timer, a salt-and-pepper-bearded former *National Enquirer* reporter named Lenny. In his downtime—when he wasn't griping about how much he hated John Kerry and his wife, Teresa—he'd regale me with stories about digging through the trash cans at Michael Jackson's Neverland Ranch during the King of Pop's first molestation trial, or digging through trash cans at Gianni Versace's Miami mansion after the fashion designer's murder, or digging through trash cans at John Bobbitt's house after his de-penising.

"Believe it or not, I miss it a little," Lenny said wistfully one night. "It was a dirty job, but it was real investigative journalism, you know? Not like this mindless repackaging of crap that we do now."

I actually found *this crap* to be pretty interesting, at least as far as the process went. I suppose it wasn't *journalism*, per se, in that we didn't do any original reporting or investigating. We'd simply take the reporting of others—most often the wire services, Associated Press or Reuters—and compress it into tidy, two-minute updates that aired once an hour.

Angie, as the producer, got to pick the stories. Two minutes was enough time for about four or five items of twenty to thirty seconds apiece. She'd pull stories from the wires and copy the text into the run-down. Lenny would go through and reword them, condensing and simplifying them so they'd sound good when read aloud.

"The key is to be concise," Lenny told me. "No big words, or words with lots of syllables. Leslie tends to trip over those."

Leslie Stuart was the anchorwoman in our unit. She was a statuesque blonde, with about an inch of height on me in bare feet. (Once you added high heels and the ludicrous beehive helmet that the stylist tortured her hair into every afternoon, she towered over me by almost a full foot.) Despite making six figures for what amounted to about sixteen minutes of actual work spread out over an eight-hour shift, Leslie seemed to be miserable in her job. She'd spend her downtime e-mailing her agent imploring him to convince the bosses to give her a better gig.[22] When she wasn't doing this, she spent her time nodding her head vigorously in agreement with Lenny's anti-Kerry barbs and, if I didn't know any better, flirting with me and some other male production assistants. (Yes, I know it sounds unlikely that the hot Amazonian anchor was flirting with me. Believe me, I was just as incredulous then as you probably are now. But years later, I saw her on TV, saying that she had been a serious alcoholic during the time I was working with her, so that would explain *a lot*.)

After more than three months on the job, I was content. I was pretty settled in and—dare I say—happy. The work was challenging and occasionally entertaining. My schedule was a little strange, but as the exact opposite of a morning person, going in to work at three P.M. appealed to me. And aside from Lenny's constant conservative patter ("I'm so sick of this horse-faced windsurfing *ass* and his bitchy ketchup wife," he'd complain), I wasn't routinely being confronted with the right-wing ideology I'd been so concerned about before I took the gig. I knew it was there, of course—on the TV screen, in the newsroom, all over the executive offices of the second floor—but I was finding it increasingly easy to ignore or laugh off.

I don't know what was more disturbing: that I felt myself slowly sinking deeper into the foxhole, or that I was no longer worried about it.

---

22 Despite being on the air during prime time, the most-watched portion of the day, evening cut-ins is generally considered to be an unprestigious shift for an anchor. It's much better to be the host of your own hour, even if it's one of the garbage-time morning newswheels.

April 11, 2012—11:55 A.M.

I hung up the phone with my *Gawker* contact and tried to calmly, rationally assess the situation. If they didn't suspect me already, I figured I had fifteen, twenty minutes max before my absence would start to raise the alarm.

My bag with the telltale iPad was still hanging off one shoulder. I had to stash it somewhere. But where? My apartment in Brooklyn was too far away, at least an hour's round trip. I flipped my mental Rolodex through various possibilities. Ask a newstand guy to hold it for me? Bribe a cabbie to drive it back to my apartment? Put it under a bench or some other out-of-the-way spot and just pray that it didn't set off a security panic, or simply get taken?

Then it came to me: Rufus.

CHAPTER 5

A White Devil in Brooklyn

N ew York City was always the place for me.

My decision to throw over any misgivings I had about working for Fox was spurred almost entirely by my intense desire to live in New York. I had been infatuated with the city from a surprisingly young age.

My first glimpse of New York must have been the movie *Ghostbusters*, which I saw on home video at a family friend's First Communion party when I was five years old. While the adults were in the backyard drinking and chatting, the kids were in the den watching movies. I wasn't a brave child—the film's climactic rooftop scene with the androgynous lady demon Gozer absolutely scared the training pants off me. But after the dust—and the melted, flaming Stay Puft Marshmallow goop—had cleared, I knew what I wanted to do with the rest of my life: move to New York City and work as a ghostbuster.

My dream-crushing mother kept insisting that it wasn't going to be a viable career option, but I would not be deterred. All I knew was that somewhere in America was a city where wisecracking paranormal-expert scientists, sarcastic mayors, Hasidic Jews, and binge-eating slime ghosts all existed in relative harmony, and I was going to live there when I was a grown-up.

My first visit was with my family when I was twelve years old. I'd been urging my parents to make the trip for years, but it was only after the invention of the Nintendo Game Boy and its child-distracting narcotic effect that they had agreed to load up the minivan and make the six-hundred-plus-mile trek. It was the summer of 1994, just a few months into the Rudy Giuliani administration, and well before his vaunted cleanup of the city's grit and grime. While I was disappointed that there were no Slimers hanging around, I was transfixed by the squeegee guys and three-card monte dealers, whom Giuliani hadn't yet chased out of Times Square.

The most indelible part of the trip for me is an incident that probably should have, in retrospect, scared me away from the place. I was walking with my family in midtown. We were on our way to see FAO Schwarz or Rockefeller Center or one of those other things that tourists dragging children around Manhattan are always on their way to see.

Moving as a family unit down the sidewalk, we approached a guy with dreadlocks, perched on a little stool on a street corner, hawking novelty umbrella hats out of a duffel bag. His business model was suspect, since it wasn't raining out, nor particularly sunny. (Though, to be fair, visitors to New York will buy all kinds of stupid headgear, as my eight-year-old sister's foam Statue of Liberty crown attested.)

"Umbrella hats! Five dollars!" the man called as we walked past, quickly and accurately pegging us as tourists. If my sister's pointy green foam visor hadn't tipped him off, my father's neck-strapped camera, calf-high white socks, khaki shorts, and neon-orange fanny pack probably did the trick.[23]

Now, the correct "New York" thing to do is to cruise past street vendors, panhandlers, and other annoyances without pausing or making eye contact. But my dad, polite to a fault, couldn't do it.

"No, thanks. None for us today, sir," he replied cheerfully, and kept walking.

I was a few paces behind him and the rest of my family, so only I heard the vendor's response.

"White motherfucking devil," the man grumbled angrily, scowling at my dad's back, which was by then twenty feet down the sidewalk. I

---

23 The early '90s were a terrible, terrible time.

stopped and stared goggle-eyed at the cursing umbrella-hat man. He looked at me and shrugged.

I ran to catch up with the family. "Hey, Dad," I said, tugging at my father's shirtsleeve. "That umbrella-hat guy just called you a . . . 'white mother *effing* devil.'"

"He did what?" My father shot an alarmed glance back at the vendor, who was still glaring after us. "All right, let's just keep moving, Joseph," my father said, shooing me along. "Where are your brother and sister?" He circled to round up my younger siblings, lest they, too, have racial invectives hurled at them by crazed, novelty-hat-peddling street people.[24]

Perversely, the incident made me want to live in New York even more. I wasn't scared. I was fascinated by the raucous, chaotic mashup of culture and people. Every other place I went to seemed sleepy and boring by comparison.

Ten years later—almost to the day—I'd finally made it to the city, albeit as a couch crasher. Sloane was a gracious host, and insisted that I could stay as long as I needed to. But after two weeks, I started to sense that her patience was wearing thin. I got the hint after the third time I borrowed her laptop only to find the Web browser suggestively cued up to the Craigslist apartment rentals section. I figured I had two options: find my own place, or seduce her. Since an awkwardly botched flirtation freshman year had convinced Sloane and me that we were better as friends, and only friends, I quickly settled on the former.

That being said, after ten minutes of online perusing of the terrifying apartments that were in Manhattan and were actually in my price range, prostituting myself for lodging was looking like an increasingly attractive option. The only thing stopping me was that I was already basically whoring myself out in my day job, so it seemed ill advised to follow the same path on the domestic front.

---

24 My dad, to this day, thinks of New York City as a dangerous place. He still gets nervous when I, a thirty-year-old adult man, tell him I'm going to ride the subway after ten P.M. "Are you sure that's safe? Why don't you take a cab?"

For the second time in a few months, Rufus Banks came to the rescue. He e-mailed me with the news that he'd gotten the job with FoxNews.com and would be moving to New York within the week. He proposed that we become roommates.

Since Rufus had spent the previous summer in the city and knew the lay of the land better, he took the lead in our apartment search. I told him that my budget was eight hundred dollars a month for my half of the rent. So we agreed that we'd look for a two-bedroom apartment for no more than sixteen hundred dollars a month in a cool Manhattan neighborhood like the West Village or SoHo. The first real estate broker we talked to—once he had finished shrieking with laughter—told us that we'd either have to double our budget, find a third roommate willing to split a one-bedroom three ways, or look in another borough.

So that's how we ended up in the northern part of Brooklyn, in a rapidly gentrifying former industrial neighborhood called Williamsburg. The area was one of the indirect beneficiaries of the aforementioned Giuliani-era cleanup of Manhattan. As crime and garbage diminished in the late 1990s and early 2000s, demand went up—along with rents—in all of Manhattan, including the East Village, a formerly affordable haven for artists and musicians. When the bohemian element of that neighborhood was priced out, they fled to the next most logical place: directly across the East River to "Billyburg."[25]

Currently, in 2013, the gentrification is complete, and rents in Williamsburg rival and sometimes exceed those in Manhattan. However, when Rufus and I moved there in the summer of 2004, the neighborhood was still a little marginal, with new construction plunked uneasily into enclaves that hadn't seen any serious development since the Eisenhower administration. We settled into a building that—judging from the wet paint and construction detritus that still littered the halls—the builders had finished working on roughly six hours before we moved in. It was a decent-size two-bedroom, and the rent was just slightly above our budget—nine hundred dollars apiece—which we found out later

---

25 Note: Only assholes called it this.

was actually cheap for the neighborhood, possibly because the block was, according to the broker, "a little ethnic."[26]

The nonethnic denizens of the neighborhood were mostly skinny, artsy-looking white kids in their twenties. The men all had facial hair and wore skinny jeans, plaid shirts, and Fidel Castro–style green military caps. The women all had severe, straight bangs and wore vintagey-looking dresses paired with heavy boots. Tattoos and chunky-framed glasses were abundant among both sexes.

These, Rufus informed me, having encountered them himself the previous summer, were known as "hipsters."

I hadn't run into this particular subculture before. My college had skewed heavily toward the preppy/jock end of the spectrum. Hipsters at Notre Dame would have been regarded with suspicion, if not outright hostility.

But now the tables were turned. I was the outsider. Walking to the subway in the morning in my work clothes, I suddenly felt like a corporate stooge in a way I never had while staying with Sloane. In Murray Hill, I was just another working stiff. In Williamsburg, I stuck out like a narc at a rock show.[27]

It's generally against the hipster ethos to rise early, so while I was still on the early shift, I had the streets mostly to myself during my five-minute walk to the subway. But after I transitioned to the afternoon tape shift, I'd head toward the subway at two P.M., passing three invariably packed coffee shops on my walk. I could sense the disdain of the customers as they gave me withering glances and eye rolls from behind the screens of their Apple PowerBooks. (If they had known who I actually worked for, they probably would have spilled into the street en masse and throttled me with their wallet chains in an angry rage.)

The weekends were a little less fraught with anxiety about fitting in. My college T-shirt collection served me well in this regard, giving me at least some faux-hipster cred. I wouldn't fool anyone up close, but

---

26 Translation: "entirely Dominican."
27 Hipsters don't call them concerts.

from a distance, at least, I didn't immediately scream "Sellout." I even briefly flirted with wearing an ironic trucker hat, shamefully giving in to a trend that in the summer/fall of 2004 still had about ten minutes of popularity left. I'm proud to say that I never did give in to the skinny jeans trend, though that probably had less to do with any aversion to being a fad chaser, and a lot more to do with my having chubby legs.

Brooklyn wasn't quite where I had envisioned myself, and there was nary a ghostbuster in sight, but none of that could detract from the fact that I'd made it: I was a New Yorker.

———

It's a cruel twist of fate for the employees of Fox News to be headquartered in New York City, the East Coast capital of smug liberalism—and I say that as a proud, out-of-the-closet smug liberal. It's terribly damaging to the psyche to have to live and socialize in a city where the vast majority of residents absolutely despise your livelihood. Strangers I met at parties or dinners were surprisingly quick to criticize my employer. Innocent, polite inquiries about my profession could suddenly turn on a dime and become angry, haranguing sermons on the evils of Fox News.

"Ugh, how can you work for those people?" someone I'd met only minutes before would ask, scowling into her wineglass. "They're, like, *practically* fascists."

The above exchange falls somewhere in the middle of the spectrum of reactions that I've gotten. The worst response I ever had was from a girl who just stared at me, horrified, then shook her head and wordlessly turned and walked away. Usually, the best I could hope for was a startled "Oh!" followed by a cautious "That's so . . . *interesting* . . . Do you *like* working there?"

The honest answer to that question was, for most of my tenure at Fox, "You know what—it's not so bad! And screw you for judging me." But try telling that to an angry liberal wielding a champagne flute just one bash on a countertop away from becoming a deadly weapon. So over the years, I practiced a variety of deflections:

- Apologetic ("Don't worry, I'm not one of them.")
- Cynical ("Hey, I'm just doing my part to make sure the misinformed people stay misinformed.")
- Jokey/conspiratorial ("Don't tell anyone, but I'm secretly bringing the place down from the inside.")
- Resigned to my fate ("Ehh, it's a living!")[28]

Finally, I figured out that my best strategy was simply vagueness from the very beginning. "I work in TV news," I'd say to anyone asking about my livelihood, hoping there weren't any follow-up questions.

Rufus, in the years that he worked for Fox, was much more confrontational whenever he got a hostile questioner. Argumentative by nature, he loved when people dared to question his employment.

"Oh, yeah?" he'd say. "Where do *you* work?"

When the person answered, invariably with some inoffensive but soulless corporate job, Rufus would grin and hit them with the kicker: "So you're not exactly saving the whales either, *are you*?" he'd say, cackling devilishly as the unwitting victim sputtered with indignation.

I found Rufus's strategy more satisfying than my own, but I usually tried too hard to be affable to follow his lead. I did love watching him execute it, though. I would smile and watch in silence as he reeled the victim in and then sprang the trap with relish.

I was unspeakably disappointed when Rufus eventually left Fox before I'd had the pleasure of seeing him get confronted by someone who *actually* worked for Greenpeace.

Rufus and I lived together, worked for the same company, went to the same bars on the weekends, had the same taste in movies and television and food; our bromance was almost perfect. But one thing got in the way: my girlfriend.

---

28 This one also works if you're an animal in the Flintstones household that's been commandeered into doubling as an appliance.

Jillian and I had been dating since junior year. She was a student at Saint Mary's College, the small all-women's school across the street from Notre Dame. SMC girls—often shorthanded as Smick Chicks, or Smickers—had a partially deserved reputation for being faster and looser than their ND counterparts (the shuttle bus that ran back and forth between the two campuses had been derisively christened the "Sluttle"), but Jillian wasn't like that. She was sweet, from a good family in rural Illinois.

Jillian wanted us to stay together after graduation, but New York City held no appeal for her. She argued that Chicago had some of the same big-city feel but was closer to home for both of us, cheaper, more livable, and just generally more within our respective wheelhouses.

But I didn't want to hear it. The Windy City left me cold. Yes, it shared certain characteristics with New York, but for me it would always be *less than*. It felt like a cop-out, a compromise. Plus, I argued (not *completely* inaccurately) that almost any media gig worth having was in New York. In the end, I didn't bother applying to a single Chicago job. Jillian, who'd studied to be a grade school teacher, reluctantly found a position at a charter school in the Bronx. With all four Catholic parents frowning at the idea of our cohabiting, she rented an apartment in Greenpoint, a neighborhood just to the north of Williamsburg.

Greenpoint had a bit of the same hipster cred as its southern neighbor but was slightly less gentrified, quite a bit cheaper, and overwhelmingly Polish. Jillian found a large one-bedroom for twelve hundred dollars a month, with a landlord who spoke broken English, and a grueling hour-and-a-half subway commute to her job in the Bronx.

She was miserable at first, a fact that I was totally, stupidly oblivious to. How could she not love the greatest city in the world? Didn't she know how lucky she was that I had dragged her kicking and screaming out of the Midwest?

"For what I'm paying here, we could rent a huge two-bedroom in Chicago," she pointed out one day when we were waiting for the subway. "Joe, we could rent *a house* in my hometown for this kind of money."

"Oh, please. You know that Streator, Illinois, doesn't have the same *cultural* advantages that we have here," I said, gesturing to the subway platform, which was empty aside from us and a middle-aged wino passed out on a bench.

Compounding Jillian's misery, I was barely around. I worked until eleven P.M. every night. She was in bed well before that, preparing to wake at five A.M. to start her lengthy trek to the Bronx. But since she "didn't move to goddamn New York freaking City just to see [me] on the goddamn weekends," I agreed to at least sleep over occasionally on weeknights. So a few nights a week, I'd take the train from the office to her place instead of mine, squeeze past the old Polish men in ribbed white tank tops, smoking pungent Marlboro Reds while sitting on her building's front stoop, and let myself into the apartment with the copy of the keys she'd made for me.

It would sometimes be after midnight, if the Subway Gods were working against me, so I'd creep into her apartment as quietly as I could, not turning on any lights, attempting to pull off my shoes and clothing in the dark of her bedroom.

My efforts were usually for naught, of course, as she'd stir awake when I slid under the covers next to her. We'd talk in whispers for five or ten or fifteen minutes, exchanging battle stories about our workdays, before she drifted off to sleep again. I'd lie awake, still too keyed up to end my day but grateful to be in a city I loved with a woman I loved and a job that, thankfully, hadn't yet asked me to turn into a storm trooper for the right or to swear allegiance to a portrait of Ronald Reagan in an occult ritual involving robes, masks, and a ceremonial chalice of pig's blood.

I was counting my chickens before they were hatched, in more ways than I realized.

April 11, 2012—12:01 P.M.

"Come on, Rufus, pick up, pick up," I said, holding the phone to one ear and plugging the other with a finger, struggling to hear over the tumult of Times Square.

His voice mail picked up for the third time in a row.

I cursed, filthily and loudly enough to draw a sharp look from a nearby mother who was otherwise engaged with ushering her two young kids away from a street performer in a ragged-looking knockoff SpongeBob SquarePants costume.

I'd decided that Rufus—whom I had belatedly remembered worked nearby at his Web developer job—was my one option for ditching the iPad. I figured I only had about fifteen minutes left before someone noticed that my "lunch break" more closely resembled a prison break. If I couldn't get in touch with Rufus, my only other choice was to abandon my gym bag on the street. I sure as shit couldn't go back into the News Corp. building with it. Who knew what kind of mole-sniffing forces had been marshaled in my absence? There was a good chance a corporate security team was going through my work computer at that exact moment.

I was mentally kicking around my previous idea of bribing a

newsstand guy or a hot dog vendor to hold my stuff, when my phone buzzed in my hand.

It was a text from Rufus: *What's up?*

I texted back, pecking out my response with shaking thumbs: *I need your help.*

CHAPTER 6

Red Bull and Kool-Aid

I could tell right away when Jim Siegendorf called me over to his desk in the newsroom that it was going to be bad news. He had a sheepish, almost apologetic look on his face. After four months on the job, I had figured out that Siegendorf, though he meant well, was a bad manager. Almost every other figure in the newsroom with any authority was brash, curt, matter-of-fact—not because they were jerks, but out of necessity. It was a matter of efficiency; they just didn't have the luxury to beat around the bush. Time was always of the essence, and we were on constant deadline, so it was expected that when orders came, they'd be barked at you, and that you wouldn't have a problem with it because that's just how things were done. *Pleases* and *thank-yous* were for people with boring jobs.

But Jim wasn't like the rest of the bosses and producers. He was polite and soft-spoken, and naturally all the PAs and editors hated his guts for it.

"Siegendorf? The guy's a total dipshit," one of the video editors volunteered to me, unprompted, during a cutting session.

Most of the newsroom probably wouldn't have been able to put it so pithily, but there *was* widespread consensus about Siegendorf's lack of competence. The main rap on him was that he was completely worthless during crunch time. When shit hit the fan, and the control room wanted a quick turnaround on some tape, Siegendorf completely lost his head, driving everyone nuts with constant demands for status updates, when he should have just been getting out of the way and letting the PAs and editors do their jobs.

My personal impression was that Siegendorf was a little bit addled but not all in all a terrible person to work for—but I also recognized that once underlings started speaking of you with that kind of contempt, your managerial grasp on employees was pretty much nonexistent.

He was still my boss, regardless of what my colleagues thought of him, so I came running when he called me over, and listened politely to what he had to say.

"Joe, I was wondering if you could help us out with something," Siegendorf was asking me, characteristically slow-walking the request. "We have a gap and we'd like you to do us a favor and fill in on the weekend overnights. It would just be for a few weeks. You'd really be helping us out of a jam."

Weekend overnights? That didn't sound promising.

"So what would my new schedule be?" I asked.

"Monday through Wednesday, you'd still be doing evening cut-ins, three to eleven P.M.," Jim said. "Then you would have off Thursday and most of Friday. That would be your weekend."

So far so bad.

Siegendorf continued: "Then you'd come in Friday night at one A.M. to do overnight cut-ins and do tape for *Fox & Friends* until ten A.M. Saturday morning. Then the same thing Saturday night into Sunday morning."

Friday and Saturday night, one A.M. until ten A.M.? That sounds horrible, I wanted to say. What I actually said was "Hmmm."

"It will only be a few weeks. Month and a half, tops," Jim said.

"Hmm," I said again.

Jillian was somewhat less circumspect.

"Are you fucking kidding me?" she asked me later that evening when I called her from my desk in the newsroom. "I never get to see you as it is. Now you're shitting on our weekends, too?"

"I didn't have much of a choice," I said. "I've barely been here for three months. I want to look like a team player."

"You look like a sucker is what you look like."

"No, this will be good, baby!" I said, unconvincingly. "Now we'll have Thursday nights all to ourselves."

Jillian stewed silently on the other end of the phone.

"And, uh, Sunday afternoons, after I've slept for a few hours, of course."

"Hmmm," she said.

"I should warn you right now—they absolutely will not use any jokes that make President Bush look bad."

Dave Krieger was looming over my shoulder, watching as I worked the controls of the video screener, fast-forwarding through a tape of *The Tonight Show*, blowing past the commercials that came between the end of the local news and the beginning of Leno's monologue.

It was 3:07 A.M. on a Friday night. Or was it a Saturday morning? I wasn't sure what to call it exactly. My brain wasn't functioning properly. Four hours earlier, I had been at a bar with Jillian and some of our college friends, enjoying myself thoroughly. And now I was at work, struggling with the temperamental shuttle wheel of a shitty, broken-down, Soviet-surplus video screener. I was already not a happy camper. And Dave's revelation, which he tossed off nonchalantly like he was just explaining where the office supplies were kept, wasn't helping my mood.

Dave was one of the younger writers for *Fox & Friends* and had obviously drawn the short straw and been assigned to supervise me, the newest production assistant with the misfortune to get shunted onto the weekend overnight shift. One of my duties, he had explained, would be to go through the monologues of all the late-night talk shows and mark down five or six jokes that the show's senior producers might want to use as bump-ins when coming back from commercial.

"Wait," I said. "What happens if a Bush joke is really funny?"

Dave shook his head. "It doesn't matter. They won't use it."

"Well, what exactly are they looking for, then?"

"John Kerry jokes are good. Lately they've been liking stuff about his wife, too," Dave said. "Oh, and Bill or Hillary Clinton jokes? They'll take those every time. Especially . . ." He looked around for eavesdroppers, and lowered his voice a notch. "Especially ones about Bill being fat or horny, or Hillary being a pain in the ass."

I frowned, just as a fast-forwarded Jay Leno popped up on the monitor in front of me, shaking hands with audience members in the front row at quadruple speed. I hit PLAY, knocking him back to his normal rate.

"Look," Dave said, apparently picking up my annoyance, "if it makes you feel any better, throw a Bush joke in there, but don't be disappointed when it doesn't make it on air. Because it won't. Ever."

He checked the red digital clock on the wall, one of dozens scattered throughout the newsroom, synchronized down to the second.

"You'd better get cracking," Dave said. "The show starts in less than four hours, and Leno's monologue is like forty-five minutes long every night."

He started to walk away, but stopped and doubled back.

"Oh, and one more thing," he said.

I looked up from the screen. "Yeah?"

"No Cheney jokes."

A month later, I was an absolute basket case, so addled by sleep deprivation that I barely had the energy to care that Jillian was mad at me. Working the graveyard shift five days a week is obviously not ideal, but that would have been a piece of cake compared to what I was doing— bouncing back and forth between second and third shift. I never had a chance to adjust my sleeping to either schedule, so I ended up just feeling tired at all times, every day of the week. Sometimes when I was transitioning between shifts, I'd be awake for thirty hours straight, the lack of sleep making me feel half drunk.

And it probably didn't help that I *started* some of the shifts three-quarters drunk. When I began the schedule, I told myself that I wasn't going to let it totally ruin my social life. So on Friday or Saturday nights, I'd go to dinner with friends, go out to a bar with them afterward, stay for a drink or two, then hop in a cab around midnight and head for the office. I didn't ever show up *completely* wasted for a shift—I was *clearly* too much of a professional for that—but the sleep schedule was starting to have strange effects on my body, and I wasn't always a great judge of knowing when to stop. My college-honed tolerance for alcohol was still pretty high at the time, so I set myself a limit of three drinks before work. But three beers can end up feeling like seven when your head is already clouded from getting only a handful of hours of fitful daytime sleep.

Dutywise, I actually enjoyed the overnight shifts. They had a certain inmates-running-the-asylum feel to them. The ship was manned by a skeleton crew, a swashbuckling band of loners and misanthropes fueled by coffee, Red Bull, cigarettes, and greasy food delivered by nearby twenty-four-hour delis. There was a light workload, and a lot of downtime; though we were technically a twenty-four-hour news network, between eleven P.M. and seven A.M. we ran nothing but repeats, interrupted only by the two-minute cut-ins at the bottom of each hour. The cut-ins were largely unneccesary, of course—just a way to keep us on our toes and to prevent us from sneaking off to one of the employee lounges scattered throughout the building and napping the night away on a beat-up couch. Ostensibly, we were there to deal with any breaking news; but realistically, news stopped breaking after ten P.M., except on the very rarest of occasions.[29]

I quickly figured out that the overnights were for three kinds of people. The first type was like me—reluctantly and ostensibly temporarily on the shift, unlucky enough to be assigned to the overnight because they were new to the job and didn't have any say in it, or a veteran under the impression that a stint on the graveyard shift would eventually advance his or her career. Those people were putting in the time, unpleasant as it was, and looking forward to eventually moving back to a better shift. The overnights were a necessary evil to them.

The second type you'd find working overnights were those sick

---

29 International stories tended to be the ones that broke late. Word of the devastating 2004 tsunami in Southeast Asia, for example, started to trickle over the wires while I was on an overnight shift. It was horrifying to watch the story develop in real time while the rest of the country slept, the casualty reports mounting exponentially each hour.

bastards who actually *liked* it. They had *requested* the shift, and in some cases had remained on it for years. These people tended to be misanthropes, people haters who would have been miserable on the day shift.

Billy Lenhardt was the first one of this type that I met. A video editor, he was a few years older than I and had a thick New Jersey accent. He'd been on the night shift for three years. He was a heavy smoker and hated to indulge his habit alone; I was a social smoker and was willing to keep him company as long as he was willing to let me bum a cigarette. We hit it off right away.

"I love the overnights," Billy told me once at four A.M. as we stood in front of the building just outside the entrance, puffing Camels. "No one's around to bother you."

"But who on the day shift bothers you?" I asked.

"Pretty much everyone," Billy said, laughing. "But especially Siegendorf. That guy's a fucking idiot."

"But don't you hate working at night? Doesn't it suck to be basically nocturnal?"

"I've got blackout curtains at home, so it's easy enough to sleep during the day," he said. "Also driving in from Jersey when I do, I'm reverse-commuting. The traffic is way better."

Another night-shifter who shared Billy's misanthropic leanings was Jeremy, a middle-aged video editor who'd been with the network since day one.

"They keep trying to stick me back on the daytime," he told me, explaining that the bosses didn't like that someone with his experience— and the high salary that went along with it—was slumming it on the easiest possible shift. But Jeremy had enough seniority that he could basically tell the bosses to go fuck themselves, which he did every few months in so many words. "After a while I guess they just figured it's easier to let me work when I want than it is to argue with me," he said.

He was a great editor, one of the best I ever worked with, but was laid-back to a maddening degree. There wasn't *a ton* of urgency on the overnights, but every once in a while, we'd get some footage in that needed a quick turnaround.

On a typical night, I'd burst into his edit room in a panic, tape in hand.

"Jeremy, this hits in five!"

He'd look up from the Minesweeper game he was playing on the computer and smile, all innocence: "Oh, I don't know if we'll make it, then. You'd better call the control room and tell them the bad news."

"Come on, I'm serious."

"All right, give me the tape."

He'd edit it, picking the shots slowly and deliberately as I watched over his shoulder and shuffled my feet impatiently.

"Hmm, I don't like that transition," he'd say, frowning at the monitor. "Do I have time to go back and fix it?"

I'd glance at the clock on the wall.

"No."

"Fine," he'd say, hitting the EJECT button and handing me the tape. "Here you go. It's a piece of shit. Just like most of the video they put out here."

Jeremy was the most openly cynical person I met in my time at Fox. I'd come across others who had misgivings about the place, but they would rarely give voice to their qualms—nothing more, at least, than a sarcastic muttered aside, or the occasional eye roll. Jeremy, meanwhile, would rail at length against everything about the company. He hated the incompetent management, he hated the conservative politics, he hated the fact that they kept trying to put him on the day shift—even though he explained to them that he loathed being around too many people at once.

"I'll never leave, though," he said, "because they're paying me too well." His theory was that the new hires were getting hosed—he howled when I told him about the twelve dollars an hour they were paying me—and that only those who had been at Fox since the early days were getting paid what they deserved. "They hired me back when they were actually handing out some real money to people."

The *third* type of person on the overnight shift was the saddest of them all—the ones who had been put there because daytime people couldn't stand *them*. They were too annoying or abrasive or strange or off-putting to work with larger groups, and were pushed into the overnights by supervisors who couldn't find cause to fire them but also could not in good conscience continue to place them with the general population.

The overnight cut-in producer I ended up working with most frequently was one of these unfortunate souls. Seth was a bit of a legend among the PAs. I had actually heard rumors of him before I even started on the overnight shift, whispers about the maniac producer who lived to terrorize rookie production assistants. He didn't quite live up to that billing when I finally met him, but he was undoubtedly salty about his exile to the evenings.

"I don't know who the fuck I pissed off to get stuck here," he'd gripe. After a few weeks on the job with him, I'd surmised that the answer was "everyone." He was one of the most abrasive people I'd ever met.

Of course like most abrasive people, Seth was wildly entertaining in small doses, especially if his ire wasn't aimed at you. He'd periodically freak out on a production assistant over some screwup, his voice rising to a high pitch as he screamed, the sound easily carrying across the mostly empty newsroom. I could see why he'd gained such a fearsome reputation among the PAs—night shift or no, he had zero tolerance for rookie mistakes (of which there were plenty, thanks to the relatively inexperienced crew that manned the overnights, present company included).

In just a month with Seth, I saw up close much of the behavior that had led the other PAs who had worked with him to solemnly inform me that they believed he was insane (he'd cackle to himself sometimes for no reason, and had an irrationally strong fear of spiders), a cokehead (he'd disappear from the control room for long stretches and return jittery and manic, sweating profusely and wiping his nose), or both.

But aside from that circumstantial evidence, I could never find any definitive proof of mental illness or drug use. He was eccentric, to be sure, but the night shift was starting to make me loopy as well, so who was I to judge? And in fact Seth was a hell of a good producer, routinely picking offbeat stories, quirky items that were interesting and unexpected, and actually seeming to have a little fun with his slice of the network's time.

"No one's fucking watching, anyway," he'd say. "Who's paying attention to the news at four thirty in the goddamn morning?"

I got the call a week before Thanksgiving 2004.

I'd been expecting it, actually. Once you started nearing your six-month mark—once the bosses determined that you weren't a total fuck-up, that you could get tape on the air with a respectably low mistake rate, that you were surprisingly willing to tolerate the shitty hours and laughable pay, that you might have *a future* with the company— the call (or, in this case, the e-mail) came down from on high (or, rather, from Siegendorf):

Nelson wants to meet with you.

Nelson Howe, the news director and a company vice president, was a tall, serious-looking man. Before I even realized what his position was, I knew he was important because he inhabited one of the only real offices in the entire newsroom. While Siegendorf, who was in charge of the entire production assistant department, and pretty important in his own right, had to suffer the indignity of hunkering down at a desk in the middle of the PA pod, Nelson had a door and four walls separating him from the unwashed rabble of the newsroom.

The older PAs had filled me in, like camp counselors telling ghost stories: A meeting with Nelson was the last hurdle of the trial period at Fox, and the most important. Siegendorf and his deputy, Nina, were the ones who decided whether you were competent. But it was Nelson, unsmiling, his eyes piercing from behind his horn-rimmed glasses, who looked into your soul and decided whether you were *a believer*, whether you bought into the whole Fox thing wholeheartedly, without reservation. Only then could you move to the next level.

The older PAs had a nickname for the meeting that was only

partially in jest: the Kool-Aid Conference. As in, *Are you fully prepared to drink the Fox News Kool-Aid?*

Aside from nostalgically conjuring up images of TV commercials from my youth—commercials featuring a bulbous, anthropomorphic drink pitcher bursting through a wall, screaming, "OH, YEAH!" as frightened children scattered to avoid the debris—the Kool-Aid Conference made me nervous. For starters, I was almost certainly going to have to hide my true feelings in order to keep my job.

Aka, lie through my teeth.

And it's not that I'm exactly Mr. Morals over here. I've long been a firm believer that a well-timed, tightly spun fib can work wonders in certain situations. But it seemed at least a tiny bit cynical of me to build my still-budding career on a bed of lies. Not to mention Nelson was supposed to be notoriously good at sniffing out the liars.

So I had a knot in my stomach the afternoon of the meeting as I trudged toward Nelson's office. I passed the War Room,[30] a glass fishbowl of a conference room where the *Fox Report* staff was meeting. I spotted my old pal Marybeth taking notes while listening to the senior producer speak.

Marybeth, a few weeks after finishing training me on cut-ins, had been snatched up by Shepard Smith's crew.

Frankly, I was jealous.

If Fox News was like high school (and in many ways it was), Shep and his gang were totally the cool kids.[31] The staff had a swagger that the other shows just couldn't match. They sat in the newsroom and wrote their show together, bantering wittily about the stories. Shep

---

30 The name, like many things at Fox, was a lot more sinister than its actual purpose. While I'm sure there's been plenty of nefarious business in the War Room over the years, it was mostly used for routine show planning meetings and pizza parties.

31 The *O'Reilly Factor* staff, with a sense of superiority derived from high ratings, were the rich kids in school: popular because of their expensive clothes and the expensive cars their parents had bought them for their sixteenth birthdays but secretly loathed by everyone else in the school. Greta's staff: the honor students. Hannity's staff: a mashup of the Young Republicans, the debate club, and the mock trial team. Cavuto's staff: the mathletes. Geraldo's staff: the stoners. Production assistants were the freshmen. And every anchorwoman was a cheerleader.

would sit with them, grabbing a desk in their pod, writing along with them in his shirtsleeves.

There was no parking lot available for them to retreat to for between-class cigarettes, but the host and a half dozen of his producers made do with the next best thing and could be spotted on a daily basis enjoying a preshow smoke outside the back entrance of the News Corp. building.

Marybeth wasn't a smoker, but she'd embraced the ethos of her new colleagues. She didn't consider herself too cool to still talk to me, however, and we'd maintained our friendship, chatting a few times a week when our schedules overlapped. In fact, she'd been one of the PAs who had clued me in about the meeting with Nelson.

She saw me then, as I was walking past the War Room, and she gave an excited little wave followed by a thumbs-up. *Good luck,* she mouthed.

Nelson's door was closed, so I knocked, entering when I heard a muffled "Come in," and closing the door behind me.

The windowless office was neat and tidy, much like the man who inhabited it. He wore a preppy navy-blue suit that hung loosely on his lanky frame, with a classic Brooks Brothers striped repp tie, and glasses with thin tortoiseshell frames. His hair was parted neatly to one side. He wore his ID on a lanyard around his neck, a somewhat nerdy affectation, especially for someone of his stature. (Wearing your ID badge, while technically required for entry into the building, was generally regarded as something that only newbies did. Mine had been relegated to my wallet since my second month on the job.)

His handshake was firm, quick, and bone-dry.

"So, Mr. Muto," he began, reading my name off a printout in front of him, "Jim speaks very highly of you. He says you're smart, you're fast, you choose good tape. The producers all like working with you."

"I appreciate him saying that," I said. "I try."

If Nelson was attempting to soften me up . . . it was *absolutely working*, as my ego completely took over at the first sign of a compliment.

"So we want you to continue here at Fox," Nelson went on. "But I just wanted to ask you a few things first."

Okay. Here it comes.

"What do you think about us being"—he met my eyes with his, studying—"fair and balanced? That's our motto. Do you believe it's true?"

I swallowed, hesitated, choosing my words carefully.

"I think that our prime-time shows obviously have a . . . point of view . . ." I started.

Nelson arched an eyebrow.

"But that's okay," I continued. "Everyone knows that they're opinion shows."

Nelson nodded approvingly.

"I think that our daytime coverage is actually *very* fair and balanced," I lied. "And our opinion shows just serve to balance out the rest of TV news, which is obviously *very* liberal."

"But what about our critics?" Nelson asked. "They say that we're biased. We're too conservative. Do you agree with them?"

"Wellllll . . ." I started, drawing out the word to buy some time. I saw a frown begin to creep onto his face. Uh-oh. *Think of something.*

"I think that our critics"—Nelson leaned forward in his chair—"probably don't actually watch us that much," I answered finally. And I had a good kicker, too: "Besides, they're probably jealous of our ratings," I said.

He smiled then, the first time since I'd come into the office.

We chitchatted for a few more minutes, before he stood to let me know the meeting was over.

"I think you'll have a long career here, Mr. Muto," he said while shaking my hand. "Can I give you some advice, though?"

"Absolutely."

"Suits," he said. "Start wearing suits."

"Aha," I said.

"This," he said, gesturing to my ensemble—jeans and a rugby shirt, "isn't going to fly for much longer. You should be wearing a suit every day. A nice, crisp one."

"Well, I don't exactly *own one* right now," I admitted, suddenly feeling like a total dirtball.

"Right, well, you should buy a couple. I mean, we pay you enough that you . . ." He glanced down at the paper on his desk, searching for the correct number. He grimaced when he found it. "Oh, well . . . you can at least go to Men's Wearhouse, right? Get a nice two-for-one?" He looked at me with a somewhat apologetic smile. "Anyway, think about it."

Back at the PA pod, Marybeth was done with her show meeting and was gathering tape at her desk.

"How'd it go?" she asked.

"I think he liked what I had to say," I said.

"Did you give him the spiel? 'Our opinion shows are *this*, but our straight news programs are right down the middle and blah blah blah . . .'"

I was shocked. "How'd you know that's what I said?"

She laughed. "That's what everyone says, dummy. That's what I said in my meeting last month. No one actually *believes it*, but everyone says it. What else can you say?"

I thought back to some of the conversations Marybeth and I had, ones where she'd said things about John Kerry that were as disparaging as anything that had come out of Lenny's mouth.

"But I thought you were a conservative?"

"I am, I guess," she said. "But I also have eyes and ears."

And that's when it hit me.

No one believed it.

Fair and Balanced. We Report, You Decide. Everyone knew it was bunk. A sham. Over the next eight years at Fox, I never met a single employee, not the truest of the true believers, who wasn't cynical about what our main purpose was.

"We all know the 'Fair and Balanced' thing is bullshit," a very conservative *O'Reilly Factor* producer told me once, late at night, after we'd had a few drinks. "We're not here to be fair. We're here to give red meat to our viewers."

"To stir up the crazies, you mean," I said.

He laughed. "Yeah, to stir up the crazies. Because outrage equals ratings."

I was home for a few days around Thanksgiving when Jim called me with the good news: "Joe, we're going to bump you from freelancer to full-time!"

I felt elated and slightly nauseated at the same time.

"You're getting health benefits!"

At least that would take care of the nausea if it turned out to be something serious.

"And a raise!"

Well, that was an added bonus.

"So you *were* at twelve dollars an hour. You'll be at twelve seventy-four now. Congratulations!"

Better than a sharp stick in the eye, as my grandmother liked to say.

Later that night, at a gathering with some of my friends from high school, I was talking to my friend Matt, a liberal who was in his first year of law school. He was planning on a career in some field of law or other that would help save the world, and was still aghast at my job choice.

"Frankly, I can't believe you're still there," he said. "It's been almost six months. I thought for sure you'd have run out of there screaming by now."

"I have a high tolerance for pain, I think. Or maybe I'm just a masochist."

Matt was even more aghast when I described to him how I'd lied about my opinion on Fox's bias to advance my career.

"So what do you think," I asked, "did I just completely trade away my integrity for some health benefits and an extra seventy-four cents an hour?"

"Oh, no, not at all," Matt said, taking a swig of his beer. "You did that already, when you took the job in the first place."

April 11, 2012—12:14 P.M.

New York is filled with hundreds or even thousands of compelling, dramatic locations for spy meetings: dark secluded bars, shadow-filled parking garages, remote park benches next to mist-covered ponds.

Meanwhile, my little pathetic flirtation with espionage had led me to a crowded, brightly lit Times Square fast-food joint. It was the first New York City branch of the Midwest stalwart burger chain Steak 'n Shake. And three months after opening, it was inexplicably mobbed— as if New Yorkers had never before encountered something as exotic as griddled ground beef stuck between two buns.

Amid all the chaos, I found Rufus at a counter seat, calmly working his way through a cheeseburger and fries and reading a book on his Kindle.

Rufus had lasted nearly three years at FoxNews.com. Unlike me— who found them at turns mildly irritating and rage-inducing—Rufus found the network's right-wing politics highly amusing. He'd laughingly tell me about his standing orders to "Foxify" stories that came across the Associated Press wire—that is, replace the headline and rewrite the first paragraph to something that was more suited to the website's conservative audience. If the AP had audaciously seen fit to bury a slightly unflattering tidbit about John Kerry in the later paragraphs of an article, Rufus would Foxify it, making the damaging portion the headline and the lede.

What eventually did Rufus in at Fox was the overnight shift, that great widow-maker, which he'd been pushed onto for the full five nights a week. But unlike TV, the dot-com overnight shifts were strictly one-man affairs—Rufus was the lone person on the job for a full six hours. Without any of the bleary-eyed camaraderie—the only thing I'd enjoyed about the otherwise godforsaken schedule—Rufus began to slowly descend into madness. All the blackout curtains and Ambien in the world couldn't make him a fully functioning member of society. So he'd left, bouncing around to jobs with various other media heavyweights—AOL, *The New York Times*—until finally settling into a well-paying gig programming the website for a premium cable movie channel.

His Times Square office left him only a few blocks from where he'd started his career, barely a five-minute walk from where I was in the process of destroying mine.

Rufus waved me over, putting his Kindle down and eyeing me quizzically.

"You're probably wondering what's going on," I said.

I hadn't told Rufus about my plans to leak the video. Standing in front of him, I realized I'd kept it from him expressly because I knew he would have tried to talk me out of it.

He was always smart like that.

"I can't go into it right now, but I can't have my duffel bag with me at work anymore. Can you stash it at your office? Or better yet, bring it home with you tonight?"

Rufus broke into a knowing smile. "What are you up to?"

I unslung the bag from my shoulder and handed it over to him.

"I can't tell you right now."

He laughed. "Why do I have a feeling I'm going to find out soon enough, whether you tell me or not?"

CHAPTER 7

Moonwalking into the Light

The theme song for NPR's *Morning Edition* jarred me awake at seven A.M. My eyes snapped open, and I mentally cursed the tune's smooth jazz guitar licks for interrupting my precious slumber.

Like any good New York liberal, my clock radio alarm was permanently set to WNYC, the local public radio station. But in March 2005, after only a few weeks on the regular daytime shift, I'd grown to resent the National Public Radio show and its dulcet-voiced anchors.

Fuck you, Steve Inskeep. And fuck you, Renee Montagne. Let me sleep, for chrissakes.

But silencing them would involve climbing out of my wonderfully warm and cozy bed, which I was loathe to do. My Evening Self, knowing that my Morning Self was not to be trusted, had cleverly placed the clock radio not on the nightstand but on the other side of the room, requiring a slog across the cold floor to turn it off. As a result, I generally spent the first ten minutes of my day lying in bed, hoping that overnight I'd somehow developed the telekinetic powers necessary to turn off the alarm remotely. And every morning, after those powers had stubbornly refused to manifest themselves, I reluctantly climbed out of the sack, smacked the OFF button, and stumbled into the bathroom.

Some mornings I'd sleep right through the alarm, and the voices on the radio would work themselves into my dreams, to often disturbing results. The average NPR news update is not something you want incorporated into your dream life on a regular basis. I don't want to go into too many details, but let's just say at age twenty-three, I'd had more nocturnal threesome fantasies involving foreign world leaders than was natural or healthy for someone my age.

I probably should have just switched over to music, except one thing was holding me back—those ten minutes in the morning listening to NPR with a pillow clamped over my face actually gave me more real news, more substantial information, a better grasp of the day's events, than my entire eight-hour shift at Fox.

I was pulled off the overnight shift in early March 2005—roughly four months after my meeting with Nelson—as suddenly and unceremoniously as I'd been placed on it. A hiring surge early in the year had flooded the newsroom with new blood, and as they covered slots in the cut-ins and overnights, my services were needed elsewhere—namely as a production assistant for the hourly shows. The duty was the same, but the rhythm was different. Instead of a handful of tapes every hour, it was an absolute deluge of tapes twice a day, once in the morning for one of the newswheel hours, and again in the afternoon for *The Big Story* with John Gibson. It was nominally a promotion, though it came, in typical Fox fashion, without a bump in title or money. The real benefit was that my day-to-day schedule was much more sane and normal, and my weekends were my own again for the first time in months, my head no longer shrouded in the fog of sleep deprivation.

A lot had happened in the months that I'd been among the walking dead.

First, John Kerry had lost. I was on duty election night. There was a festive atmosphere in the newsroom when I showed up to start work at six P.M.—not necessarily because Bush was narrowly favored to win, though that was probably contributing to the high spirits for a lot of people—but because for politics nerds and cable news jockeys, election nights were like Christmas, New Year's, and the Fourth of July all rolled into one. They were the culmination of months of work and anticipation, a glorious hours-long orgasm after the foreplay of the endless months of primaries, debates, and campaign ads.

Also, the bosses had ordered pizza for everyone.

They sent out a group e-mail when the pies arrived, triggering a stampede of perpetually perk-deprived producers, editors, and PAs toward the break room to gorge on the free food, a mass of starved humanity clamoring and grabbing and piling slices onto flimsy paper plates, two and three at a time, or snagging entire boxes to carry triumphantly back to the newsroom, and in general acting as if they'd never seen food before.

Anchors and producers from DC had come up to New York for the occasion because the network had decided to run election coverage from NYC's larger studios. There was a long-simmering tension between the two factions. The DC bureau produced the six P.M. *Special Report* show and generated the majority of the network's political coverage, while New York did almost everything else. DC thought of themselves as an elite offshoot, a more journalistically credible team of heavyweights that outclassed the populist muckrakers and ratings chasers in Manhattan. They happened to be *right*; but we New Yorkers still resented them for their attitudes.

The visiting snooty Washingtonians had taken over large chunks of our newsroom real estate. I joined a contingent of PAs who had gathered in the back corner by the vending machines to voice their displeasure.

"Some punk kid from DC is sitting in my regular desk," Camie was complaining as she fed a dollar bill into the machine.

"He says his producer said he could sit there, and he's 'way too busy' to move seats. Jerk-off." She jabbed a button, and a can of Diet Pepsi clunked and clattered its way down to the slot.

"What are you complaining about?" I said. "You're not even supposed to be here tonight."

It was true. After training me on scripts, Camie had gone on to do tape for one of the newswheel hours. She was strictly daytime and hadn't been called in for duty that night, but she'd shown up at seven P.M. and asked Siegendorf if she could just hang out, off the clock, and help where needed. It was a bold move, but I was happy to have her there, if only to have someone else with whom to bitch about the interlopers from the Beltway.

"They act like all we do here is cover car chases and murder trials," I said.

Even the always polite Southerner Red Robertshaw was put off by the DCers, whom he admitted were being "a little pushy."

The DC people may have had a point, however, about the New Yorkers being relative lightweights. The usurpers did almost all the heavy lifting the entire night, leaving nothing for the home team to do except cut b-roll of victorious members of Congress—tapes that went mostly unused as the bulk of the night's coverage focused on the biggest prize: the presidency.

Around one A.M., Fox was the first network to declare Bush the winner of Ohio, giving him 269 electoral votes, just one shy of victory. But after getting burned in 2000, inadvertently awarding Bush the win over Gore with Florida still very much in doubt, Fox and the other networks were understandably gun-shy about calling the race, and the extremely close tallies in New Mexico and Iowa meant the winner would not be known until the morning.

I left work at three A.M. with the victor still undetermined, though it was looking decidedly grim for John Kerry. I invited Red to walk over to Rockefeller Center with me, where NBC News was finishing up their coverage for the night.

As a certified Bush hater, I probably should have been more bummed out. But I'd never been a huge Kerry fan, preferring Howard Dean—even after his campaign-destroying scream speech. Kerry had run a lackluster campaign and had never really made a strong case for himself outside of "I'm not Bush." And as Mitt Romney found out in 2012, if you want to unseat an incumbent president, you have to give people a reason to vote *for* you—not just *against* the other guy. So I couldn't get too worked up at the prospect of the Massachusetts senator losing.

Also, a nagging voice in the back of my head was telling me that even though I'd been with Fox only for a few months at that point, I was at least partially complicit for mounting the network's case against Kerry. I shoved that voice down and tried to enjoy the sights in front of me. Fox's coverage was relatively bare bones, old dour white guys in a windowless studio, but NBC had gone all out, lighting up 30 Rock's limestone facade with red and blue spotlights, and painting a fifty-foot-wide map of the United States on the famous ice-skating rink below. A team of workers had spray-painted each state red or blue throughout the night as the winners were called.

I don't know if I was punchy after being cooped up in the newsroom all night, or if my anguish at having to endure another four years of Bush was manifesting itself in strange ways, but I suddenly felt overwhelmed by it all, and began to geek out as only a politics nerd could.

"Isn't this great?" I said to Red, feeling myself get misty-eyed and swallowing a lump in my throat. "I mean, I don't even care who wins at this point. America is just so *great*. We're so fucking lucky to even *be here*."

Red eyed me skeptically.

"Maybe you should go home and get some sleep," he said.

Another development in the months that I'd been on the overnights: Jim Siegendorf, executive producer in charge of all the production assistants, had been fired in late January. They'd done it very publicly, too, in the middle of the day, in the most humiliating fashion imaginable. I showed up for my three P.M. shift to find the PA pod buzzing. I'd missed the whole sordid spectacle by an hour or two.

"Dude, I saw the whole thing go down," Frankie, a wiry, Eminem-looking PA was telling me. "It was the most awkward shit I've *ever* seen. Siegendorf got up to go to a meeting, then came back, like, an hour later with two security guards following him. They watched him pack up all his shit, then escorted him out of the building."

I stared at Frankie in shock. "What were you doing the whole time? You were just watching this?"

He shrugged. "I was still working, actually, the whole time. I was crashing on tape for the two P.M. I couldn't just stop cutting. Meanwhile, Siegendorf's ten feet away, cleaning out his desk." He shook his head, cringing with the memory. "It was fucking awkward."

Word filtered down that Siegendorf had been the fall guy for our lackluster ratings during the coverage of the Southeast Asian tsunami aftermath. We'd still beaten the other networks, but just barely. Meanwhile, CNN had seen their ratings explode, and the boost in viewers and publicity had helped launch a new star, Anderson Cooper. Ailes was furious that we'd failed to capitalize more on the event, and blamed the video department for not getting more compelling footage of death and destruction onto the screen. Since Siegendorf was responsible for the production assistants, and we were responsible for picking and choosing the video, it was his head on the chopping block.

There was an unseemly amount of jubilation in the PA pod following Siegendorf's sacking. I hadn't loved the guy myself, but I thought he'd gotten a raw deal, especially for someone who'd been with the network almost from its founding. Also, even though video was technically ultimately his responsibility, it wasn't his fault that CNN was eating our lunch. They had more than eighty people on the ground in the region, and were able to dig up all the best video and keep it exclusively for themselves. Meanwhile, we had sent fewer than a dozen producers and correspondents, and were almost entirely reliant on whatever footage the wire services fed us.

On the plus side, they'd replaced Siegendorf with his deputy, Nina, who was universally beloved and wise enough to realize that a man of my talents was being wasted on the overnights. When she told me that I was being switched to daytime for good—no more evenings, no more weekend overnights—I almost cried with relief.

My girlfriend, Jillian, when I told her the good news, actually did cry a little. She was thoroughly tired by that point of spending her Saturday and Sunday afternoons watching me snore in her bed 'til four P.M., poking at me occasionally to get me to wake up and pay attention to her.

"Are you ready for this?" I asked the video editor. "It's going to get *really loud.*"

He looked up from his edit rig, turning his head to glance back at me over his shoulder.

"Do your worst," he said.

"Okay. You asked for it."

I clicked PLAY on the computer, and the iconic guitar riff filled the edit room, rattling the small pair of speakers arranged on either side of the monitor.

"This is too good!" I yelled. "We've got to share this with everyone." I reached over and flung the edit room door wide open. Heads started turning as the music spilled out into the newsroom.

Then the singing kicked in—that familiar high pitch, alternating between smooth as silk and rough as a cat's tongue, somehow both masculine and feminine at the same time.

Michael fucking Jackson.

I took my baby on a Saturday bang. . . .

Nina bounded over, poking her head into the room.

"Muto, what's going on in here?" she shouted.

"It's verdict day! I'm getting everyone psyched up," I shouted back, clapping along with the music.

If you're thinkin' 'bout my baby, it don't matter if you're black or white.

"Do you think you can 'psych people up' without deafening the entire newsroom?" Nina asked.

"You got it, boss lady," I said, easing the speaker volume down a few notches.

"That's better," she said, retreating to check in with the PAs in the other edit rooms on either side of mine.

She needn't have bothered, though. It was June 13, 2005. We'd just gotten word that the verdict in the Michael Jackson molestation trial would be revealed within the hour, and the entire Fox News operation had ground to a screeching halt. In fact, it felt like the *entire world* had ground to a screeching halt, as every news channel—even the networks—had switched over to live coverage, blowing out their regular programming for wall-to-wall Jacko coverage.

Fox had been following every contour of the increasingly bizarre proceedings for months, breathlessly reporting each new development in the testimony and documenting every one of the pop star's courthouse entrances and exits. Michael, always the showman, did his part to make the lengthy trial a spectacle: showing up every day in a different faux-military, Dracula-by-way-of-Sgt.-Pepper outfit; entertaining fans outside the courthouse by dancing on the roof of his SUV while holding an umbrella, like a demented Gene Kelly; and constantly expressing indignance that anyone would *dare* find anything untoward about a world-famous fortysomething multimillionaire having pornography-and-alcohol-soaked sleepovers with thirteen-year-old boys.

In short, it had been an entertaining clusterfuck, and I was sad to see it go. We all were—not that you'd know it from the carnival atmosphere of the newsroom that day. I wasn't the only one playing DJ with Michael's back catalogue.

Not to be flippant about child molestation, of course. It's a horrible thing, and on the small chance that there is actually a hell, I'm sure there's a particularly nasty circle of it reserved for those who hurt kids. But working in the news tends to coarsen you, and gallows humor becomes a coping mechanism. I was just shy of one year on the job, and I'd already been subjected to hours of raw footage from Al Qaeda beheading videos, suicide bombings in Israel, insurgent attacks on U.S. troops. I'd seen the heartbreaking Southeast Asian tsunami aftermath, with bodies laid out in horrifyingly long rows, and absolute devastation filling every inch of the frame. I'd endured the seemingly never-ending, simultaneous death watches for Pope John Paul II and Terri Schiavo, the woman in a vegetative state whose case became a macabre tug-of-war between pro-life congressmen and a husband who wanted her to die with dignity. Don't get me wrong—I'm not complaining; I knew I'd signed up for this stuff. Mayhem and misery were practically in the job description. My point is simply that sometimes the only way to cope with all the awfulness of the world is to laugh at it. You just had to joke about all the horrible things. It was either that or break down crying. It was utterly absurd that an eccentric pop star standing accused of doing unspeakable things to children could ever be considered a lighthearted romp of a story, but compared to the other things we'd been dealing with lately, it sort of was. Hence, the semi-party taking place in the newsroom.

As the news choppers tailed Jackson's caravan of SUVs winding its way toward the courthouse, a small group of PAs and editors—with no work to do, thanks to the live coverage—had gathered in my edit room.[32] We were discussing the best song to play after the reading of the verdict. The consensus was that "Man in the Mirror" was a properly somber, introspective choice in the case of a guilty judgment—though at least one wag in the room[33] suggested we go more for dark comedy and play either "P.Y.T. (Pretty Young Thing)" or "Beat It."

We had more trouble deciding on a song in the case of an acquittal. Was it right, we debated, to pick something celebratory? Why didn't Jackson's repertoire include any tunes that would properly express our ambivalence, the fact that we were extremely disappointed in him and yet somehow also relieved that a man who had provided us with so many years of entertainment—batshit though he may be—would not have to rot away in prison, slowly and sadly getting even stranger looking after being permanently cut off from his supply of white pancake makeup and wigs that looked like they came from an Asian ladies' beauty supply shop?

Cameras weren't allowed into the courtroom, but there was a live

---

32 One of the benefits of being a PA for an actual news hour instead of the cut-ins—you got your own room and editor assigned to you for a full two hours. No more having to beg, borrow, and steal edit time. I never forgot my roots, though, and made a point of not giving the cut-in PAs a hard time when they tried to horn in on my editor.

33 Okay, it might have been me.

audio feed. As the jury forewoman read off the counts—all of them "not guilty"—the newsroom was completely silent, save the sounds of the juror's voice and the occasional gasp from a producer. Cameras outside the courthouse captured the assembled fans cheering and celebrating; a crazed-looking elderly woman released doves from a cage, one by one, as each "not guilty" rang out.

When the juror finished reading, I opened the playlist on my computer and cranked the volume on the song that I'd decided was the only one appropriate for the situation, wherein a very rich, famous, and powerful man potentially got away with a horrible crime.

You've been hit by, you've been struck by, a smooth criminal! Jacko sang, as I told my editor to cut a video of the crazy dove lady.

My producer would be wanting that.

With the move to daytime, I felt like a new man. There's something invigorating about working a regular nine-to-five, something that had been lacking with the evening and overnight shifts. Getting up every morning, fighting your roommate for the shower, elbowing your way onto an already overcrowded subway car, pushing through a caffeine-deprived mob to get to the coffee shop counter—the mere act of getting to your desk became an accomplishment in and of itself, a tiny triumph to start the day.

Most important, my career felt like it was back on track. And I was thinking of it as a *career* now, not just a job. I'd pledged from the beginning that I would stay at Fox only long enough to eventually hop somewhere else, but somewhat to my chagrin, I wasn't feeling any motivation to leave. Sure, I wasn't making any *money*—but would I really get paid more somewhere else? And certainly I was sometimes disagreeing with the network's content, occasionally watching segments on our air that made me grit my teeth in anger—or, more likely, shake my head with bemusement. But if I went to CNN or MSNBC, would I really agree with everything said on those channels?

Looking back with the benefit of hindsight, my decision to stay baffles me. I don't know if it was overrationalization or Stockholm syndrome–style brainwashing or what, but in the course of about a year, I'd gone from a die-hard liberal crusader to a cog in the wheel of the most powerful name in conservative media, *and I was perfectly okay with that fact.* I think the most likely explanation was that I was simply comfortable. The job was challenging, and occasionally stressful, but unlike many of my friends who'd graduated from the Notre Dame film and television program, I was actually working in the industry. True, it wasn't quite what I envisioned my career would be—but how many of my fellow graduates could honestly say they were getting their work in front of millions of people on a daily basis? Not many, I was willing to bet. But I was! (Anonymously, to be sure, since none of the Fox News programs had credits at the end, but still . . .)

There was always a niggling voice in the back of my head, whispering that I'd betrayed my progressive roots. I did my best to pacify that voice. Small things, to be sure, but symbolically important enough that I could feel I hadn't completely gone over to the dark side.

For example, I'd marched in the giant protest the weekend before the 2004 Republican National Convention convened at Madison Square Garden. It was on a Sunday, and I'd just pulled an all-nighter at work. I wanted nothing more than to crawl into a bed, any bed, and sleep the day away. But I forced myself to take the subway down to the staging area, walking the entire route in the August heat. It was not, as I'd feared, entirely a hippies-and-bongos affair (though that element was present in very large numbers) but a gathering of hundreds of thousands of average, peaceful people, people who, I realized mid-march, would probably peacefully beat me to death with their BUSH LIED/ SOLDIERS DIED placards if they knew who I worked for.

I found small but satisfying ways to rebel on the job, too. In bold defiance of my directive, I'd include late-night Bush jokes on the list I submitted to the *Fox & Friends* producers. They never used any of them, but I hoped that they at least felt a twinge of shame when they passed them over in their rush to get to the hilarious Leno jokes about Bill Clinton chasing bimbos.

And sometimes when a producer asked for a file footage montage of President Bush, I'd make sure to include at least one shot that made him look unpresidential: tripping on the steps as he dismounted his helicopter, grinning like a goofball after making a bad joke, and—my favorite— taking a walk while inexplicably holding hands with the Saudi crown prince. It wasn't the most mature thing I'd ever done on the job, but it was so oddly gratifying. And I never got caught . . . except once.

The producer called me from the control room immediately after one of my videos rolled, a quick shot showing the leader of the free world taking a lover's stroll with an elderly Middle Easterner in full robes and turban.

The producer was laughing, fortunately. He was amused. I think he knew exactly what I was trying to do.

"Muto, do me a favor and make the Bush video a little less colorful next time," he said.

"Sorry," I said. "I have no idea how that shot got in there."

"Yeah, well, you'd better pray Roger wasn't watching, or the next phone call you get is going to be from him. And trust me on this—he won't be laughing."

April 11, 2012—12:37 P.M.

I was back at my desk on the seventeenth floor, significantly calmed down. It seemed I might actually be okay. The incriminating iPad was safe with Rufus. There'd been no News Corp. storm troopers waiting at my desk for me. Even Tim Wolfe, the producer in the desk next to mine, didn't seem suspicious that my lunch break had lasted about three times longer than normal.

Could I actually be getting away with this?

CHAPTER 8

Crime Does Pay, But Not Particularly Well

On my first day as a crime fighter, I showed up in an outfit guaranteed to strike fear into the hearts of lawbreakers everywhere: khaki pants, a baggy, ill-fitting button-down shirt, and a cheap tie.

Who knows what evil lurks in the hearts of men? I did, after spending several hours prowling the men's accessories department of the Burlington Coat Factory on Sixth Avenue and Twenty-Third Street in Manhattan. Ties were cheap there, most less than ten dollars a pop, and I picked out six new ones to supplement the one or two I already had in the closet at home.

My rationale: Even though it had been made explicitly clear to me that my new gig—the video production assistant for Fox's new weekend crime show—was *not* a promotion, I figured that maybe if I dressed the part, I could *will* a promotion into being. So the faded jeans and open-collar shirts I'd favored as a newsroom PA were out; it was dress pants and ties for me from now on.

"Who's that handsome young go-getter in the sharp polyester tie?" an executive would probably say. "How is it possible we're still only paying him twelve dollars and seventy-four cents an hour? Give him a raise immediately, and put him in charge of his own show!"

It was January 2006. I'd been at Fox a year and a half, and I felt I was a rising star, my ego—and pride at being recognized for my talent—easily supplanting whatever misgivings I had about advancing at a company I wasn't sure I wanted to be working for in the first place.

Before I reported to my show's home base on the seventeenth floor, I swung by the newsroom to show off my new duds to Camie.

She was highly amused.

"All you need to add is an oversize blazer and you'd look like a high school freshman going to his first dance!" she squealed with delight. "I keep expecting you to pin a corsage on me."

My pride was stung. "You're just jealous because I'm up on seventeen now with all the anchors, and you're stuck down here," I said.

"Yeah, well, enjoy your new weekend show," she shot back. "I'm sure your girlfriend just *loves* it that you're gonna be stuck here 'til ten every Saturday night."

She had me there. Jillian had not reacted well to the prospect of having her weekends ruined again, barely a year after my reprieve from the dreaded overnight shift.

"I can't believe you're doing this to me!" she'd fumed when I told her, a few hours after Nina had told me.

"And it's not even any more money? That's insane, Joe. These people are taking advantage of you!"

She had a point, I realized, but I certainly couldn't let her know that.

"Yes, but it's more *responsibility*," I explained. "It could lead to a promotion down the line."

"Well, I still think it's bullshit," she said, folding her arms.

"Hey, we'll still have Fridays together, baby," I said soothingly, rubbing her arm.

She rolled her eyes and walked away.

Jill's completely salient and reasonable points notwithstanding, I was enthused about the gig. I'd be helping to launch a brand-new show. I'd separated myself from the newsroom scrum, where two dozen PAs struggled in virtual anonymity, hoping to distinguish themselves and get off one of the career-dead-end newswheel shows. And as the only production assistant on the show, I'd have complete control over my domain—sole responsibility for every piece of videotape that ran during my hour.

I settled into my desk on the seventeenth floor. For the first time since I'd started at the network a year and a half ago, I had a space that was mine and only mine. This was a huge difference from the unassigned "hot desk"-style seating in the newsroom, a long-running game of musical chairs in which you'd take whatever seat was available in the morning when you showed up, fighting your fellow PAs for the choicest workstations.

Also different from the newsroom—there were windows! Sort of. The outer ring of the floor was taken up entirely by offices for the on-air personalities, or the "talent," as they were known in industry parlance. The talent all had windows in their offices, floor-to-ceiling portals that let in that rarest of commodities, sunlight. And if one of them left their door propped open, one or two precious beams might even reach us!

In practice, the talent spent very little time in their offices, and what time they did spend was mostly with the door closed, doing God knows what,[34] but if we were lucky we'd get an hour or two of indirect sunlight a day. Still not great, but a huge improvement from the Morlock-like existence I'd escaped. (I'd still be spending show days, Saturdays and Sundays, slinging videotape in the newsroom, but even escaping it for 60 percent of my week felt like a small victory.)

It was strange to be on the talent floor. I'd had limited contact with the on-air people in the newsroom—they rarely ventured down there—but now I was surrounded by them. It was absolutely surreal to sit at my desk and watch Geraldo Rivera on my TV, only to bump into him ten

---

34 One anchor spent almost all his time with his door not only closed but *locked*. His assistant told us that when she knocked to deliver something that needed his attention, he'd often take a suspiciously long amount of time to unlock it and let her in, and would appear disheveled and red-faced. The rest of the floor speculated wildly about what he could possibly be doing in there. The assistant, for her part, was convinced that he was surfing porn sites on his computer and *handling his microphone*, if you catch her drift—which, to be fair, might actually be an understandable tension release for someone who is about to go on television in front of millions of people.

minutes later as he politely waited for me to finish using the vending machine. ("Do they stock that thing with mustache wax for him?" Camie asked when I excitedly told her about my encounter.)

The first thing I discovered about the talent: They're just like us! I expected diva-like behavior but saw surprisingly little. Part of this owes to the fact that most of them, aside from some of the big names (O'Reilly, Hannity, Geraldo), are virtual unknowns in the town where they live and work. Any one of these anchors, had they been in a smaller market, would have been in the top tier of local celebrities—right up there with the pro athletes and the car dealership owners who insisted on appearing in their own commercials. However, since Fox News is headquartered in Manhattan, where the attitude toward Fox News generally ranges anywhere from ambivalence to outright hostility, a huge chunk of our on-air talent could easily pull one million viewers on a daily basis, then leave the office and wander the streets of midtown in virtual anonymity.

"That guy with the giant head looks familiar," a person passing Gregg Jarrett or Jon Scott on the sidewalk might say to their companion. "Is he the weather guy on the CBS morning show?"

And the male anchors did all have giant heads. It must be some sort of corollary of the old maxim *The camera adds ten pounds*; the camera also apparently subtracts ten inches of head circumference. How else to explain how anchors who, in person, had melons that looked like they should have ropes attached to them as they float above Thirty-Fourth Street on Thanksgiving, could go on TV and look totally normal? Perversely, the rare anchor or reporter with a head that was normal size in real life went on camera looking like a pinhead from a 1920s circus sideshow.

The female on-air personalities were, on the other hand, generally average-skulled. They made up the difference in hair size, however. The stylists would spend thirty minutes giving one of our ferocious blond pundits a massive beehive worthy of a John Waters film, using four cans of ozone-killing hair spray, all so the woman could walk into a studio and call Al Gore an asshole for believing in global warming.

Fox News developed, over the years, a reputation for preferring blondes, and that was an accurate assessment—we had more than our fair share. But as you can see from the chart below, hair color was relatively low on the list of criteria for female talent:

CRITERIA FOR BEING A FEMALE ON-AIR PERSONALITY AT FOX NEWS CHANNEL (IN DESCENDING ORDER OF IMPORTANCE)

- Hotness
- Ability to string two words together
- Ability to summon outrage and berate a guest at length
- Blondness
- Conservative views (or the ability to convincingly fake them)
- Journalistic credentials

That's not to say that our ranks were filled with bimbos. I absolutely don't want to sell the women of Fox News Channel short. Plenty of them were hardworking, smart, dedicated journalists who just so happened to be hot. (Megyn Kelly, who is as of this writing in fall 2012 an anchor of two morning hours, would be an example of that.) And although being attractive was arguably the *most important* criterion the bosses kept in mind when hiring new talent, it was by no means a deal breaker. (Greta Van Susteren, though relatively plain in appearance, remains one of the biggest stars and highest-ratings getters at the network.)

That being said, we weren't totally devoid of bimbos, either. One former reporter springs to mind. She was literally the best-looking human being I've ever seen up close in real life, to the point where I temporarily lost the faculty of speech one time when she offhandedly said hello to me in an elevator. Her epic hotness eventually helped her claw her way to a relatively prominent on-air position—a surprise to at least one producer who worked with her and had acclimated himself to her looks, swearing to anyone who would listen that he was about 75 percent certain that the reporter was functionally illiterate.

It was an undeniable fact that simply being attractive could get your foot in the door at Fox to a degree that didn't seem to be the case at MSNBC or CNN, our competitors who placed a much lower priority on flashiness.

And this was actually all part of Roger Ailes's governing philosophy. He believed that in a world where all the networks were working from basically the same set of facts and chasing the same stories, the channel with the most exciting presentation would win. That's why Fox had all the graphics that swirled and whooshed across the screen with beeping and buzzing sound effects; that's why we had almost uniformly gorgeous female anchors and commentators, all with pouffy hair and heavy makeup, wearing short but professional skirt suits that revealed a ton of leg; that's why the camera operators and directors conspired to work in as many wide shots as possible to show off said leg. Fox was sexy and exciting, in a way that the other networks simply could not match. That, I would argue, almost as much as the conservative politics, was what made Fox so popular with viewers. After all, right-wing talking points could only get you so far. There was no Republican position to take in the Michael Jackson trial. It was just a voyeuristic, sensationalistic, celebrity train wreck, and it garnered ratings that dwarfed most of the political stories we were following. Much of the time, I think flashy tabloid stories would actually trump political stories. If it ever came down to a choice between covering some dry scandal that made a Democrat look bad and covering an exciting car chase, Fox would pick the car chase any day of the week.

Which brings us to the anchor of my new show. She was named Kimberly Guilfoyle, and despite her unfortunate (but oh so silky) dark brunette hair, she was being groomed as the Next Big Thing at Fox News. In regard to the aforementioned chart, she was absolutely off the scales for #1, instantly becoming one of the most beautiful women at the network. She was also quite good on #3—summoning outrage and berating guests—a helpful trait for the type of true-crime show she was going to be doing. Whether she possessed any of the other traits was still an open question, one that we, as her new staff, would have to help answer.

Kimberly's résumé would have made a great premise for a TNT network hour-long dramedy series. Half Puerto Rican and half Irish, she had worked her way through law school as a Victoria's Secret underwear model. She started her career as a San Francisco assistant district attorney, along the way marrying Gavin Newsom, a movie-star-handsome winery entrepreneur turned politician who was eventually elected San Francisco's mayor. (*The Lingerie Lawyer* Thursdays at nine on TNT!)

On paper, she was actually a bad match for the network. Her marriage to the archliberal Newsom—and subsequent stint as First Lady of a city that Fox hosts routinely took delight in skewering as a radical, hippie, left-wing, pot-riddled cesspool—should have disqualified her. But she'd moved to New York to do analysis for CNN and Court TV and eventually filed for divorce from His Honor, and someone on the second floor at Fox took notice.

She was poached from the competitors and given a hefty contract and a promise to build a weekend show as a vehicle for her. The concept was that she'd function as a sort of Saturday/Sunday version of Greta Van Susteren—none of the investigative journalism chops, but about forty times the sex appeal.

The Second Floor saw it as a can't-miss proposition.

"Does anyone have any other comments about the show so far? Anything they think is *really* working?" the executive asked. "Or anything they think"—she looked around the room dramatically—"is *not* working?"

The staffers of *The Lineup* with Kimberly Guilfoyle shifted awkwardly in our seats. A month after the show's debut, it was clear that a lot of things weren't working, but no one wanted to say so in front of Suzanne Scott, a company vice president and a powerful programming executive who was only a level or two removed from Roger Ailes.

Even though she half scared the shit out of me, I had to admit she was an impressive figure. She'd started with the network as a personal assistant to one of the anchors and had quickly worked her way up through the ranks from there, eventually rising to become the senior producer for Greta Van Susteren's show, before corporate noticed her and brought her into the fold. She was intense, as you'd expect someone with her ladder-climbing ability to be, and more than a bit icy. She was also taking special interest in our show, since her background with Greta meant she was an expert on the crime beat.

Our production team was disconcertingly small. I was the youngest, and also the only guy. In addition to me, there were two bookers in charge of recruiting guests to come on the show; a line producer, who was responsible for keeping track of the time while we were on air; a senior producer, who was ostensibly in charge of the whole endeavor but, as near as I could tell, did absolutely nothing all day; and finally, the brains behind the whole operation, Lizzie, the producer.

Lizzie was a short, profane, raucously funny New Jersey broad. She was ultracompetent and very good at her job, and had zero patience for anyone who wasn't—which, as far as she was concerned, was everyone around her. In the weeks leading up to our first show, I watched Lizzie's frustration grow as she bristled at what she saw as the constant meddling from Suzanne and the other executives, who had started second-guessing her on every single detail.

And the details were endless. Decisions had to be hammered out for every show element: graphics, music, animation, an opening title sequence, ideas for "signature" segments (i.e., "Kimberly's Court," during which the host was supposed to give her own verdict on one of the criminal cases in the news that week); the list went on and on.

But the details that gave Lizzie the biggest headache, the details that everyone—from the executives on down to the makeup and wardrobe department—agonized over, were all related to the personal appearance of our beautiful host. *How should Kimberly be lit? Did we want soft, Barbara Walters–style lighting, or should we go for a more dramatic and mysterious setup? And what should she wear? Something professional like she'd wear in court? Or something a little sexier, to get our money's worth— like a miniskirt and a blazer without a shirt underneath, revealing a tasteful amount of cleavage?* ("We should put her in robes, like Judge Judy,"

I half joked at one of the early production meetings, only to be met with cold *you're not being helpful* stares.)

And the hair and makeup. *Oh, God*, the hair and makeup. Kimberly was strikingly beautiful in person—disconcertingly so, as a matter of fact—but if she wasn't coiffed and primped and painted properly, her severe features would warp under the harsh studio lights, making her look like the world's most glamorous transsexual. And even on some days when the makeup was right, the hair people still went overboard, giving her a shellacked beehive that the Second Floor worried made her look like a Fembot.

But that's not what Suzanne was asking about that day. She was probing us for weakness, testing us to see if we'd dare diagnose what was ill about our fledgling show.

"Is there anything you think we could do to improve the show?" Suzanne said, urging one of us, any of us, to break the awkward silence that had settled over the meeting.

There was only one person in the room dumb enough to rise to the bait.

"Well, . . ." I started, and all heads in the room swiveled toward me. I met Lizzie's eyes. She had a *what the hell are you doing* look on her face.

Undaunted, I stupidly pressed on. "I'm not sure that we're doing a good job of emphasizing the whole 'victim's advocate' angle that we discussed."

During preproduction for the show, that had been the buzzphrase tossed around by everyone—victim's advocate. *Kimberly will be a victim's advocate!* Or: *This segment idea is great, but how can we approach it from more of a victim's advocate angle?* It's the hook that would supposedly separate her from Greta, her weeknight counterpart, though I never knew quite what they meant by it.

It was only later that I figured out it was all just a euphemism for *Be more like Nancy Grace*. Grace was a CNN Headline News host with a grating personality who had her own inexplicably popular crime show. A former prosecutor herself, she had juiced the ratings of the formerly moribund also-ran network by creating her own brand of angry perp-berating Southern charm. That's what the Second Floor wanted from Kimberly.

But after a month of shows, I wasn't seeing it.

It was only after I opened my mouth to say so that I realized I wasn't offering constructive criticism so much as throwing our whole team under the bus. After all, any failure to emphasize the agreed-upon theme reflected as poorly on the staff as it did on the host.

When we got back to the seventeenth floor, Lizzie wasn't quite mad. But she wasn't thrilled with me, either.

"Hey, Muto," she said. "In the future, if someone asks you if you can think of anything about the show that sucks . . ."

"Yeah?" I said.

"How about you just keep your friggin' trap shut next time, okay?"

A few weeks later, when Lizzie got back from something like her *sixth* meeting on the second floor, where the topic was solely Kimberly's makeup, she flopped down at her desk in exasperation.

"Can somebody friggin' shoot me?" she said, miming a gunshot to the head. "If I have to go to one more of these meetings about her makeup . . ." She trailed off. "You know, if we spent half the goddamn time planning what's going to go on the show as we did talking about how she friggin' looks, we'd have the number one show on the friggin' network."

Ratings were actually pretty decent at that point, due to a resurgence in a type of story that we began referring to as "MPWW"—Missing Pretty White Women. This had always been a fertile topic for the network (remember Laci Peterson, the murdered pregnant lady I'd almost botched my job interview over), but the spring of 2006 was sort of a renaissance of the genre.

Leading the charge was Natalee Holloway, who I began to think of as Queen of the MPWWs. Natalee was an eighteen-year-old from Alabama who disappeared on the final night of her high school senior trip to Aruba. The last people to see her alive were three local boys with whom Natalee had hitched a ride after leaving a bar. From a crime show producer's standpoint, the story had it all:

- The victim was a beautiful blonde who was seemingly the picture of teenage innocence.
- Her mother, Beth, was telegenic, wildly sympathetic, and extremely candid in interviews, which she gave frequently to almost any outlet that asked.
- The local authorities came off as cartoonishly incompetent buffoons who were clearly bungling the case, arresting and releasing almost a dozen different suspects during the course of the investigation.
- The main suspect, a local boy named Joran van der Sloot, was sleazy-looking and politically well connected, with a father who was in line to become a local judge (and was later accused of aiding his son in a cover-up).
- There was an endless parade of salacious rumors about the victim (*She was high on drugs that night! She was secretly a slut!*) and her ultimate fate (*She was sold into white slavery! She was murdered and fed to the sharks! She decided to go for a night swim alone and simply drowned!*). The rumors were completely unverifiable, entirely unable to be disproven, and endlessly discussable.
- And most important, there was a ton of video: Natalee looking cute performing in color guard at a football game, on the dance team at a basketball game, and in a car chatting with her friends; perp walks of all the suspects in handcuffs with their heads bowed; and hours of footage of searchers combing the beautiful beaches of Aruba.

The Holloway case was pure, uncut cable news crack cocaine. And despite having almost no new substantial developments, we managed to cover it for several months, some nights giving up as much as two-thirds of the show to the topic.

But even we were amateurs compared to Greta Van Susteren. We had only two nights a week to fill. Greta managed to talk about little else besides Holloway for five nights a week, and even ventured down to Aruba on several occasions. ("I hear Greta's buying a friggin' time share down there," Lizzie cracked.)

Mindful that the Natalee Holloway story could (and probably should) peter out at any moment, we scoured the news every day for other missing-girl cases that could possibly catch fire and become our next ratings bonanza. There were a few that seemed promising, but none of them ever took off the way Natalee did.

We (the media, I mean) took a lot of flack at the time for focusing only on the missing girls who were pretty and white, but the fact of the matter is that we covered plenty of cases that involved the homely and minorities. The ratings just never followed.

And we were shameless ratings chasers.

I'd never realized the full extent of it until I was on *The Lineup*. When I was just a production assistant in the newsroom, I was completely insulated from all the hand-wringing over ratings. PAs were left out of those meetings. We were transients anyway—free agents who shifted from show to show based on the needs of the day's schedule. It didn't concern us one iota if the ten A.M. hour beat the eleven A.M. by 15,000 viewers. *Who gave a shit?* But when I joined *The Lineup*, I was on a true team for the first time in my career. The number of viewers suddenly became one of my paramount concerns.

Fox has an entire department devoted to doing nothing but crunching the ratings data. The unlucky souls who toil there—constantly wrestling with columns of numbers destined to be glanced at by about three dozen people—would e-mail us every Tuesday with spreadsheets breaking down our viewership into fifteen-minute increments, as well as breaking down the proportion of our audience that was in the coveted age twenty-five to fifty-four demographic (very attractive to advertisers) or the dreaded, shunned fifty-five and older grouping (might as well be corpses propped in front of the TV). It was crude and imprecise at best, but it was the only tool we had to gauge our success or lack thereof, and we clung to it like a drowning man grasping for a life preserver.

And what the ratings told us in early 2006 was that viewers were just not interested in any missing women who weren't young, pretty, and white.

"It's racism, pure and simple," Amy, one of the bookers, posited on a Wednesday morning as we all looked at the previous weekend's ratings. We'd done three segments on Natalee, followed by one on a missing black girl, and the numbers had plummeted when we made the switch. "The viewers just don't care about someone not like them," she said.

"I don't think that's what it is necessarily," I chimed in. "There's something special about the Holloway story. It's like they can picture her as their daughter."

"Nah, it's that they want to fuck her," Lizzie said, laughing. "You know these horny old farts at home are getting off on that video of her in the cheerleading outfit."

"Want to fuck who?" a voice said loudly from the hall next to our pod. We all looked up and it was David Asman, an anchor, who'd apparently overheard while passing by.

"Natalee Holloway. You know, the Aruba girl," Lizzie said, wonderfully unperturbed to get caught by an anchor working blue in the office.

Asman rolled his eyes. "Oh, brother, *that thing* is still going on? The poor girl is clearly dead. Can we stop talking about it already?" He walked off, shaking his head.

True story: I joined Facebook specifically to befriend an accused rapist.

Back in 2006, years before Mark Zuckerberg's little experiment became your aunt's favorite way to share pictures of her cats, Facebook was still mostly for college kids. In fact, it was strictly limited to those with .edu e-mail addresses. Since I was the only one on the staff who had one, it was decided that I'd join.

The mission: Convince members of the Duke lacrosse team to spill their guts.

In March 2006, an exotic dancer named Crystal Mangum claimed she had been raped while she and a colleague were performing at a house party attended by several members of the Duke University men's lacrosse team. She picked three players out of a photo lineup, telling police they had trapped her in the bathroom and sexually assaulted her. The story was an instant media sensation, thanks partially to the overzealous Durham, North Carolina, prosecutor Mike Nifong, who denounced the lacrosse players in several interviews, and vowed to secure convictions. It was also irresistible cable news fodder—a powder keg of race and class issues: The accuser was black and poor, while the suspects were white and from affluent families.

I had a mixed opinion of the case. On the one hand, the players came across as total dickheads—fratty, entitled jocks who had mistreated the performers they'd hired. (One of them reportedly yelled, "We asked for whites, not niggers," as the strippers drove off. Another wrote a nasty e-mail to his teammates after the party, vowing to hire more strippers but this time "killing the bitches" and "cut[ting] their skin off while cumming in my duke issue spandex"—apparently an ironic reference to the book *American Psycho*, a nuance that was lost on most cable news viewers.) My alma mater, Notre Dame, actually had quite a bit in common with Duke: Both were academically well-regarded schools whose student bodies primarily consisted of well-off white kids; both were situated in economically depressed towns with large minority populations that had a sometimes tense relationship with the university; both schools aspired to cultivate an Ivy League reputation but were hampered by powerful athletic programs that sucked up all the oxygen on campus, giving rise to a drunken, privileged jockocracy that was worshipped by the other students and given free rein by the administration. So I could sympathize with those who said the chickens had come home to roost for the Athletes Gone Wild.

But on the other hand, the case stank to high heaven.

The accuser had been extremely intoxicated on the night in question; cops had found her passed out in a parked car. Then she had picked the suspects out of a photo spread that consisted *only* of members of the lacrosse team, with no random faces in the mix—a clearly illegal procedure that even the police admitted would probably not hold up in a trial. And two out of the three suspects she had identified ended up producing airtight alibis, proving that they weren't even at the party at the time of the alleged assault.

The evidence that the accuser was lying kept adding up, and eventually became overwhelming. Even though we at *The Lineup* could tell the case was bogus, our status as victim's advocates—and the continued high ratings we were pulling—meant we had to keep pursuing it.

And that's how I found myself Facebook messaging dozens of college athletes, with a surely enticing proposition: We know you turned down the *Today* show and *Good Morning America* and *20/20*, and dozens of other high-profile shows, but we thought you might be interested in coming on a small cable news program that no one's ever heard of, because the host is a super-hot lady, and the production assistant is young and hip and speaks your language, as proven by his reaching out to you through Facebook, a site he joined just a few days ago for the express purpose of contacting you.

Unsurprisingly, the responses did not come rolling in. My messages were completely ignored, with the lone exception of a freshman midfielder, who was kind enough to get straight to the point:

dude fuck you. seriously.

If only he had seen my sweet tie, he probably would have changed his tune.

On Saturday night, Geraldo Rivera strutted down the center aisle of the newsroom as if he owned it. Which, for all intents and purposes that evening, he did.

Flamboyant, and more than a little eccentric, the seasoned anchor and reporter stood out in the buttoned-down world of Fox News. In 2006, he was in his early sixties but looked barely a day over forty. He had a thick, jaunty mustache, a luscious head of hair, a smoking-hot wife, a fully stocked bar in his office, and a waterfront mansion in New

Jersey that he sometimes commuted from in a speedboat. Basically, he was James fucking Bond. The rank and file adored him in all his ridiculous glory. That Saturday night, he wore a skintight black muscle shirt, the better to show off a pair of powerful guns that put my flabby, decades-younger arms to shame. Even though it was nighttime, and he was indoors, he was wearing sunglasses with lenses tinted an absurd shade of bright amethyst.

He had been mostly absent from the newsroom the past few months, working on the syndicated weekday tabloid show that had been birthed as a vehicle specifically for him—*The Lineup* had actually been created to take over the weekend time slot that he'd vacated. But when the war between Israel and Lebanon started in July 2006, it proved unexpectedly popular with the viewers, who were apparently suckers for the Bruckheimer-esque, explosion-filled rocket attack footage the wire services were feeding us on a daily basis. The bosses decided that a heavyweight presence was needed to handle the weekend coverage. When it turned out none was available, they went with Geraldo. The staff of *The Lineup* had been pressed into service to support his efforts.

Geraldo was both widely beloved and widely mocked by the other employees. Something about his personality, *his very presence*, was so silly and so over-the-top that it was as impossible to dislike him as it was to not ridicule him. He was arguably the only on-air personality in the entire network who didn't owe his success to Fox News and Roger Ailes—he had been famous long before Fox even existed. As a consequence, he was given more leeway than almost any of the other talent and was the highest-profile, openly liberal anchor we had. But he never let his personal politics trump his tabloidy love of drama and spectacle. And since nothing was more dramatic and spectacular than war, he was totally in his element with the Lebanon coverage.

It was actually a perfect time for the Mustache Man to reclaim his weekend perch: Kimberly Guilfoyle was out on maternity leave a few months after eloping to Costa Rica with her baby daddy, the heir to a high-end furniture company fortune; and there were no compelling crime stories in the pipeline—the Duke lacrosse story had cooled off after the DA's case had more or less imploded, and even the old standby Natalee Holloway case had entered a dormancy period.[35]

After the show that night, we all went to Langan's, a bar on Forty-Seventh Street, just a few steps away from the office. The Irish pub was a popular after-work hangout for Foxies, to the point where we'd jokingly refer to it as Studio L, as if it were an off-site extension of headquarters. The bar had garnered a reputation for being a journalists' haunt even before Fox adopted it, catering for years to hard-drinking *New York Post* writers. (The longtime columnist Steve Dunleavy, a legendary lush, had passed out in the joint so many times that they'd formally dedicated a stool to him and etched his likeness into a commemorative frosted-glass plaque that hung above the bar.) And now my staff, along with the staff of our sister show, *The Big Story Weekend*, which aired in the hour after us, had commandeered it as our unofficial clubhouse, heading there every Saturday and Sunday after the show was finished taping, and often staying until closing time.

That night, Geraldo and some of his crew had come with us.

"First round's on me, guys!" Geraldo shouted as soon as he walked into the joint, setting off applause and high-fiving from the twenty or so producers and production assistants who had commandeered an entire corner of the room. Geraldo slid his AmEx "Black" card across the bar top and ordered a whiskey on the rocks for himself.

It was only after I started working for *The Lineup* that I understood the forces that drove newsmen to drink. We sacrificed our entire weekends and any semblance of a social life, chasing down cripplingly depressing stories about murder, rape, and mayhem. We simply *had* to drink together after work, as a release valve more than anything. And it wasn't that none of us had other friends, or other places to be. But more often than not, we shunned those other commitments in favor of the

---

35 The Holloway case would heat up at least two or three more times over the years, mostly thanks to Greta Van Susteren's dogged, tireless pursuit of a resolution. As of the fall of 2012, the exact circumstances of Natalee's disappearance remained a mystery—though the main suspect, Joran van der Sloot, was serving a twenty-eight-year prison sentence in Peru for an unrelated 2010 murder.

post-show bacchanalia at Langan's. And our non-Fox friends, if they knew what they were missing out on, probably would have thanked us for it, because frankly, after coming off a show taping, we were down-right unpleasant to be around—stir-crazy from being cooped up all day; cracking dark, demented jokes about missing teenagers; and so eager to inhale any and all booze in sight that the bartenders sometimes had to pretend they'd run out of our favorite liquor to stop us from taking yet another round of shots.

As the year wore on, the drinking situation spiraled out of control. The war in Lebanon had wound down, and Geraldo went back to his syndicated show full-time. We returned to the crime beat—some of us more reluctantly than others—and welcomed a new fill-in for Kimberly.

Megyn Kelly was, at the time, the Fox News Supreme Court re-porter. She was headquartered in DC but was on loan to New York for the occasion. Like the woman she was filling in for, she was a trained lawyer. But that's where the similarities ended. She was blond and sunny where Kimberly was raven-haired and fiery. And she was refreshingly free of diva-like behavior: She took the subway or hailed a cab to the office instead of demanding the company pay for a car service; she sug-gested good story ideas and did her own research; and instead of head-ing straight home after the show, she'd come to the bar with us, sometimes outlasting some of the die-hards.

There was a sense that Megyn was a rising star at the network—a sense only reinforced when rumors later swept the DC bureau that she was sleeping with Brit Hume, the crusty six P.M. anchor who was al-most three decades her senior. It was widely agreed in the New York office that the rumors had been started by someone jealous of the plum assignments she'd been getting. (My personal theory was that Hume himself had started them, but I could never get anyone else to sign on to that viewpoint.) Either way, the chatter was a signal that she had ar-rived, and a few years after I worked with her, she was imported to New York for good and was given a two-hour daytime block, for which she adopted a highly aggressive archconservative persona. My first thought on seeing her in action was *She's faking it*. And my second thought was *She's a genius*. Creating a new persona for herself was somewhat cynical but was overall a brilliant career move. She was smart, talented, and beautiful, but that would only get you so far at Fox—Ailes wanted to see a point of view as well. So Megyn started to act a little less smart and a lot more Republican when she was on-air, and suddenly there was chatter in the hallways that she was in the running for Greta Van Susteren's prime-time slot.

But in 2006, that later version of Megyn Kelly was just a glimmer in the eye of the cool, laid-back reporter sitting on a stool at Langan's, drinking a glass of white wine and trading dirty jokes with the staff of the network's second-rate crime show.

Megyn was not there, fortunately for her, for an especially memorable bender of a weekend in October that I consider both the apex and the nadir of my post–crime show drinking career.

First, on Saturday night, Danny, a booker for *The Big Story*, got bounced after picking a fight with the bartender, an affable, goateed man whose only crime was swearing to an incredulous Danny that the joint was completely out of Jack Daniel's. Next, Lizzie, exhausted from shouldering the demands of a diva host, a micromanaging phalanx of executives, and an immature staff that needed constant hand-holding (and possibly under the influence of between four and nine margaritas), drifted into unconsciousness mid-conversation, toppling from her barstool all the way to the floor. After determining that she didn't have a concussion, we called the car service that the network had on retainer for shuttling guests to and from the studio, and piled her into it for the long trip to New Jersey.

But Saturday turned out to be just the warm-up act for Sunday, when barely an hour into the festivities, two producers probably senior enough to know better, slipped out of the bar with the intent to smoke a joint in a dark alley somewhere. When no dark alleys presented themselves, they settled for a partially dimmed doorway on Forty-Seventh Street, steps from the bar entrance and barely fifty yards from the blazing lights of Times Square. When word filtered back to the bar what they were up to, we laughed at their audacity.[36]

Unfortunately for them, the NYPD found it a lot less amusing.

It was only the intervention of a fast-thinking, sweet-talking, and breathtakingly gorgeous reporter—fortunately, she had accompanied us to the bar that night after appearing in a segment on the show—that spared my two colleagues from getting an uncomfortably close firsthand view of the criminal justice system they'd been covering. She worked her magic on the pair of New York's Finest who had been driving their cruiser down Forty-Seventh Street and had easily spotted my poorly concealed colleagues toking their faces off, miraculously convincing the cops to give up one of the easiest busts of their careers and let the two producers go with just a warning.

---

36 I wish I could tell you I had been far too smart to join them, but I had simply been in the bathroom when they hatched the plan—otherwise, I might well have been with them.

April 11, 2012—1:03 P.M.

As a high-powered professional television journalist, I spent many of my workdays deeply immersed in some of the most complex, serious, consequential issues facing the American public.

As I browsed the surprisingly comprehensive Wikipedia[37] entry for *The Beverly Hillbillies*, I was forced to admit to myself that this was not one of those days.

I was writing the Great American News Quiz, O'Reilly's weekly opportunity to channel his inner Merv Griffin and play game show host.

The division of labor for the quiz segment was simple—O'Reilly would pick a topic, I would write twenty multiple-choice questions based on said topic, the host would pick the five he liked best, and the next day he'd pose them to two Fox News personalities: smirky *Fox & Friends* cohost Steve Doocy and good-natured blond morning anchor Martha MacCallum.

It wasn't exactly Pulitzer fodder, but it was a fun-to-watch, highly rated segment. As an added bonus, writing the questions was an enjoyable task for me, a nice change of pace from my normal duties.

Some days the writing was painfully slow going, but that day, of all

---

37 I would never trust Wikipedia as a source for an important news story, but it turned out to be a valuable repository when it came to trivial nuggets of information about beloved sitcoms from the 1960s.

days, the questions were absolutely flowing out of me. Part of that had
to do with the week's topic: sitcom legends. (At one point the News
Quiz actually had been a quiz about the week's news, but under my
watch, it had slowly morphed into a quiz about whatever the hell captured O'Reilly's fancy.) But I think the other explanation for my suddenly prolific quiz-question production is that I was grateful to have an
activity, something to take my attention away from the thought that
had been growing in the back of my brain all day: *I think I've really
fucked myself here.*

An hour later, I put the finishing touches on my last quiz question
and hit PRINT. Wandering over to the laser printer a few feet from my
desk, I gathered the still-warm pages and leafed through them. It wasn't
my finest work—but considering that I'd spent much of my morning
in a state of sweat-drenched near-panic, it could have been much worse.

I stapled the sheaf of paper, stuck it in a manila folder on which I
had written *NEWS QUIZ* in fat Sharpie, and walked the twenty feet
from my desk to Bill's office. He hadn't arrived for the day yet, but his
door was wide open. His personal assistant, Margaret, had prepped the
room for him: The day's newspapers, books requiring his autograph,
and various other items that needed his attention were arranged in a
neat pile on his desk. I put the quiz folder on top of the pile.

Back at my desk, I dropped heavily into my rolling chair, only to
hear a familiar booming Voice, shouting questions at my fellow producers. The Voice was fifty feet down the hallway and coming ever closer.

He was here.

CHAPTER 9

The Calling

My first meeting with Bill O'Reilly lasted all of thirty seconds. I was already technically his employee at that point, having been recruited by one of his lower-level producers, interviewed by his executive producer, and approved by the Fox News human resources department, all in the course of a few months, and all without seeing hide nor hair of the Big Dog himself.

It was January 2007, just about two and a half years after I began at Fox News. My rise had been disconcertingly meteoric. I had started as an overnight-shifter, unsure I even wanted to be there, and now I was about to join the network's most popular, highest-profile show.

The meeting took place in Bill's office. I was escorted in by Stan Manskoff, one of the executive producers of *The O'Reilly Factor*. The door was open, but Stan stopped to knock anyway, rapping lightly to get Bill to look up from some papers he was studying at his desk.

"Bill," he said when he had the anchor's attention, "I've got the new radio guy here. Can he come say hello for a second?"

O'Reilly sighed, as if we were inconveniencing him terribly. "All right," he said. "Bring him in."

We stepped into Bill's office, a different part of the seventeenth floor from where my soon-to-be-former *Lineup* colleagues sat. It was a corner office, naturally. In keeping with the Fox News low-budget aesthetic, it wasn't that large or flashy, maybe about fifteen by twenty feet, with plain-looking institutional furniture. Two other corner offices on the seventeenth floor belonged to Sean Hannity, who barely used his (he preferred to spend most of his time at the offices of his radio show, located at WABC studios above Penn Station, about fifteen blocks away), and Geraldo, who used his plenty. The fourth corner office had been inexplicably claimed by the wardrobe department and was filled with racks and racks of dark, sober men's suits and brightly colored women's blouses, skirts, and jackets.

Bill's desk was placed so that he faced the door, with his back to the windows, large floor-to-ceiling ones that gave a decent, if partially obstructed, view of Times Square a block to the west, and the Hudson River and New Jersey beyond. The walls were decked with framed memorabilia: a congratulatory magazine ad from the company that syndicated his old tabloid show *Inside Edition*; a photo montage of Bill reporting from various exotic locations; yellowed copies of famous newspaper front pages (DEWEY DEFEATS TRUMAN, JAPAN SURRENDERS, MAN WALKS ON MOON). Across the room from his desk was a couch, with three flat-screen TVs mounted on the wall above—a large one tuned to Fox News, and two smaller ones underneath tuned to CNN and MSNBC, respectively. All three were muted.

Bill didn't rise to greet us. His eyes followed me, sizing me up as I took the four or five steps from the door to his desk. I was suddenly self-conscious about my appearance. After getting off to a strong start with my plan to wear ties, I'd reverted to my old ways. And now, in front of Bill, I was worried that my lightly faded jeans were too unbusinesslike, and that my two-day-old facial scruff pegged me (correctly) as someone who was too lazy to shave every day.

I stopped front and center and grasped the giant meat hook that he'd stretched across the desk. His shake was firm enough but wasn't the pulverizing, I'm-more-macho-than-you death grip I'd expected from him. His hand was surprisingly soft.

"Joe Muto. Nice to meet you," I said.

"Mmm-hmm." He nodded, his gaze still not breaking from my face.

"Joe's coming to us from *The Lineup*," Stan offered.

Bill glanced over at Stan, his face registering a look of confusion.

"The weekend crime show," Stan said. "With Guilfoyle, Mayor Newsom's ex-wife?"

A look of recognition from Bill. "Ahh, Guilfoyle." His eyes snapped back to me suddenly, startling me.

"Anyway," I said, hoping I hadn't flinched visibly, "I'm excited to come aboard. I can't wait to start next week."

Bill nodded again.

"Work hard," he said, then looked back down at his paperwork.

I stood there confused. *Was that it?* I felt Stan's touch, light on my shoulder, and looked back at him. He gave a little jerk toward the door with his head. *Let's get out of here.*

"So that's it?" I asked when we were back in the hall.

Stan shrugged. "What did you want, a parade?"

Sam Martinez had been the first O'Reilly-ite to approach me. I knew Sam from my newsroom days. He'd been the PA for *DaySide with Linda Vester*, cutting video for the infamous news show that had both a live audience and a host who seemed to hate live audiences.

Sam was unmissable in the newsroom. For starters, he was enormous, built like an NFL lineman, over six feet tall and pushing three hundred pounds. But for all his size, he was surprisingly agile and light on his feet. When he did a Death Run from the edit room to playback with a tape that was in danger of missing air, he wove gracefully around obstacles, taking corners and barreling toward playback at a speed you wouldn't think a man of his mass would be able to attain. Smaller PAs dove out of the way when they saw him coming, flattening themselves against cubicle walls with a look of absolute terror. But he never crashed into any of them, delivering the tape without incident every time, puffing heavily and sweaty-browed from the effort, but triumphant. Sam was also the most gregarious PA in the newsroom, spending his downtime not huddled at his computer surfing websites like everyone else, but roaming from desk to desk, chatting with the other production assistants, slapping backs and bellowing greetings in his loud tenor.

He was in full yelling and backslapping mode when I bumped into him one night in late 2006, at an after-work happy hour at (where else?) Langan's, celebrating the birthday of another PA with whom we were both friendly. I was still on *The Lineup*, and he had left *DaySide* for a position with Bill O'Reilly's radio show.

"Muto!" he yelled as I walked into the bar, raising his beer glass in a salute. "Get over here and take a shot with me!"

I bellied up next to him. "I'm in. What are we doing? Tequila?"

He looked at me with mock outrage. "Why do you think I want tequila, huh? Is it because I'm brown?"

Sam was Mexican American, one of the few minorities in a newsroom that was heavily white, and he didn't let anyone forget it.

"A Mexican guy always has to drink tequila, is that it?" he continued, laughing, punching me good-naturedly on the shoulder.

"Mexican? I thought you were Samoan," said a woman's voice behind us. We both turned. It was Camie.

"Okay, now I'm offended for real," Sam said. Though with his bulky build and the thick black goatee he was sporting, he *did* look a little like he was from Samoa.

"Aww, quit being a baby and let's take a shot," Camie said. Then to the bartender, "Three shots of Patrón."

The barkeep lined up three shot glasses and filled them from a squat bottle of clear liquid. We picked up the glasses and clinked them together.

"Viva Mexico," I said, and we knocked back the smooth, pleasantly burning elixir.

An hour later, nicely buzzed, Sam and I were nursing beers at a table.

"How do you like your job, man?" he asked. "I walk past your desk sometimes. It looks like you're not really doing much." I almost got indignant but realized he was probably right.

"I like the people," I said. "But I have jack shit to do during the week. And I'm pretty bored of the crime beat."

"You know . . ."—Sam lowered his voice conspiratorially—"we have an opening coming up on Bill's radio show. I could put your name in. I think you'd be good for it."

And just like that, it was moral dilemma time for me again.

Working for *The Lineup*, I could at least pretend I wasn't involved in promulgating the worst of Fox's conservative tendencies. I gave myself plausible deniability. *After all*, I told myself, *there was no ideology in the crime stories. There's no liberal or conservative—just guilty or innocent.* But if I started working for O'Reilly, that fig leaf I'd been grasping on to for the sake of my own conscience would disappear entirely. There'd be no pretending anymore that I was somehow separate from the Fox News right-wing outrage-manufacturing complex. Instead, I'd be at the very center of it.

Then again, was there really that much difference in what I was doing and what Sam was doing? I'd already compromised by taking the job with the company in the first place. Once I was in the building, taking a paycheck, did it really matter what specific show I was affiliated with? Wouldn't it actually be better to be on a show with some clout instead of stuck on a dead-end weekend show that was slowly bleeding viewers and was on the verge of going down the tubes? And couldn't I, as I'd originally vowed when I took the job, change the network from the inside a lot more effectively if I was in the belly of the beast? Wouldn't keeping the famous, feared Bill O'Reilly honest actually be a much higher calling than tracking down missing blond teenagers?

"Yo, you still with me, man?" Sam snapped his fingers in front of my face. "You drifted off or something."

"All right," I said. "Let's do it."

"Fuck, yeah!" Sam yelled, pounding the table. He jumped out of his chair, waving his hands over his head to get the bartender's attention. "Shots! Now!"

Two weeks later, I was sitting in Stan Manskoff's office. He was quizzing me on my duties for *The Lineup*, feeling out if I was going to be a good fit for the O'Reilly team. It wasn't an ideological litmus test like the Kool-Aid Conference two years earlier. It felt more like an assessment to see if I was competent enough to handle the pressure of working for a demanding, high-profile host. Stan must have liked whatever it was I said, because another week after that, he called me back into his office.

"We'd like to offer you the job as the new production assistant on Bill's radio show," he said.

The O'Reilly empire at the time consisted of three distinct teams that worked closely together: TV, radio, and website. TV was the biggest, and in Bill's eyes the most important, employing about fifteen people. Radio was smaller—only five people at its peak. And the website team was basically just two guys, with some additional support staff on the West Coast. The three staffs were intertwined, all attending the same meetings, all under Stan's supervision, and all expected to do whatever they could to further the O'Reilly cause. Stan was offering me a chance to join the team. The Dream Team, really. It was the pinnacle of working for Fox. If I was going to go all in, this was my chance.

I thought for a few seconds.

"Thanks for the offer, Stan, but I'm going to have to say no."

The next day, I was in a meeting with Brigette, our head of HR, in her second-floor office.

"I'm confused," she was saying. "I thought you wanted this job. You interviewed for it. Stan said you seemed very eager in the interview. Why turn it down?"

"I do want the job," I said. "But not if it isn't a promotion."

The offer was for me to be a production assistant. It was just a lateral move. If I took it, I was guaranteed at least another year—or even two—before I was eligible for a bump up to associate producer, a title I craved desperately by that point. If I stayed with *The Lineup* for another few months, I was virtually guaranteed to get that promotion.

I explained this to Brigette in so many words, and she nodded along as I spoke.

"I totally get where you're coming from," she said when I'd finished. "But this position just isn't at that level."

"Look," I said. "I know that O'Reilly is the big leagues and that my show right now is basically the minors. And I want to come work for O'Reilly. It's like getting called up by the Yankees. But I'm on the verge of becoming a cleanup hitter for my current team, and you guys are asking me to join the Yankees as a batboy. I'd love to join the Yankees. But not if it means I'm taking a step backward in my career. Or even a step sideways."

Brigette sighed. I could tell I was losing her.

"I know that the metaphor is tortured," I said. "But does it make sense to you?"

"Sort of," she said. "But I'm a Mets fan."

Ouch. Swing and a miss.

Two months passed. Sam had been so disappointed when I told him I'd turned down the job that I began to second-guess myself. Had I blown an opportunity that I'd never get another stab at? As much as it would suck to be trapped as a PA for another year or two, the position would be so high profile that it might just be worth it. And I'd at least be off the weekend shifts and get out of the increasingly toxic cycle of post-show debauchery at Langan's that I couldn't quite seem to tear myself away from.

The schedule and the drinking had finally taken their toll on my personal life. Jillian and I broke up, to the surprise of absolutely no one who knew us and had witnessed the increasingly ugly fighting that marred the last few months of our relationship.

In retrospect, I had been a terrible boyfriend. Jillian had never bought into the whole New York thing, and I grew to resent her for it, in essence choosing the city I was obsessed with over the woman I had once loved.

With my love life in tatters, and my career seemingly at a dead end, I pondered doing the unthinkable. Something so foul and despicable that it gives me chills to this day, knowing how close I came to the brink.

The law school brochure was actually in my hands when the call came.

I was home on a Monday afternoon (the first day of my "weekend"), trying to figure out if any law programs were craving students who had managed only a 2.8 GPA in the world's easiest major and who were in the midst of washing out of a cable news career. My cell phone rang.

It was Max Greene, the executive producer of the entire weekend prime time. He was a great boss, mostly because he wasn't afraid to climb into the trenches with his troops; he'd been a mainstay at Langan's, heroically picking up rounds and thus earning our loyalty forever. But I hadn't heard from him in weeks—he'd developed a reputation as a turnaround art-ist and had been temporarily pulled from the weekends and lent out to Geraldo's syndicated show, which was floundering in the ratings. He'd never called me at home before, so I knew something big was up.

Max got right to the point: "Joe, I heard that you've got an offer from O'Reilly."

I didn't know how he'd found out. I hadn't told anyone on my staff what I was up to.

"Max, I interviewed with them, but I didn't take the job. It wasn't a promotion."

"I just got off the phone with HR. It's a promotion now."

I was speechless.

"Look," Max said. "I know it's tempting to go to O'Reilly. It's a big deal. But if you stay with us, I'll give you the promotion, too."

Two minutes after he hung up, my phone rang again. It was Stan Manskoff, offering me the job. I told him I'd have to think about it, and would have an answer for him at the end of the day.

I called Max back. "Honestly, I'm torn," I said.

But I wasn't torn. The truth is, I was scared.

I knew I was very good at what I did. And I had no doubt that I'd greatly impress O'Reilly with my skills, possibly to the point where he'd declare me his successor, or write me into his will, just like a cartoon rich guy. But in all my previous positions, I'd always been secure in the knowl-edge that I had at least a tiny bit of leeway to be a fuck-up and a slacker; the shows were low profile, the bosses forgiving. If I came into work hungover or late, if I screwed up a tape or missed a deadline, I knew I could ultimately get away with it. I knew I'd have no such luxury with O'Reilly. The show was as high profile as it got, and the boss was any-thing but forgiving. That's what was scaring me more than anything.

Taking this job meant, above all else, that I had to grow up.

"Joe, you know I really want to keep you," Max said, "but you've got to do what you think is best for your career."

I was worried he'd say that.

April 11, 2012—3:33 P.M.

"Muto, get in here!"

I jumped out of my chair and trotted the short distance to Bill's office. Five years of working for him had put me on a hair trigger, training me to pop out of my chair whenever he called, lest he get annoyed at my tardiness.

I poked my head in. "What's up, Bill?"

He wordlessly held up the News Quiz folder that I'd left on his desk. I walked in and plucked it from his hand.

"Thanks," I mumbled, and beat a hasty retreat.

Back at my desk, I went through the pages of questions. He'd used his pen to scratch a neat check mark next to each of the five he wanted to use.

Out of the corner of my eye, I saw a grim-faced Stan Manskoff leave his office and walk into Bill's, closing the door after him.

That wasn't a good sign. Bill, for all his standoffishness, rarely closed his door. As the network's top star, he knew that no one could challenge or rebuke him, and he conducted the majority of his business without regard for who might overhear. Everything from dressing down a producer to calling his wife on the phone to dictate precisely what he wanted her to cook for dinner ("Some chicken, side of potatoes, maybe a vegetable . . . let's say green beans") was done within full earshot of whoever was sitting outside his office or happened to be walking down the hall.

But Stan had closed the door, which meant he had something unpleasant to tell Bill.

And I had a pretty good idea what it was.

CHAPTER 10

Radio Days

You never see the truly crazy ones coming.

Sure, some of the crazies are easy to filter out. You can hear it immediately over the phone line; they're nervous, stuttering, halting in their speech. They can't make a coherent point. They curse, or use a racial slur in the very first sentence out of their mouths. You know within two seconds—*no fucking way* you're putting this guy on air.

So you spin a little lie, and you hang up on them before they have a chance to protest: "Hey, buddy, I'm really sorry, but there's another guy on the line who wants to say the exact same thing as you, and he's been waiting twenty minutes." *Click*. Or "I'm really sorry, but we're almost out of time. We're not taking any more callers this hour. Give us a shout another time." *Click*.

Some of the callers will heap abuse on you. Call you an asshole, demand that you put them through to Bill immediately, accuse you of being too scared to take their call on-air. Some callers are persistent. They call back ten minutes after your little fib-and-click routine and accuse you (accurately) of wanting to get rid of them.

With those callers sometimes you get a little vindictive and just leave them hanging on the line indefinitely. Pretend that their angry harangue or their third callback has successfully led you to change your mind about them; they've shown you the error of your ways, and you're going to put them through to Bill! He'll take their call right after the commercial break, so just hang on the line and don't go anywhere because he could take the call at any moment!

And so you end up leaving some people twisting in the wind for the entire show. Two full hours some of these poor bastards sit on the line. Then the show ends, and they're still hanging on the line, not even getting it that there's no way they're making it on today, and in fact Bill has already left the radio studio and headed back to his office. Getting rid of these geniuses who think that the best way to get on a radio show is to curse at the call screener is always a wonderfully cathartic way to end your day, to wield the one small bit of power you have. Sometimes you'll get on the line to say good-bye, maybe subtly taunt them a little with a polite and cheery "Sorry you didn't make it on air this time. Call us tomorrow!" *Click*.

And sometimes you'll just pick up the line, listen to them breathing for a second, and hang up without saying anything. *Click*. Either way is satisfying.

It sounds cruel, toying with people like this, but it's completely necessary. You have to be a hard-ass. You have to be ever vigilant. Sometimes you have to be kind of a dick.

Because it's your neck if one of these callers gets through.

The call screening interface is deceptively simple. You have ten phone lines, each of which rings constantly, starting fifteen minutes before showtime, and continues ringing throughout the entire program. The phones are hooked up to a computer. You just need to strap on a headset, and then you can answer calls simply by clicking your mouse. After that, it's a matter of filling in the boxes of text. Name, hometown, and whatever the caller wants to say to Bill. The host has a monitor in front of him, right next to his microphone, and his monitor mirrors your monitor exactly. He sees what you type, and that's how he knows what caller he wants to go to next. So you'd better be specific and let him know exactly what each caller is going to say. No surprises, please.

Of course there's a very limited amount of space in those text boxes, so you have to be as concise as possible when you take down the POV, leaving some details on the cutting-room floor. John from Tulsa says immigrants are ruining the country. Mike from Columbus says Democrats are traitors. Anne from Coral Gables says she's tired of homosexuals flaunting it in everyone's faces. That's all the information you give the host to work from. Based on these limited descriptions, each of these calls could go either way. Bill is trusting you to not put through any complete maniacs.

And make no mistake: He can tell within two seconds if you've put him on the line with what he refers to as a "kook" or a "loon." He knows the signs as well as you do—the breathlessness, the agitation, the crackpot theories spilling out all at once. He picks up the call and immediately knows he's trapped, and he'll politely let the kook squeeze out one or two sentences before cutting him off. Meanwhile he's glaring daggers at you through the glass partition that separates the radio studio from the control room.

You need to get that glare only once before you figure out that you don't want it a second time.

That's why the *real* crazies are so dangerous. The dirty little secret of talk radio is that you can prank any show in the world—you can get past the best call screeners in the business—and all you need to do is not sound like a stuttering moron for a grand total of thirty seconds. If you can coherently give a producer your name and hometown, and then string together three or four sentences describing what you plan to say on the air, without saying anything overtly racist or blurting out the F-word, then you're in.

Those guys are the truly dangerous ones. You don't even see them coming. They can be spouting off about something innocuous, then suddenly they say it.

The worst word they could possibly say.

The name that must not be mentioned, under any circumstances.

The name of the enemy.

I'd started as an associate producer for *The Radio Factor* with Bill O'Reilly in January 2007. I was a salaried employee for the first time in my career, making $42,000 a year. I was excited to ditch my time card, until some back-of-the-envelope calculations revealed that, with the loss of the substantial amount of overtime I'd been pulling, I'd actually be making less money than I had previously.

The radio show was on five days a week, noon to two P.M. (Bill had made the dubious decision to go up against Rush Limbaugh, the nation's most popular radio personality, who had a lock on that time slot at virtually every top-tier talk station in the country. So while *The Radio Factor* was in every market, it was almost always on the second-rate station, or tape-delayed to a less desirable slot on the better station.) The studio was on the eighteenth floor, almost directly above the area on the seventeenth floor where my former *Lineup* colleagues were sitting. It was small, just two rooms separated by a thick pane of soundproof glass. On one side of the glass, an oval table with four expensive-looking microphones on swivel arms. On the other side, a massive control board with switches and sliders and levers and glowing buttons, and three workstations for producers arrayed behind it. The walls in both rooms were covered in sound-dampening foam panels, soft surfaces studded with dark gray pyramid shapes that swallowed your words. After the din and chaos of the newsroom where I'd spent much of my past two years, it was both eerie and oddly relaxing.

The staff of *The Radio Factor* with Bill O'Reilly was small—five, counting me. When we weren't in the eighteenth-floor radio studio, we occupied a small area just outside Bill's seventeenth-floor office.

There was Stan Manskoff, the executive producer, who was actually important enough to have his own office next to Bill's. He was there for adult supervision but was mostly checked out of the proceedings, occupying his time with the sundry TV-related issues that cropped up throughout the day. Stan was responsible for the entire empire, overseeing radio, television, and the website. He was the steady hand at the tiller of the USS *O'Reilly*, the practical second in command to the volatile Captain Bill. Stan was a details man by nature, sweating the small stuff that the Big Guy couldn't be bothered with. He was a reluctant hatchet man when necessary, carrying out deeds that were too distasteful or unpleasant for Bill to dirty his hands over. And he was the main go-between for Bill and the Second Floor, the broker for a relationship that was tense even on good days, and downright apocalyptic on bad ones. It was probably the most stressful job this side of Fallujah, and to this day I have no idea how Stan was able to survive every day without guzzling a bottle of Pepto to deal with the grapefruit-size ulcer from which he undoubtedly suffered.

He was the same age as my parents, graduating college in '72. But unlike my parents, who'd attended a sleepy Midwestern Catholic college that had barely been touched by the 1960s counterculture (my mother swears—unconvincingly, if you ask me—to this day that she never once attended a party where someone was smoking pot), Stan had spent his university years behaving like—to coin one of Bill's favorite phrases—a "far-left loon," protesting U.S. military actions, occupying various administrative buildings, and (I'm guessing, based mostly on a contemporary picture showing him with long, straggly hair and a beard) ingesting copious amounts of marijuana. I loved the guy immediately.

Manskoff had built an impressive career as a producer at ABC News, which is where he'd met O'Reilly, who was a correspondent for that network in the late '80s. Years later, when Bill was already established at Fox News and needed a heavyweight presence to run his burgeoning empire, he tapped Stan, luring him away from his cushy network gig with what was rumored among the staff to be a huge pile of money. If Stan had any misgivings about betraying his radical leftist past to come work for a TV host who could only be described as a living caricature of The Man, he kept them to himself. (Though I did catch him occasionally emitting some world-weary, Danny-Glover-in-*Lethal-Weapon*-I'm-too-old-for-this-shit type of mumbling when he thought no one was listening.)

Next in line on the radio crew was Sam Martinez, associate producer, head call screener, and the guy who'd recruited me. At twenty-six, he was one year older than I was and had a year and a half of O'Reilly experience under his belt. He was happy to have me aboard but also warily guarded his turf from my encroachment, taking umbrage at any indication that I was on the verge of usurping him. His worries were unfounded. I knew my place, and I had no intention of trying to overtake him; I was perfectly fine with my status as the little brother. But like any good little brother, I sometimes took delight in tormenting my work sibling and his insecurity about his place in the hierarchy.

"Hey, Sam, when you were out sick yesterday, Bill told me that he liked the way I screened calls better than the way you do it," I'd lie.

"What? Bull*shit*!" he'd say. "You're totally full of shit, Muto." Then, quietly: "He didn't actually tell you that, right?"

I'd let him dangle for a few minutes before confessing. When I did, he'd grumble and begin planning his payback, to be sprung on me at a later date.

Sam's unease was surprising. Anyone could see that his position on the staff was secure. He was by far the hardest-working producer on the O'Reilly team, and conceivably in the entire building. He also had one of the most impressive personal stories I'd ever heard. He was born in California, the grandson of Mexican immigrants. His father died tragically when Sam was only six years old, leaving his mother suddenly alone with three young kids to support. Sam grew up and worked his way through Arizona State, turning down scholarships from more prestigious schools so he could stay close to home and help on weekends in the restaurant that his mother owned and had built from the ground up. After graduation, he came to New York with barely a dime in his pocket, staying at the YMCA until he could find an affordable apartment. He'd overcome so many hardships to get to his position that it sometimes made me ashamed of my easy, comfortable, white-bread, middle-class upbringing.

Sam was middle-of-the-road politically, not a hard-core conservative like some of the other staffers. But he was absolutely in awe of O'Reilly, and terrified of disappointing him.

Also in the radio unit was Richie, the sound board operator and engineer. Thin and bespectacled, he was in his fifties, but through some sort of bizarre Dorian Gray/Benjamin Button supernatural intervention, he appeared to be not a day over thirty-five. I asked him his secret once. "Clean living," he said, taking a bite of the apple that most days was the only thing he ate for lunch.

And finally there was Eric, another associate producer, who was brought on a few months after I came in. (His predecessor, in an ill-fated career move, had left the show in early 2007 to work on Rudy Giuliani's presidential campaign.) Eric's background was in sports radio; dealing with the irate maniacs who'd call into those shows made him almost *over*qualified to handle our tame-by-comparison callers.

We were a merry little band, tight-knit in a way that can only come from being locked in a small enclosed space for several hours a day—it's a miracle none of us went nuts, as in *The Shining*, and ax-murdered our compatriots, the foamy walls dampening the sounds of our screams and the sickening wet thuds of the ax cleaving human flesh.[38]

The secret to Bill's success, the reason why he's such an imposing inter-viewer, is something that doesn't fully come across on television: He's one of the most physically intimidating people on the planet. Cameras don't do him justice; all the HDTVs in the world can't replicate the experience of standing in his presence; the sheer size of him cannot be limned from mere pixels.[39] He's a force of nature that has to be experienced in person to be appreciated, like Niagara Falls or the Grand Canyon.

He's six feet four but somehow seems taller the nearer you stand to him. He's equipped with the classic anchorman's giant head, but unlike many of his colleagues, it doesn't look odd on him—probably because it sits upon equally giant shoulders. A former athlete, he still carries himself with that unmistakable jock swagger. He's softening around the middle ever so slightly but is otherwise in remarkably good shape for a

---

38 Wow, this got dark suddenly.

39 Arguably, this is the reason why his radio show never fully took off. We rarely had guests in the studio. Bill interviewing someone over the phone just didn't have the same impact. Similarly, with the TV show, you'll notice a marked difference in the segments where the guest is in the New York studio with Bill versus the segments where the guest is coming in via satellite; most notably, the satellite guests are less afraid to talk back.

man in his early sixties. I have no doubt that I, three decades his junior, would lose a fight with him, and lose badly.

And that voice. That golden voice, powerful and terrible, thick, rich, and warm like butterscotch syrup fresh off the stove, deep and smoldering like a lion's growl, sounding as if he's perpetually on the verge of breaking into a shout, even when he's whispering.

Everyone on the staff did the voice. Never in front of him, of course. And not to make fun of him, either, not really.[40] It's just that the voice was so infectious, so pervasive in the workplace, that it became simply impossible to tell a story about the boss without dropping your voice a couple octaves while reciting his dialogue.

Sam was a particularly gifted mimic and would have the whole control room howling, recounting the various times Bill had dressed him down.

"So Bill looks at me and he goes 'MARTINEZ!'" Sam would say, nailing Bill's clipped staccato delivery. "'ARE YOU SURE YOU CAN HANDLE THIS JOB? IF YOU'RE NOT, TELL MANSKOFF AND WE'LL GET SOMEONE IN HERE WHO CAN.'"

Sam took a lot of heat in my first few months, most of it unfairly, because Bill was big on assigning blame for things. If there was an issue, no matter how small, he always wanted to know whose fault it was. As the new guy, I was still under O'Reilly's radar (I wasn't sure he actually knew my name until at least my third month on the job), so Sam took the brunt of the punishment for any of my minor transgressions.

And I do mean minor. The issue with Bill wasn't that he flew off the handle for no reason—there was *always* a reason. The problem was that he had no sense of scale. In his book, every foul-up, no matter how big or small, was an occasion for a shouting jag. He'd get just as mad at the producer who had failed to book a desirable guest as he would at his assistant if she forgot to get mustard on his sandwich. He'd get just as angry about being given a stat that turned out to be wrong, leading to

---

40 Well, okay: *sometimes*.

his embarrassing himself on the air, as he would about being given a research packet with the wrong font.

And when he turned on the rage, all six feet four of him towering, red-faced, wild-eyed, and screaming, jabbing a finger in the face of whoever was unlucky enough to have provoked his ire, it was a truly terrifying experience. It was also oddly exhilarating—thrilling, even—as long as you weren't the target. One of my fellow producers compared it to watching a tiger at the zoo mauling someone who'd wandered into its enclosure.

"You're powerless to stop it," she said. "All you can do is watch and hope that he eventually loses interest and wanders away."

The radio crew was an autonomous unit, separate from the TV staff, but we were all under the O'Reilly umbrella, so there was some crossover. We were all in on the same morning conference calls and the same twice-weekly pitch meetings. Also, about once a week, I was roped into producing a TV segment in addition to my radio duties. The associate producer was responsible for every aspect of a segment from start to finish: booking the guests, arranging transportation and a studio space, researching the topic and assembling all the information into a concise, neatly formatted document for Bill to look at, and finally cutting any tape that was needed. It was much more involved and challenging than being a production assistant, and required a lot more effort; I liked it but was also relieved to have to do it only a couple times a month, usually on days when TV was short-staffed.

Otherwise, most of the time, Sam, Eric, and I were left alone to run the radio show as we saw fit, which was fine with us.

I backed up Sam on the call screening as often as I could, because sparring with the crazies was the most fun way to spend the show's two-hour length—but my main job was to wrangle sound bites, using digital recording and editing software to chop words from politicians and newsmakers into palatable twenty-second morsels for Bill to play and comment on. I'd start at seven A.M.—an ungodly early hour for me, but one I found myself enjoying because I had the whole seventeenth floor almost to myself—scouring the morning's news for anything that caught my ear, whatever I thought was interesting or funny or that Bill might want to hear.

At nine A.M. we'd all pack ourselves into Stan's small office, and he'd dial Bill's house on the speakerphone. O'Reilly would tell us what he wanted to focus on that day, picking a different topic for each hour of the show, making guest suggestions, and requesting any specific sound bites relating to the topics. After the call, I'd scramble to assemble any extra bites he'd asked for, and half an hour before the show's noon start time, I'd print out a multipage sound sheet with transcriptions of each bite.

Making the sound sheet was a trial-and-error process, especially the first few months. Sound bites that Bill had specifically asked for were obviously on it, but you couldn't stop there. You had to find extras, ones he hadn't asked for, to pad out the total number of bites on the sheet. If you didn't have at least twelve for him to choose from, he'd complain, not to me, who had put the sheet together, but to Stan—making sure that Sam and Eric and I were in earshot when he did so.

"Sound sheet's a little light today, Manskoff," he'd say. "What's the problem?"

He'd actually do this a lot, complain to Stan about a specific producer's work while seemingly oblivious to the fact that the producer could very clearly hear him. I could never figure out if the oft-used move was indicative of some sort of subtle, genius, next-level management/motivational technique or rather a sign of a passive-aggressiveness so severe that it was on the autism spectrum. Either way, we'd overhear his complaint and fly into a panic, overcompensating and grabbing sound bites at a frantic pace, delivering him a supplemental sound sheet that was three times longer than the original, and setting him off with even more complaints: "You're giving me too much information," he'd fume. "Look at all this paper I have on my desk!"

Too little information was bad; so was too much. He was the Goldilocks of cable news.

Another obstacle with the sound sheet was figuring out which bites to give him. I knew the ones I found interesting were not necessarily going to be the same ones that would grab Bill's fancy, and vice versa. I had to attempt a mind meld with him, anticipating what he'd want. And asking him was out of the question—he hated to be bothered with requests for information or clarification, even ones that were entirely pertinent to the task at hand. Nothing bugged him more than questions he assumed you should know the answer to, even if knowing the answer would have required telepathy. The entire staff was terrified to ask him anything, and would do so only as an absolute last resort. Over the years, I watched my colleagues jump through multiple hoops, spending hours of work tracking down answers to questions that could have been satisfied with a ten-second phone call, or a quick head-pop into Bill's office.

Another one of my duties before the show started was to sweep through the radio studio to make sure everything was copacetic. Other people used the studio when we weren't in it, and they sometimes left it in disarray, which Bill hated. I checked the thermostat, making sure it was set to exactly 72 degrees, Bill's preferred temperature. The trash can on the floor next to his chair had to be emptied of anything that might potentially give off an odor, lest a banana peel or empty yogurt container offend his sensitive nostrils. There had to be an array of his favorite pens (Bic Atlantis, blue, with the soft cushion grip) in front of him, so he could scrawl notes during the show and sign books during the commercial breaks.

Each workstation in the control room was outfitted with a DUMP button, a glowing red rectangle about the size of a small box of matches, covered by a clear plastic flip-up safety guard to avoid accidental presses, like the LAUNCH button on a nuclear submarine. The show was on a delay of about eight seconds; each press of the button obliterated a chunk of that time. The listeners at home would most likely notice the omission, hearing a strange digital hiccup in the audio, but that was better than the alternative—allowing a burst of profanity to get on the air.

Or even worse—Keith Olbermann's name.

By the time I started on *The Factor*, Bill O'Reilly's feud with the then-MSNBC host had been simmering for a few years. Olbermann had started it, punching up at his higher-rated eight P.M. competition, making Bill a frequent subject of his Worst Person in the World segment. Bill foolishly took the bait, railing against Olbermann by name on several occasions. In 2006, a year before I joined the staff, O'Reilly devised an online petition to get Olbermann fired, urging his three-million-plus viewers to sign it. Keith responded with a mocking segment showing him and his whole staff lining up at a computer to sign the petition, one by one.

The upshot of all this was that Olbermann's ratings soared. He still wasn't beating *The Factor*, but on some nights he was getting one-third or even half of O'Reilly's audience—phenomenal numbers at the time for then-third-place MSNBC.

Just before I joined the staff, O'Reilly seemed to come to the conclusion that fighting back was only giving material and oxygen to his hated nemesis. So he did what any rational, mature TV host would do: He stopped referring to Olbermann by name, only obliquely making references to him with the euphemism "Elements at NBC News." As in "Elements at NBC News spew out far-left propaganda on a daily basis." The staff obligingly played along with the euphemism, and our in-house nickname for Olbermann became simply Elements, as in "Bill, you'll never believe what Elements did on his show last night."

The O'Reilly/Olbermann feud was, of course, a deeply ridiculous spectacle. Two famous millionaires who worked for multinational corporations taking petty swipes at each other on a nightly basis was profoundly embarrassing for all involved. The most amusing part is that neither man seemed to realize he was fighting a fun-house version of himself. O'Reilly and Olbermann were two sides of the same coin. They were Batman and the Joker, mortal enemies who were linked to each other through obsession but had more in common than either would admit.

And the similarities are startling. They're both tall men with deep voices who got their big breaks on populist entertainment shows—Bill on the tabloid show *Inside Edition*, and Keith on ESPN's *SportsCenter*—before moving to (only slightly) more serious news programs. Both were known for abrasive relationships with coworkers and management. Both had limited self-awareness and a next to zero sense of humor about themselves.

To give Olbermann a bit of credit, he actually did seem to be having fun poking at Bill, referring to him derisively as Bill-O and doing a mocking impression of Bill's voice.[41] When MSNBC moved their headquarters from Secaucus, New Jersey, to Rockefeller Center, just two blocks away from Fox headquarters, Olbermann procured a life-size cardboard cutout of O'Reilly (it had been used as promotional material for one of his books) and propped it up in a window of his office. The window was several floors above street level, so whatever Olbermann had scrawled in the word balloon next to Bill's head wasn't legible from the ground, but it was almost certainly not polite.

While I'm not sure if Olbermann's enmity for Bill was real, or just feigned for the ratings, O'Reilly, for his part, was completely sincere in his hatred of Elements. As far as Bill was concerned, it was not just a media feud done for show. Olbermann was O'Reilly's obsession—his white whale—and Bill was determined to stab at him from hell's heart with his microphone harpoon.

Olbermann's mockery continued, and even with Bill's strategy of not mentioning him by name, his ratings continued to rise, so O'Reilly took a new tack, ignoring Olbermann completely and going after his corporate bosses. The average O'Reilly viewer was probably confused when Bill suddenly started attacking NBC head Jeff Zucker and Jeffrey Immelt, the CEO of General Electric, NBC's parent company at the time. That marked a new degree of escalation, and eventually a secret truce was arranged by Immelt and Rupert Murdoch themselves. Word came down from above: Knock off the NBC/GE attacks. After a long, closed-door meeting with Stan, and an even longer phone call with Ailes, Bill reluctantly agreed.

---

41 See? What'd I say? Totally infectious.

The detente lasted less than two months. Word of it leaked to *The New York Times*, and Olbermann angrily denied it on his show, denouncing the *Times*, Murdoch, and O'Reilly. Bill couldn't let the truce-breaking go unanswered, and struck back a few days later, reporting that GE was under investigation for selling parts that were ending up in roadside bombs used by insurgents in Iraq.

The grudge match ended for good in 2011, when Olbermann flamed out in spectacular fashion, leaving MSNBC for unknown reasons (rumors were that management was simply sick of dealing with his prima-donna ways) and taking a job with Al Gore's fledgling liberal news network Current TV. He was, in turn, fired by them less than a year after he started.

But we didn't know any of that in early 2007, when I started on the radio show.

All we knew was to keep our ears on the program, our fingers on the DUMP button, and our eyes on Bill scowling at us through the glass.

The radio show ended its seven-year run in the spring of 2009. It had never taken off to become the juggernaut its TV counterpart had become. The radio industry was too competitive, and Limbaugh's show was too strong and entrenched. But that's not what killed *The Radio Factor* in the end. After all, the show was profitable—even without the powerhouse Limbaugh stations, the syndicators were still making money, and Bill was still getting paid very well. Ultimately, what killed O'Reilly's radio show was O'Reilly himself. Or, rather, his indifference. The show was a lot of extra work for him, and not much payoff. I'm sure that the seven-figure checks it put in his pocket each year were nice, but money had long ceased being a motivating factor for him. What he wanted more than anything was to win, and when it became clear he couldn't do that with the radio show, he picked up his ball and went home.

April 11, 2012—4:22 P.M.

Stan e-mailed me in the late afternoon: *Intern is out today. Can you handle green room?*

I e-mailed back: *No problem.*

The O'Reilly Factor studio is a surprisingly small room on the ground floor of the News Corp. building. The windows look out onto Sixth Avenue, but they were usually covered by retractable screens. This was done mostly to disguise the fact that the show wasn't live at eight P.M., when it's normally dark outside, but actually prerecorded at five in the afternoon, when the sun is still shining.[42] Also, unlike the *Today* show, which is able to attract a diverse, sizable mob of Midwestern tourists and New Jersey soccer moms to wave excitedly outside its windows, the only people drawn to the Fox windows, on the rare occasion when the

---

42 This isn't a huge secret in the industry, but it is largely unknown to the average viewer, since there's a totally seamless handoff from the live seven P.M. show to the taped eight P.M. The seven P.M. anchor, usually Shep Smith, simply says something like "That's it for me tonight. Now here's O'Reilly," and the guys in master control hit PLAY on the pretaped *Factor* episode. If they do it right, it will go straight from Shep to Bill saying his typical show-opening catchphrase: "*The O'Reilly Factor* is on tonight!" with little or no delay.

Pretaping actually causes several logistical headaches, which is why *The Factor* is the only show on the entire network that gets away with it—Bill was the only one with enough clout to demand it in his contract. There are a variety of reasons why he wanted to pretape, but the two most important were (1) he likes being able to fix mistakes after the fact; (2) he likes getting home early to see his kids. Fair enough, on both points. And it got me out of there at a decent hour, so I wasn't complaining about it either.

screens were left open, were elderly retirees with black socks pulled up to their knees, and irate, middle-finger-brandishing locals.

Next to the studio was an equally small "green room," a waiting area for show guests. In keeping with the Fox low-rent ethos, it was nothing fancy—a couch, a few battered old chairs. Two tiny alcoves curtained off in the back of the room had lights and mirrors and chairs set up for hair and makeup. There was a wall-mounted TV in the front of the room, tuned to the closed-circuit broadcast of everything taking place in the studio on the other side of the wall.

While the show was taping, there was always a producer or intern in the green room to manage the traffic of the guests passing in and out, to convey any messages from the control room, and, most important, to handle Bill's packets—the folders of information that a producer prepared for every segment.

The packet was a manila folder labeled clearly with a thick Sharpie, containing several printed pages of information about the guest, a bullet-pointed summary of the topic at hand, and any relevant stats, charts, or articles. As segment producers, we sweated over these packets, sending them through round after round of sometimes excruciating fact-checking with Gayle, the fastidious executive producer and fact-checker of the TV show, making sure Bill had them a full two hours before showtime—only to have the host ignore them for most of the afternoon, finally pick them up ten minutes before he headed to the makeup chair, glance at the first page of each, and toss them aside.

Regardless of how little attention he paid to the packets, he still needed them in front of him during the show. But instead of keeping them all in a stack and grabbing the appropriate packet when needed, he insisted that there be one and only one packet in his eyesight at all times.

That's where I came in. There weren't even any guests in New York City that day—everyone was coming to us via satellite—so the only reason for me to be down in the green room was for packet-switching duties. The work was mindless enough that it was usually assigned to an intern, but on the days when there wasn't one available, it was assigned randomly to a producer.

When I got down to the green room, it was completely empty. No guests, no hair or makeup artists. Just me and a sad deli tray of bagels left over from that morning's shows.

In retrospect, I should have realized: I was being separated from the herd.

CHAPTER 11

Stand and Deliver: Rage, Ridicule, and Sexy Ladies, Twice a Week

J esus CHRIST, Muto," he yelled, pounding a clenched fist on his thigh for emphasis, causing two of the more nervous producers to flinch. "Do you WANT me to lose two hundred thousand viewers in the middle of the program? Hmmm? IS THAT WHAT YOU WANT?"

Now, I don't claim to be any sort of expert on workplace relations—in fact, as the mere existence of this book proves, I'm sort of the *opposite*. But I'm well versed enough to know that when your boss is angrily and loudly accusing you of wanting to intentionally sabotage his television show, that's an indication that the meeting is not going well.

I began this book with a rare instance in which I knocked it out of the park at a pitch meeting. This chapter is going to be about what happened most of the rest of the time.

In this particular case, the story that had spurred O'Reilly's rage seemed fairly innocuous to me. A friend who worked in PR for a publishing house had sent me a book, a memoir by an aging actor, hoping to get the author on the show. The celeb's career was nonexistent at the time, but he'd been a pretty big name in the '70s, the star of a hit TV show. I thought he'd be a good guest and that Bill would be happy to get at least a glimmer of celebrity wattage.

I was wrong.

"Muto, this guy is what, a hundred and seventy years old?" Bill was saying. "He's old and gray. No one's heard a thing from him in twenty years. And you want me to put him on the show? Do you honestly think that's going to help us? We'll lose half the demo in the first thirty seconds. Either that or he'll drop dead live on the air."

Stan, who was seated across the semicircle from Bill, looked up from his BlackBerry. "Well, that actually might help the numbers, you know. If he dropped dead, I mean." Everyone but Bill and I laughed. Stan was a cool customer, and as executive producer, he was the only one on the staff with the stature to stand up to Bill. Sometimes when Papa Bear really got on a roll against one of us, Stan tried to jump in as a human shield and absorb some of the onslaught. But Bill wasn't having it this time.

"Look, Muto, you can't be coming to these meetings with shit like this."

Stan caught my eye and gave a little shrug. *Sorry, I tried.*

I opened my mouth to protest: "Bill, I just—"

He raised his hand to cut me off. "No, I don't want to hear it. Use your head next time." He swept his gaze across the rest of the semicircle. "And that goes for the rest of you. You've all been giving me junk lately, and I'm TIRED OF IT. I won't have it anymore."

Silence from the rest of the group. It was a surprisingly small staff, less than fifteen of us total, radio and TV combined, with the bulk of us being associate producers under thirty like me.

Bill took a deep breath, composing himself, rubbing his temples with a hand.

"All right. Anything else, Muto?"

I'd actually led off with the actor's book, thinking it was my strongest pitch. I still had two more ready to go, gripped in my now profusely sweating hands. But I knew there was no way in hell he'd take them now, no matter how good they were. I'd poisoned the well.

"No, Bill. I think I'll quit while I'm behind."

He nodded. "Yeah, good idea." More laughter from the other producers, mostly out of relief that it wasn't them this time. They'd all been on the receiving end before, and they all knew they would be again. It was only a matter of time.

"Okay, Brooks," Bill barked. "You're up."[43]

Naomi Brooks, the producer to my right, shot me a look. *Thanks a lot for getting him pissed off.* She knew she was screwed, too. When one of us put Bill in a foul mood, all our pitches suffered. And sure enough, Naomi struck out, whiffing on three stories that were quickly dismissed by the still-salty host. No one got a story accepted for the rest of the meeting.

After the last producer had his last pitch shot down with a dismissive "I don't think our viewers care about that story one bit," Bill took the opportunity to admonish the group one more time: "I don't want you people coming in here again with stories like today's. If you're at all confused about what sort of stories we're looking for, talk to Stan."

Stan looked up from his BlackBerry again. "Who, me?" he said with mock surprise.

During a pitch meeting, you had to package and present a story idea for an audience of one: Bill O'Reilly. The stories he was looking for had to be ones that would, first and foremost, get him viewers. That was the number one criteria. No matter how newsworthy or journalistically sound a story was, if he thought it would cause people to change the channel, he wasn't interested. Beyond that, he was looking for stories that supported his worldview: that American culture and society was under assault by the forces of secular liberalism, and that he, Bill O'Reilly, was the only thing standing between the secularists and the total dissolution of the nation's moral fiber, the only journalist brave and steadfast enough to stand up for the folks.

That's a heavy burden to place on stories that most of us found during fifteen minutes of Web surfing during our lunch breaks, but there

---

43 Bill called all of us, even the women on the staff, by our last names. We just called him Bill. It was very egalitarian of him, actually, but led to some confusion at times. For example, whenever a female producer got married and took her husband's name, Bill, a creature of habit if there ever was one, would still call her by her maiden name for months, and in some cases years, after the wedding.

were certain guidelines I developed over my five years on the show that I noticed improved my chances of getting a pitch through.

Rule 1: Size Counts

Getting a story onto the show was a complicated threading of the needle. The story had to be small and obscure enough that Bill—who read several newspapers cover to cover and listened to the CBS News radio broadcast on his way into the office—hadn't yet heard of it. But it also had to be *big* enough that he thought it was worth covering in the first place. A pitch that fell into the former category was usually met with an impatient "Yeah, yeah, we know all about it," while a pitch from the latter might get dismissed with a curt "Too small."

Rule 2: Delivery Is Everything

"It's all about confidence," Max Greene had told me before I left his weekend unit for the greener pastures of O'Reilly Land. "If you're not confident in the story, he'll hear it in your voice immediately, and he'll shut you down."

Max was right. Confidence, even if it was false, was essential for the successful pitch. If you sounded self-assured, it put Bill at ease and made him more receptive to whatever you were about to say. If you sounded nervous and halting, it made him nervous in return, and he was more likely to start asking tough questions and nitpick your story to shreds.

Concision was also important. A flood of convoluted details was not what he was looking for. He wanted a narrative that was short, simple, and able to be explained to him in a sentence or two—ensuring that it would, in turn, be easy to explain to viewers. The best pitchers would weave a story for Bill, something that was easy for him to grasp in a matter of seconds. So the best strategy for the producer was to speak in headlines, save the details for later, and always put the most sensational elements of the story at the beginning of the pitch.

I would practice in my spare time, condensing well-known stories into their essential, pitchable elements, keeping in mind to massage them to fit Bill's chosen narrative:

Adam & Eve: "Bill, a liberal feminist extremist tricked her husband into consuming drugs, and then told authorities that a talking snake told her to do it."

The Nativity: "Bill, a ruler in the Middle East ordered the murder of thousands of infants based on the advice of some liberal astrologers."

The Boston Tea Party: "Bill, a far-left antigovernment, anticapitalist group in Massachusetts attacked a ship belonging to a corporation they didn't like, destroying millions of dollars' worth of merchandise."

The Civil Rights Movement: "Bill, radical black activists in the South are carrying out a campaign to damage the teeth of police dogs."

A clear, concise, well-plotted pitch could put an otherwise weak story over the top, while a convoluted pitch could kill a relatively strong story in the crib. Every once in a while, the story was so good that delivery didn't matter, but those stories were few and far between. Most stories were firmly on the bubble, and the proper framing could tilt them one way or the other.

Rule 3: Stoke the Fires of Outrage

As far as content, the most nearly surefire way to get your pitch onto the show was to stir Bill's sense of outrage. In theory, that sounds as if it would be a relatively easy thing to do, but in reality it was quite difficult. Since he was already constantly operating at a low level of outrage twenty-four hours a day, it took a lot of additional rage inducing to move the needle even a fraction. Bill was actually inured to outrage, in the same way that I assume Hugh Hefner, after five decades of horndoggery, is immune to normal means of arousal. Just as Hef, I imagine,[44] needs a half dozen nubile nineteen-year-olds covered in baby oil performing gymnastics for him to get it up, Bill needed extreme circumstances to raise his ire enough to draw him into a story.

Man rapes a teenager? *Sad, but not for us.*

Man—who had been let out of jail two days earlier by a mix-up in paperwork—rapes a teenager? *Not bad. Call the local sheriff and find out what the hell happened. Maybe we can do something with it next week.*

Man who had been let out of jail two days earlier—because a liberal judge had ordered him freed—rapes a teenager? Bingo! *Lead story and Talking Points Memo tonight. We're doing three blocks on it. And send Jesse out to ambush the judge.*[45]

Rule 4: Establish a Villain

"So who's the villain in this story?" It was a question Bill asked a lot. He felt that any good outrage-stoking story needed a tangible target for said outrage, a name and preferably a photo that could be splashed on-screen for the host to point to and say, *This is the bad guy. This is the guy hurting you.*

That's why the aforementioned hypothetical teenager rape scenario was a slam dunk when the element of the liberal judge was added. An unelected egghead judge who was unbeholden to the people made for a perfect villain—to the point where the "Bad Judge" story became a genre in and of itself, and the stories were particularly fertile ground for us. "We've got another Bad Judge," Eugene—our head booker, and the one guy who always seemed to get at least one pitch through per meeting— would say periodically. Bill would rub his hands together in anticipation: "Excellent. What is it this time?"

But judges weren't the only game in town. Some other good villains:

---

44   And yes, I imagine this sort of thing a lot, in case you were wondering.

45   For more on ambush *artiste extraordinaire* Jesse Watters, please see chapter 13. Or, you know, just keep reading 'til you get there.

- Liberal college professors
- Liberal journalists
- Liberal politicians
- Liberal Hollywood celebrities
- Anyone who resided in the state of Vermont (especially liberals)

Of course, any good villain story needed a hero as a counterpoint. In most scenarios, the hero was naturally Bill himself, the only one brave or bold enough to call out the villain; but in a pinch, a local politician or law enforcement official could be the designated hero. Some ideal hero archetypes: the gruff, plainspoken, cowboy-hat-wearing small-town sheriff; the wholesome family-values-oriented local politician; the passionate, attractive young female activist—speaking of which . . .

Rule 5: Sex Sells

This will come as a surprise to absolutely no one, but people in the TV industry think young, sexy ladies make for good television. That's why almost every reporter and anchor on Fox is a blond sexpot dressed in a skirt that barely extends past her labia. That's why Greta Van Susteren practically renounced her American citizenship and became an Aruban national in her pursuit of the case of missing teenage beauty Natalee Holloway. And that's why one of the best ways to fast-track a pitch onto *The O'Reilly Factor* is to find something that involves a sexy lady.

My favorite of these types of stories was something we referred to as Sexy Teachers, a euphemism that sounded much better than the unfortunately more accurate Statutory Rape Teachers. In the world of cable news morality, there was a clear double standard when it came to these stories. A male teacher's sex with underage female students was always rightfully treated as unforgivable, predatory behavior. But when it came to a female teacher seducing her male charges, the coverage took a tone of mild disdain with a strong undercurrent of winking titillation— doubly so if the teacher was hot.

Consequently, we knew never to show up for a pitch meeting with a teacher sex story unless we also had a picture of the hopefully attractive perp.

"What does the teacher look like?" Bill would ask, and we'd dutifully hand over the printouts of her mug shot, or (if we were lucky) sexy Facebook photos, or (if the Cable News Gods were truly with us that day) bikini model photo-shoot proofs. (This actually happened with a teacher named Debra Lafave, a twenty-two-year-old blond *Playboy*-caliber stunner who had moonlighted as a bikini model before becoming a high school English teacher and eventually making a man out of a fourteen-year-old boy.)

But the quest to get sexy ladies on the air was not limited to sex-offending educators. Bill was also constantly on the prowl for guests who were "demographically friendly," which was a polite way of saying "fuckable." One of his pet theories was that viewers were turned off by the average cable news expert commentator, most of whom tended to fit into the category he disparagingly called Old Gray White Men. OGWMs were virtually banished from the show, to be used only as a last resort.[46] So when a producer pitched an expert who was young and beautiful, even if her credentials were otherwise suspect, or her field of expertise was of dubious newsworthiness, she was always given at least a tryout.

This focus on getting eye candy on-screen had its upsides and downsides. On one hand, it launched the careers of several talented political analysts and commentators who otherwise would probably have been dismissed as too young or too lightweight. On the other hand, it saddled *The Factor* with several segments that should have had no place on a "news" show, including an inane segment featuring a blond "body language expert" examining the hand gestures of a politician or public figure, and an especially unfortunate experiment—the existence of which I am not making up or even exaggerating—called Hot for

---

46 Exceptions were made for the recurring cast of regulars who appeared on the show every week, like Dick Morris, Karl Rove, and Bernie Goldberg, each one older, grayer, and whiter than the last.

Words, an *etymology* segment featuring a huge-breasted Russian immigrant explaining the origin of common words and phrases. Alert the Pulitzer committee!

Rule 6: Get Him on the Bandwagon

Bill rightfully prided himself on his ability to identify stories that would catch on with the viewers, and to catch them early, getting in on the ground floor and enabling him to say later that he had broken the story.[47] But as much as he loved being one of the first to grab on to a story, he also hated being one of the last. If you could convince him that he was in danger of being late to the party, he'd fast-track a story to air.

"Bill, the right-wing blogs are really going crazy for this one,"[48] you'd start your pitch. Or "They've been doing this story all day on our network." Or, most effectively, "This story is topping *Drudge* right now."

Matt Drudge, the proprietor of the *Drudge Report* website, despite not being on the Fox News payroll, was one of the most powerful people at the network. Every producer in the building, myself included, checked his site ten times an hour to see what stories he was pushing. It was the first thing I looked at when I turned on my computer in the morning, before I even glanced at my e-mail, and the first thing I clicked over to after any major news development, just to see what Drudge's take was.

Drudge is a reclusive, slightly mysterious, fedora-wearing figure who

---

47   In the mainstream journalism world, the widely accepted definition of *breaking* a story means that you're the first person to report it. In Bill's mind, however, breaking a story simply meant that he was the first person to talk about it on television. It didn't matter if the story had been kicking around on blogs for six months—as long as Bill was the first to put it on TV, he would take credit for breaking it.

48   Not that Bill wanted to follow the lead of the right-wing blogs too closely. He held the conservative blogosphere at arm's length, not considering himself part of it, and going so far as to reject any story he saw as excessively partisan, lest it taint the aura of fairness he seemed to think he'd managed to hold on to. For example: He never embraced the Birther movement, refusing to give any oxygen to those who questioned President Obama's birthplace. It was only when Donald Trump started dabbling in Birtherism in 2011 that O'Reilly finally started giving the issue a prominent place on his show.

made his bones during the Monica Lewinsky scandal: He was the first to publicly report on it, posting an item revealing that *Newsweek* had prepared—and then spiked at the last minute—a story on the intern's relationship with Bill Clinton. Drudge runs a website that's both proudly low-tech, with a design gone largely unchanged since the '90s, and wildly successful, with millions of visitors a month and a reported seven-figure revenue. His sensibility—right-leaning, populist, and biased toward muckraking and sensationalism—tended to align perfectly with Fox's. When he promoted a story, complete with a headline putting his own gloss or spin on it, it would, like clockwork, pop up on the network, with spin intact—often within an hour or two of going up online.

Bill was uncharacteristically respectful of Drudge's power to drive a story, so throwing his name into a pitch was a surefire way to get the boss's attention, and usually his approval. It was not uncommon for Bill to reject a story, sometimes with extreme prejudice, on a Monday, only to turn around and embrace the exact same story on a Tuesday simply because he was told that Drudge was now pushing it.

Rule 7: Fit It to the Narrative

Certain stories barely even needed pitching—they fit into Bill's repertoire that had been established and had been successful on multiple prior occasions. I've already mentioned Bad Judge stories, and Sexy Teacher stories, but the ur-example, the ultimate ongoing narrative and the one perhaps most closely associated with O'Reilly, is the "War on Christmas."

By the time I joined the show, the War on Christmas had been going for a few years, the first shots having been fired in 2004, when Macy's had the temerity to ditch the phrase "Merry Christmas" in its advertising and in-store displays, in favor of the more inclusive "Happy Holidays." This, of course, represented an unconscionable attack on Christianity, and Bill, along with the FNC five P.M. host John Gibson and numerous right-wing Christian groups, launched a salvo against Macy's, accusing it of caving to secular forces of political correctness.

The following year Macy's, apparently deciding that making a few Jews visiting their store uncomfortable was preferable to poking the hornet's nest of outrage-prone American Christendom, announced that they'd bring back "Merry Christmas." But Sears, Kmart, and Walmart hadn't been paying attention, and hence became that year's targets. They, too, caved the following year. Then Best Buy stepped in to take their place and was also summarily smacked down. And so on.

By the time I came on board *The Factor*, the War was all but won, with every major corporation cowed into compliance, terrified to attempt a holiday advertising campaign that didn't incorporate the word *Christmas*. O'Reilly declared victory, then continued fighting just for the thrill of it, opening a new, more localized front, railing against states, cities, and municipalities that refused to acknowledge the reason for the season, or seemed poised to strip Christ from Christmas.

"These things come earlier and earlier every year," Eugene would say when he announced his first War on Christmas pitch of the season, sometimes as early as mid-September. The details would change from story to story, until every incident eventually blurred together into a sort of bizarre Yuletide Mad Libs:

> A well-meaning, but liberal (governor/mayor/city council /atheist activist) would try to get (a manger scene/a tree/ Christmas lights/Santa Claus/any mention of Jesus) removed from (City Hall/the public park/a school), because they say (it offends non-Christians/it violates the Constitution/there's not enough money in the budget for it). The controversy leads to a backlash from the (community/Catholic Church/ parents of the schoolchildren), and eventually (an outraged public hearing/angry protests/death threats).

I suspect that even Bill knew how silly the War on Christmas narrative was, but the canard was simply too fertile for him to abandon entirely. (The liberal watchdog group Media Matters calculated that in the month of December 2011, *The Factor* spent almost forty-two minutes talking about the War on Christmas, compared to just over thirteen minutes of screen time devoted to the *actual* wars in Iraq and Afghanistan.) Personally, as a lapsed Catholic, I never took offense that corporations were trying to make the holidays more generic and secular; rather, I found it offensive that the whole premise of the War on Christmas narrative was that any attempt to *include* non-Christians was inherently offensive.

Of course, I kept all that to myself. If anyone else on the *Factor* staff (which was roughly 50 percent Jewish) found Bill's blithe dismissal of the non-Jesusy religions insulting, they also wisely kept it to themselves.

Rule 8: When All Else Fails, Appeal to His Ego

In college, while trolling eBay for funny things to hang on the wall above the bar in the off-campus house I shared with six other guys, I came across a small light-up sign advertising Colt 45. The sign featured the suave actor Billy Dee Williams nattily dressed in a white dinner jacket with a red bow tie, cracking open a tall can of the foul malt liquor, while a smiling Phylicia Rashad look-alike, with big hair and a dress with shoulder pads so tall they almost reached her earlobes, stood behind him, caressing his shoulder and gazing lovingly at his face. The text on the sign read THE POWER OF COLT 45: IT WORKS EVERY TIME!

I mention this because I thought of that sign, and that slogan, whenever I came across a pitch that fit Rule 8—aka the Billy Dee Williams Rule. If someone on another network mentioned Bill's name, all a producer needed to do was to show that clip at the pitch meeting and it meant almost automatic inclusion in the show. If the mention was complimentary, great. If it was an insult, even better!

To draw from some recent examples of pitches that were accepted without a second thought, there's the tale of a savvy racehorse owner who named one of his colts The Factor, ensuring several days of coverage on the show as the animal came close to running in the Kentucky Derby. Or Ellen Barkin, a boilerplate liberal celebrity, who insulted Bill on Joy Behar's Headline News show, becoming the lead *Factor* story on an otherwise slow news day.

Works every time.

<hr>

It took me five years of failure to learn those rules. I say failure, because knowing the types of stories O'Reilly was looking for is a completely different thing from actually *finding* said stories.

I wasn't enough of a masochist to frequent the right-wing blogs my colleagues combed for good politics-related pitches, so I decided to dedicate myself to an unrelated niche that my fellow producers (smartly, as it turns out) wouldn't touch: Sexy Outrage stories.

It did not go well.

"Bill, there's a new website called H-Date that people are very angry about," I pitched one day.

"Oh, yeah?" Bill said. "Why are they so mad?"

"Because it's a dating website specifically for people with herpes."

His hands went immediately to his temples, the gesture of weary annoyance that I unfortunately knew quite well.

"Are you kidding me, Muto?" he asked, suddenly as angry as I'd ever seen him. "You honestly want me to put that disgusting fact on television?"

I stood in place, knowing from experience that interrupting him at the beginning of a tirade I had set off was a very bad idea.

"This is a family show," he continued. "It airs at eight P.M. People are eating dinner. I will not bring a discussion about . . . *herpes* . . . into America's living rooms."

I probably should have learned my lesson there, but a few months later, I came across another story that I somehow got into my head would be a slam dunk.

"Bill, people are outraged because the Iowa State Fair is planning to hold an erotic corn-dog-eating contest," I said.

"Jesus, Muto!" Stan blurted out as the rest of the producers groaned or laughed nervously.

But Bill was confused. "I don't get it," he said, frowning. "What's an erotic corn-dog-eating contest?"

"Come on, we don't need to hear this," Stan protested, but Bill silenced him with a wave of the hand.

"Go on, Muto," Bill said.

"Well," I started, "I don't know the exact way it's going to work, but my understanding is that they're going to bring women on the stage, and then have them eat corn dogs . . . in a sexy way."

At this point, Bill had a look of utter disbelief on his face. *Is this pitch actually happening?* I, of course, misinterpreted the look as confusion, wrongly thinking that he still didn't grasp what I was describing, so I plowed on.

"I believe that the objection is that the contestants are going to treat the corn dogs like they're, uhhh, you know . . . male . . . genitals—"

"YEAH, WE'VE GOT IT," Bill said, cutting me off.

After the meeting, Stan pulled me aside.

"Erotic corn dogs? What's the matter with you?"

I shrugged. "Worth a shot, right?"

"I don't know about that," he said, sighing. He took off his glasses and rubbed the bridge of his nose, then replaced them and leveled his gaze at me. "Maybe in the future you should run your pitches by me before the meeting."

"What for?"

"So I can save you from yourself."

April 11, 2012—5:51 P.M.

Bill glanced at me out of the corner of his eye as I stole up from behind, snatching the folder marked E-BLOCK off the anchor desk in front of him and sliding the F-BLOCK folder into its place. He nodded and mumbled his thanks. I slipped out of the studio and reclaimed my seat in the empty green room.

I'd made it through almost the entire show. Just one more block to go before I could leave. I was anxious to go, too, because the *Gawker* people were waiting for me at a downtown bar to plan our next move.

I had half a mind to walk into the bar and tell them I was done, to call it off right there on the spot. I hadn't been busted yet, but I had no idea how much longer my luck was going to hold out.

Also, I wasn't thrilled with the tenor of the postings. Everything was coming out all wrong. When *Gawker* had asked me to write an anonymous column from inside the company, I'd envisioned it as a sort of mischievous prank, something fun and light and silly, something that would get a little attention on some obscure media blogs but would go largely unnoticed by the larger world. But I had misjudged *Gawker*'s ability to stir the shit. They were absolutely brilliant at it, and the story was getting way more notice than I'd ever imagined, with mainstream publications like *The New York Times* starting to weigh in. But with the added scrutiny, the story had gotten away from me, and the light tone

I was hoping for had somehow morphed into something sinister and dark.

I won't deny that a small part of me was exhilarated by seeing the fuss I had kicked up; but mostly I was terrified by the slow realization that I was dealing with forces I didn't understand, and consequences that I'd underestimated.

I was rapidly coming to the conclusion that my best bet was to cut my losses while I was still anonymous, wait a week or two for the heat to die down, then give my notice.

I'd just about made up my mind when the green room door opened. I looked up. It was Stan, who should have been in the control room supervising the end of the show. He had a grim look on his face.

He didn't need to say anything. I knew I was fucked.

CHAPTER 12

Loofah, Falafel, Let's Call the Whole Thing Off

On a list of days that will live in infamy, October 13, 2004, is, for most people in the outside world, probably pretty close to the bottom. If we consider dates like December 7, 1941, November 22, 1963, and September 11, 2001, to be at the top of the Infamy List, then 10/13/04 would have to fall somewhere between March 6, 1969 (Major League Baseball introduces the Designated Hitter rule), and May 19, 1999 (George Lucas releases the first Star Wars prequel).

But that was just for the outside world.

In the insular, gossipy microcosm that was Fox News, the day that saw the release of a salacious sexual harassment lawsuit against Bill O'Reilly—our biggest star and most fearsome newsroom presence—had the same effect as Lee Harvey Oswald flying a Japanese Zero into the World Trade Center.

I was still in my early green days then, doing videotape for the afternoon and evening cut-ins. I showed up to work like normal at three P.M. and grabbed a desk next to the rest of the team. As I was logging in, I noticed that something was amiss in the newsroom. It was quieter than usual. Instead of the sound of workers talking on phones or shouting questions to colleagues seated across the room, people were huddled in small groups around desks, talking in muted tones, occasionally stifling giggles or gasping, and periodically looking around nervously. It reminded me of a bunch of schoolkids furtively attempting to share a hilarious passed note but not wanting to get caught by the teacher. All the small groups appeared to be looking at the same website, because the same bright orange background appeared on all the monitors.

"What's going on?" I asked Barry, a cut-in writer I was friendly with who was occupying the desk next to mine. He was, I noticed, also reading the orange website as intently as the rest of the newsroom. "What's everybody looking at?"

"Oh, my God. You haven't heard?" Barry said, minimizing his browser window and turning to me with a gleeful look. "Go to *The Smoking Gun*. Right now. Immediately."

The Smoking Gun is a website that posts government documents, lawsuits, mug shots—anything in the public record that might be entertaining. I'd actually looked at the site a few weeks prior, laughing at the section featuring leaked concert "riders"—backstage demands that musicians inserted into contracts with promoters. (My favorite: macho conserva-rocker Ted Nugent's 2002 request for tropical-fruit-flavored Slim-Fast in his dressing room.)

But a secretly effete rock star's beverage preference was not the topic du jour at *TSG* that day.

O'REILLY HIT WITH SEX HARASS SUIT, the site's headline screamed.

The story went like this: An associate producer named Andrea Mackris had accused O'Reilly of sexual harassment and asked for sixty million dollars from him and Fox to keep quiet about it. (The sixty-million-dollar figure was the amount of revenue Mackris and her lawyers estimated *The Factor* brought in for Fox each year.) O'Reilly and the network reportedly negotiated quietly at first but then balked, and sued Mackris for extortion. She countersued for harassment, and filed a salacious twenty-two-page lawsuit that *The Smoking Gun* posted, and that two-thirds of the employees in the newsroom currently had their noses buried in.

"This is some pretty racy shit," Barry said.

And so it was. I'll spare you most of the horrific details since I'm not a sadist (and since this is 2013 and you all have access to Google if you want to see the damn thing for yourselves), but the gist of it is: Mackris claimed that, over the course of several dinners and phone calls, Bill repeatedly made suggestive remarks, tried to convince her to buy herself sex toys, and on at least three occasions called her while he was pleasuring himself. The lawsuit never says so explicitly, but Mackris apparently had audio recordings of some of the phone calls, because at some points, it quotes O'Reilly verbatim and at length.

One of these word-for-word passages features Bill monologuing a fantasy of showering in a hotel on a tropical island with the producer. He repeatedly mentions his desire to scrub her down with "one of those mitts, one of those loofah mitts."

Let me interject at this point and defend my former boss on one point.

I'm not sure if his scenario qualifies as *erotic*, per se—though if getting a soapy caress from a volatile middle-aged millionaire floats your boat, this is pretty much the pinnacle. What it is, however, is extremely *hygienic*, and also *practical* in its use of specific props likely to be on hand. This was clearly a well-thought-out fantasy, showing a lot of planning and dedication. (As I would later learn working for him, Bill's a detail-oriented guy. The lawsuit doesn't say so, but I wouldn't be surprised if he had a specific make and model of loofah in mind.)

Unfortunately for Bill—and fortuitously for late-night comedians and Keith Olbermann—soon enough, the thread of his tropical fantasy gets away from him, and he temporarily forgets the name of his ersatz sex toy, confusing it with a word for a delicious Middle Eastern food made from fried chickpeas.

And that's how the entire Fox News organization and the world at large discovered that the number one host in cable news had allegedly told one of his producers that he wanted to massage her lady parts with a "falafel."

I had just finished the falafel section of the lawsuit, and my jaw must have been hanging open, because Barry sounded panicked when he quietly hissed at me: "Dude!"

I turned to him and saw that his monitor was no longer displaying *The Smoking Gun*. No one's was. A hush had fallen over the newsroom, the chat groups had evaporated, and everyone was back at their own seat with their heads buried in their screens, suddenly *very* interested in whatever duty they had been shirking in favor of gossip. I looked around, puzzled. Barry caught my eye and gestured with his head toward the newsroom entrance.

It was O'Reilly.

He stood framed in the doorway, tall and stone-faced, surveying the room like some sort of cable news golem, seemingly daring anyone to make a peep.

No one did.

He pushed into the room, walking briskly down the main aisle toward the *Factor* pod, as producers unlucky enough to have a desk in his direct path ducked their heads even farther, trying to make themselves invisible.

He came within twenty feet of my desk. I risked a peek out of the corner of my eye as he blew past. I had misjudged his countenance from a distance. It wasn't the impassive stone face that I had originally thought. It was a clenched jaw and a mask of pure, unadulterated fury.

Just fucking try me, his face said. *Make my fucking day.*

The fallout was swift and severe. Bill usually started every show with a segment called the Talking Points Memo, an editorial monologue about five minutes long. Normally he'd spend it commenting on some political issue, giving his opinion while his words appeared, bullet-pointed and paraphrased, in a graphics box floating next to his head.

The Talking Points segment that night, a few hours after the charges broke, was anything but business as usual. Bill vaguely referred to the allegations, saying, "This is the single most evil thing I have ever experienced, and I've seen a lot." But where Bill was vague, the late-night comedians were happy to be much, much more specific, as I discovered that weekend going through the shows for my *Fox & Friends* duty. Conan O'Brien may have been the most merciless, doing a recurring bit where a Bill sound-alike called into the show to chat and ended up soliciting Conan for sex. Tina Fey, who was still behind the Weekend Update desk on *Saturday Night Live* at the time, was also brutal, uncorking a fast and furious monologue that mixed righteous feminist anger with penis size speculation, entitled "Don't Forget Bill O'Reilly Is Disgusting." Even the normally bland Jay Leno got in on the action, cracking a joke about a "fair and balanced" set of breasts.

Reaction among the newsroom staffers was surprisingly gleeful. Schadenfreude reigned, as most people agreed that Bill had it coming. I hadn't been around long enough at that point to have had any significant run-ins with him, but there was no shortage of producers, video editors, makeup ladies, and security guards he had rubbed the wrong way over the years; some of these folks were now positively crowing, filling the air with speculation about O'Reilly's future. Interestingly, not one person I spoke to thought Fox would go so far as to pull him off the air. He was just too valuable. If one lowly producer had to endure his masturbatory phone calls on a regular basis, that was the price the suits on the second floor were willing to pay for the five million viewers and countless ad dollars he brought in every night.

And as if to underscore this, O'Reilly's ratings spiked by 30 percent during the crisis, even though—aside from the initial Talking Points Memo—he wasn't saying a single word about the lawsuit. ("His ratings are going up faster than his dick," Barry cracked after we saw the first round of post-lawsuit numbers.)

In the midst of all this, Bill disappeared entirely from the newsroom. He had habitually made one or two appearances per day in the subterranean space. But following his day-of, glare-filled excursion when we almost made eye contact, he hadn't returned even once, reportedly sequestering himself all day in his seventeenth-floor office with the door closed, emerging only to tape the show in his ground-floor studio.

Rumors flew. Everyone had a theory, none of them fueled by anything other than wild speculation and hearsay. Even the O'Reilly staffers, when buttonholed by information-starved staffers on other shows, protested that they were as much in the dark as everyone else. The tabloids had a field day, with the News Corp.–owned *New York Post* floating innuendo about the accuser, and the liberal-leaning *Daily News* breathlessly reporting the more salacious O'Reilly-damaging details.

Then, just as suddenly as it began, it was over.

A little more than two weeks after Mackris filed the lawsuit, she settled with O'Reilly and Fox out of court. He announced it on the show that night, again during his Talking Points segment. The statement was a carefully worded masterpiece of blame diversion, complete with complaints of being the target of "media scorn from coast to coast," and claims that the reason for all the scrutiny was dislike of him and Fox News. He recited the meticulously lawyered phrase "There was no wrongdoing in the case whatsoever by anyone." He cast doubt on the most salacious tidbits without directly addressing them: "All I can say to you is please do not believe everything you hear and read." And finally, he attempted to close the books on the topic: "This brutal ordeal is now officially over, and I will never speak of it again."

No one in the newsroom had any such inclination toward dropping the subject, however; it was all we could talk about for the next week.

"*The Washington Post* is saying that Mackris got at least two million dollars in the deal," I announced to my cut-ins team the day after the news of the settlement broke, reading off the paper's website.

"I heard she got four million dollars," my producer, Angie, said. "One of the tech guys swears he bumped into her at a bar downtown last night, and she was wasted. She was apparently celebrating because she's rich now and doesn't have to work here anymore."

Lenny, the former *National Enquirer* writer, shook his head. "I heard it was even more. My buddy at the *Post* said he's hearing it was six or even eight mil. And that O'Reilly refused to pay it out of his own pocket. Ailes agreed to pick up the tab to keep him happy."

Angie grimaced. "I'll remember that at my next review when they tell me money is too tight for a raise." She deepened her voice, launching into a surprisingly accurate impression of Nelson Howe, our fastidious news director: "'Well, Angie, we'd love to give you that whopping three percent raise this year, but we had to pay for O'Reilly to get his rocks off over the phone with one of his employees. I'm sure you understand.'"

The speculated money shortage never materialized. But the company-wide consequences were still annoying enough to garner a round of *I-told-you-so*s from the peanut gallery that had blasted O'Reilly from the beginning of the scandal. A few weeks after everything had settled down, we got a mass e-mail from human resources about mandatory sexual-harassment and diversity-sensitivity classes.

Lenny, who by that point had been switched from the evening shift into full-time on the overnights, did not take the news well. "What is this horseshit?" he griped after reading the e-mail. "I start work at goddamn eleven at night, and they want me to come in at two in the fucking afternoon for a *sensitivity* class? I'm still asleep then, for chrissakes!"

"Maybe they'll let you have an exemption because of your schedule," I said. "I don't think you really need the classes anyway."

"Nah, I know this place. They'll make me come in, and they probably won't even pay me for the hours, the cheap bastards." He gestured in frustration in the direction of the executive offices, two floors over our heads. "And all this because fucking O'Reilly can't stop polishing his knob over the hired help. Pathetic."

Personally, I was delighted to attend the harassment class. The company did, in fact, pay for the time, so that was three hours of overtime I wouldn't have gotten otherwise. I chose one of the available slots that allowed me to take the three-hour class, then hang around—still on the clock—for an extra hour and a half before my actual shift started.

I showed up for the session on a Tuesday afternoon in a nondescript conference room on the third floor only to find a feeding frenzy under way. There was a snack table at one end of the room set up with sodas, cookies, chips, and candy. The twenty or so attendees who had arrived before me, unaccustomed to such displays of culinary generosity from our stingy employer, were in the process of mobbing it, piling food onto flimsy paper plates with abandon. Never one to pass up a free meal myself, I elbowed my way up to the table, grabbing a lukewarm Diet Coke and a handful of pretzels.

Snack in hand, I turned to the large table, looking for a friendly face to sit with, figuring that the three hours would go faster if I had someone next to me to whom I could safely make snide remarks. (Normally, I'd have no reservation making sarcastic asides to a stranger, but I figured that a sexual harassment seminar was no place to try my luck with a potentially unreceptive audience.) I recognized a few people from the newsroom, but, disappointingly, I didn't see any friends. Cutting my losses, I picked a seat next to a long-haired, Ramones T-shirt–wearing tech guy, assuming he'd be the best partner in crime.

He grinned at me as I lowered myself into the seat next to him. "Not too bad so far, is it?" he asked, with a mouthful of Pringles. "Free food, right?"

Before I could answer him, one of our second-tier anchorwomen sat in the vacant chair on my other side. She smiled and nodded at us. "Hey, guys."

I decided it was best to keep my mouth shut for the duration of the class.

Without my ability to be a wiseass during the session, the three hours dragged on. To their credit, the man and woman leading it— lawyers who apparently specialized in schooling office drones on workplace conduct—were affable, and copped an apologetic, *we're on your side* attitude about the whole thing: *We know this is all nonsense, but please bear with us and we'll all get out of here eventually.*

They explained the criteria of what does and does not constitute harassment, criteria that I discovered are surprisingly vague. Obviously, if your boss says, "Sleep with me or you won't get that promotion," that's a textbook case. Open and shut. But anything shy of that depends a lot on interpretation, intent, and circumstance. The lawyers introduced us to the concept of "hostile workplace," meaning that an employer could be held responsible if an employee felt the office atmosphere was pervasively offensive but the managers refused to do anything about it. (By that standard, I probably could have scraped together a case after my first two weeks of listening to the banter in the control room.)

After about an hour of lecturing from the lawyer duo, we broke off into small groups, and were given worksheets to read and discuss among ourselves. The sheets had several poorly written and far-fetched role-playing scenarios for us to evaluate:

> Susan is a production assistant. Her supervisor, Derek, a senior producer, approaches her one day and tells her that the rest of the staff is going to a strip club after work to unwind. Susan feels uncomfortable, but she decides to go anyway, because she worries she won't get a promotion if she refuses.

My small group agreed that the scenario was unrealistic, not because there were no senior producers pervy enough to bring their team to a titty bar—there certainly were plenty of those—but because any news staff worth its salt would balk at after-work drinks that were as pricey as a strip club's yet didn't include a selection of free hot appetizers.

My group was heatedly debating the relative merits of chicken wings versus pigs-in-blankets on bar happy-hour steam table buffets, when the lawyers signaled that the group discussion time was over and that we'd be doing a Q&A to end the session.

"We just want to see if anyone else has any situations, hypothetical or otherwise, that they need clarification on," the female lawyer said.

To my left, the anchorwoman's hand shot up. "Yeah, I'm wondering . . . uhhh, hypothetically . . . if your boss tells you that you have to wear short skirts instead of pants on the air because they want viewers to see your legs more, does that count as harassment?"

When the class's round of nervous laughter died down, the anchor persisted: "No, seriously, though. I'm not saying anyone said that to me, but if they had . . . ?" She trailed off.

"As a matter of fact," the male lawyer said, "they can ask you to wear whatever they want. The law says that since your on-air appearance is basically their 'product,' they can control how you dress." He cleared his throat. "There's a lot of legalese that I won't get into, but long story short, they can pretty much ask you to wear anything."

"So if they want me to do the news wearing a bikini . . . ?"

"Yup." He nodded. "Theoretically, they could ask you to do it naked."

The anchor sighed, then broke into a smile of resignation. "Couldn't hurt the ratings, I guess."

———

I went to the sensitivity class three more times during my career at Fox. If the program ever differed from that first session, I wasn't able to tell. It seemed like the same lessons, the same information, the same outlandish hypothetical scenarios each time. It was as if someone in the Fox legal department decided that, to inoculate the company from lawsuits, we all needed to renew our training every two years or so, like some bizarre sexual harassment DMV. And just like getting a driver's license, the class was interesting the first time—due to the novelty more than anything else—and a huge pain in the ass on every subsequent occasion.

Making matters worse, by my third go-round through the training in 2007, I was working for *The O'Reilly Factor.* At the beginning of the class, the lawyers had us go around the room, giving our names and our positions. When I announced who I worked for, I could hear some grumbling coming from the back of the room.

It's your boss's fault we're stuck in here again.

The taint of Bill's alleged transgressions clung to his staff, sticky and thick like hummus spread on a pita. The lawsuit was still fresh enough in everybody's mind in 2007 that it was the first thing I was asked about by multiple people when I told them I was taking the *Factor* job.

"What are you going to do," Camie asked me about two weeks before I started, "if he calls you late at night?"

I laughed. "Do you know how much money Mackris got? For that kind of cash, he can talk dirty to me all he wants."

She wrinkled her nose in disgust. "Ewww."

"Hell," I continued. "For that kind of money I might take a cab to his hotel room and finish him off myself."

Camie punched my arm with surprising strength. "You're disgusting!"

The *Factor* old-timers, those who had been working on the show when it all went down, were a lot less willing to joke about it than I was; most of them were reluctant to even talk about it. I got the impression that it had been a very unpleasant couple of weeks for everyone involved.

"There were closed-door meetings every day," one of them told me. "And Bill was in a horrible mood the entire time. We were all walking on eggshells."

And there was at least one long-term effect on the staff that I personally found debilitating—we were severely hindered from eating the Middle Eastern entrée *that shall not be named*.

The *Radio Factor* crew would sometimes order lunch from a great little Israeli place near the office. The owner was incredibly surly (and, according to some online reviews, mentally insane) and some days when he answered the phone, he'd just flat-out refuse to make a delivery for no apparent reason. But the matzoh ball soup was so good that we gladly took his abuse.

One time during a commercial break, we were calling out our meal choices to Eric, who was writing them down in preparation to phone in our order. (We figured that Eric, who was fluent in Hebrew, had the best chance of coaxing the reticent restaurateur into cooperating on days when he was being difficult.) I was studying the menu, not paying attention to the goings-on in the studio, when I found the dish I wanted.

"Eric, put me down for the combination plate with hummus, Israeli salad, and falaf—"

"MUTO!" Sam said, sharply cutting me off. "Let me see that menu real quick!"

I looked up to see panic written on Sam's face. I followed his gaze and saw the door between the control room and the studio swinging shut. Bill, normally safe behind soundproof glass, had been hanging out in our half of the studio, chatting with Stan.

"What was that all about?" I asked.

Sam shook his head. "Dude, you don't even know. You almost said the F-word in front of Bill."

"The F-word?" I asked, incredulous. "You mean *falafel*?"

"Jesus!" Sam yelled, throwing up his hands in despair. "Quit it! Stan, tell him to quit it."

Stan looked up from the e-mail he was writing. "Muto, you should probably listen to Martinez."

"How the hell am I supposed to order lunch, Stan?"

Stan smiled. "Order something else. Or find something else to call it."

"Like what?"

"Eric, put Muto down for some fried chickpea patties," Stan called out. He paused for a second. "Me, too, actually. Fried chickpea patties on a pita. Extra hot sauce."

So our closing question is: Did he do it? Is he guilty of sexually harassing one of his underlings?

My closing answer is: Hell, I don't know.

We do know that he almost certainly *said* some of the things he was accused of saying. The lengthy transcripts in the lawsuit point to the existence of audiotapes. Plus, some of the moments in the lawsuit seem simply too O'Reilly-esque to be fake. For example:

> "Immediately after climaxing, Defendant BILL O'REILLY launched into a discussion concerning how good he was during a recent appearance on *The Tonight Show* with Jay Leno: 'It was funny, they used a big clip of me . . . Right after [NBC News anchor Tom] Brokaw, and Brokaw was absolutely the most unfunny guy in the world, and the audience got a big charge out of my . . . It was good.'"

Bragging about how funny he was, and taking delight in showing up a fellow newsman, especially one with more mainstream cred than him—this is all classic Bill. The fact that he is supposed to have done it immediately after completing phone sex makes it both disgusting and hilarious, but it seems too true to his personality to be made up.

So, if we assume he said the things he said, doesn't that make him guilty? It would seem so. But there's one thing holding me back from declaring O'Reilly's guilt: My former boss is many, many things, but he's not a stupid man. And to say the things he allegedly said to an employee without believing she was fully on board is a colossally stupid thing to do. So the most charitable explanation for him is that he deluded himself into thinking that Mackris was into it as much as he was.

Believe it or not, I do have some residual affection for the guy, and I want to believe that my interpretation is correct, even though I completely recognize that it's an incredibly weak defense to say something like "He can't possibly be guilty—he thought she wanted it!" (Not to mention that it comes perilously close to victim blaming, as if it's her fault for not making it clear enough that the advances weren't welcome.)

I can honestly say that there was at least one positive that arose from the whole debacle—my harassment class–derived paranoia meant that I completely shunned any pursuit of workplace relationships. That's not to say that a few didn't fall drunkenly into my lap over the years, but they were never premeditated, which was just as well, because in my experience they were always more trouble than they were worth.

And as Bill found out the hard way, hitting on a coworker is all fun and games until somebody's picture ends up in the *Daily News* with the headline A LOOFAH AFFAIR.

The elevator ride with Stan was awkward, to say the least.

He hadn't said much when he'd come to fetch me from the green room: "Some people want to talk to you about this Fox Mole stuff," he'd said. "I need you to come with me." I followed him from the green room through the lobby to a bank of elevators, which my still-in-shock brain curiously noted was almost the same path I used to take when running scripts in those early months.

Stan punched the key for the fifteenth floor, and the elevator started rising. He stared straight ahead, while I leaned against the back wall of the car, my head swimming, my legs suddenly weak.

I snuck a glance at Stan. He looked tired. I realized I had barely seen him in his office all day. No doubt he'd been at meetings with God knows who, dealing with my fuckery.

I felt horrible for dragging him into it. He was a good boss, and a decent person. He put up with acres and acres of shit every day, the likes of which I could barely imagine, and here I was adding to his burden.

The silence in the elevator was beginning to get oppressive. I had to say something. Anything.

"Stan, I think there might be a misunderstanding here."

He looked at me, smiling a sad smile.

"Let's hope so."

The elevator doors opened and I followed him out.

CHAPTER 13

I Loved You in *A League of Their Own*, You Far-Left Loon

N ow the one thing you never, never do is turn off the camera," Jesse said.

I nodded without looking at him. I was bent at the waist in my seat on the train, fiddling with the bag at my feet. It was full of video equipment, on loan to me from some storeroom deep under Fox headquarters.

"Hey, look at me," he said, snapping his fingers in my face. I straightened in my seat, gave him my full attention. He looked me in the eyes.

"Never turn it off. For any reason."

Jesse Watters was another *Factor* associate producer, a few years older than I, but still shy of thirty. He had somehow worked his way into Bill's good graces enough to become the show's resident ambush interviewer, regularly sent out with a camera crew and a handheld microphone to capture any reluctant guests unfortunate enough to stir Bill's ire. It was a position that held some esteem—ensuring the frequent reception of kudos from the boss, and the chance to be on air every once in a while.

Jesse had done dozens of these ambushes before, so this was old hat for him. But I'd never been. It would be my first time, and I was nervous. Meanwhile, my partner was decidedly not nervous. He lounged in his seat, looking relaxed and not at all like someone who was about to publicly interrogate a famously volatile celebrity. It was October

2007, late afternoon on a Friday. Our commuter train was rolling toward Huntington, a Long Island bedroom community and the site of
a book signing that, unbeknownst to the author, was about to get rudely
interrupted by an ersatz camera crew from the number one program on
cable news.

Our target: talk show host, comedienne, provocateur, and Sworn
Enemy of Bill: Rosie O'Donnell.

The marching orders had come just the day before, during the pitch
meeting. Jesse had informed Bill about the signing. Rosie would be
autographing her new book, *Celebrity Detox*—an account of her brief
stint cohosting, and controversial departure from, the syndicated lady
chat-fest *The View*—and the event would be open to the public.

"How about an ambush?" Jesse asked.

"Let's get her," Bill said, smiling with anticipatory delight.

Bill and Rosie had been feuding for months. The first incident came
in March 2007, when Rosie, then still in her position as the lead host
on *The View*, went off on a rant about an incident involving British
sailors getting seized by an Iranian naval ship. Her theory was that it
was a Bush administration plot to spur the U.S. into war with Iran.

"I have one thing to say: Gulf of Tonkin. Google it," Rosie had told
the studio audience, which consisted largely of middle-aged housewives, most of whom were doubtlessly uninterested in her geopolitical
conspiracy theories. That alone would not have been enough to draw
the attention of *The Factor*, but a few days later, Rosie started with the
9/11 Trutherism:

> "I do believe it's the first time in history that fire has ever
> melted steel. I do believe that it defies physics for the World
> Trade Center Tower Seven, building seven, which collapsed
> in on itself, it is impossible for a building to fall the way it
> fell without explosives being involved, World Trade Center
> Seven. World Trade Center One and Two got hit by planes.

Seven, miraculously, for the first time in history, steel was melted by fire. It is physically impossible."

It was an over-the-top, bonkers rant, one that Rosie had to have known would set off alarm bells at Fox News headquarters, sending hosts and producers scrambling for the red wall boxes that are on every floor, clearly marked IN CASE OF LIBERAL CELEBRITY SAYING SOMETHING OBJECTIONABLE, BREAK GLASS.

Enter Bill O'Reilly.

He weighed in with a Talking Points Memo calling Rosie a "fanatical leftist" and "irresponsible," accusing her of "actively supporting Iran over her own country" and calling on ABC to fire her from *The View*.

Rosie, no shrinking violet, punched right back on her show the next day, referring to Andrea Mackris and the harassment suit.

Sam and I were watching live when she said it, and our jaws dropped. We couldn't believe she'd gone there. It was the nuclear option.

What's even more startling is that it worked. Bill decided that the budding feud had already gone too far. E-mails went back and forth. Phone calls were made. Someone on our staff talked to someone on Barbara Walters's staff. A settlement was hastily negotiated: Bill wouldn't call for Rosie's firing anymore as long as she stopped referring to Mackris.

It was all supposed to be hush-hush, but Rosie, in typical fashion, pulled back the curtain a hair, cryptically writing on her blog that she'd been told she wasn't allowed to talk about the lawsuit again. Bill, meanwhile, kept his end of the bargain, reluctantly dropping the on-air feud but privately holding on to the grudge, keeping it in his pocket for a rainy day.

As it turns out, all the behind-the-scenes machinations were mostly a moot point—ABC announced barely three weeks later, in late April 2007, that contract negotiations had failed, and Rosie would not be coming back for a second season of *The View*.

Bill declared victory, temporarily breaking the terms of the feud settlement to engage in a little on-air gloating. A few days later, Rosie got into a brutal live TV shouting match with her conservative cohost

Elisabeth Hasselbeck and ended up leaving the show several weeks earlier than planned.

O'Donnell dropped out of the spotlight after that, apparently taking time to regroup and write her book. Without Barbara Walters to protect her, she was again fair game. And so a few months later at the pitch meeting, when Jesse presented the opportunity for the ambush, Bill was chomping at the bit, practically bouncing in his chair with glee.

Jesse explained that the layout of the bookstore was such that a full crew—his usual accompaniment, consisting of two guys to handle both the camera and a large multidirectional microphone—wouldn't be able to infiltrate. He'd need to go in stealthily. Instead of the large shoulder-mounted camera, he'd need someone with a small camcorder that could be concealed in a bag until the absolute last moment.

"So we need a volunteer," Stan said. "Who wants to go with Jesse tomorrow?"

Sam's hand shot up.

"I'll do it," he called out.

O'Reilly looked him over, coolly assessing him, his height, his bulk, his unruly facial hair.

"Hmmm . . . I don't know, Martinez," Bill said. "I think you might scare some people too much."

The semicircle of producers exploded with shocked laughter, as Sam sputtered, red-faced with indignation.

"No offense, of course," Bill said, smiling somewhat cruelly. "It's just that they'll see you coming from a mile away. I think we need someone more . . . subtle."

My hand crept up.

I wondered immediately if I'd made a mistake. I'd never been on an ambush before. I'd never even been on a field assignment. I had zero qualifications, aside from the fact that my college film experience left me arguably more adept with a camera than some of my colleagues.

But I was still, at that point, the newest staff member, and I was eager to make my mark with Bill. Nine months into the job, despite my constant presence at a desk just outside his office, and two hours a day spent staring at him through the radio studio's glass partition, I still wasn't entirely sure that he knew my name; as near as I could tell, he was under the impression that I was a summer intern who had overstayed his welcome.

I had another reason for volunteering, a less selfish one: I wanted to take some of the heat off Sam. I could tell by looking at him that Bill's offhand dismissal had made him angry—rightfully so, I should add. But Sam was a bit of a hothead, and I worried that his immediate reaction would be to say something to Bill that he wouldn't be able to take back.

"I can do it," I said.

Bill turned to me, studying me through narrowed eyes.

"Yeah, I think that would work," he finally said. He turned to Jesse. "Watters? Is Muto good for you?"

Oh, he did know my name. Bonus, I guess.

After the meeting, Bill pulled Jesse and me aside to give us some instructions. "Be low-key," he said. "Don't just barge in there. Wait in line with everyone else to get your book signed, then—BAM!—pull out the camera and hit her with the questions."

Jesse and I nodded.

"You have to be respectful," Bill continued. "Dress nice. Khaki pants and a blazer," he said, probably more for my benefit than Jesse's; the ambush specialist was wearing his normal work attire of suit pants and a tie with a preppy print, while I was wearing my usual beat-up boat shoes, jeans, and button-down.

"What do you want me to ask her?" Jesse said.

"Ask her about the 9/11 thing," Bill said. "Does she still believe that it was a conspiracy? That kind of thing."

Jesse nodded, and scribbled in a notebook.

I wondered what I'd gotten myself into.

———

The next day I wore, as instructed, khaki pants and a blue blazer. Sam, who had calmed down by then, howled when he saw me.

"You look like King of the White People," he said. "Are you even allowed to hang out with Latin folk like me anymore? I feel like you're about to ask me to clean your house or something."

"I don't know what you're talking about," I said. "I look damn good. But now that you mention it, my apartment is looking a little dirty. . . ."

I ducked, laughing, as he whipped a yellow highlighter at my head.

Jesse and I left the office before the TV show even started taping, and headed to Penn Station. Even in the early afternoon, a full ninety minutes before rush hour, the station's lengthy underground concourse was a shit-show mélange of confused tourists wheeling massive suitcases, disgruntled commuters stocking up on sixteen-ounce tallboy cans of beer for the train ride home, and rowdy groups of teenagers from Long Island stumbling up the stairs from the train platforms, hooting and high-fiving in anticipation of a Friday night in the big city.

I followed Jesse as he wove expertly through the crowd. He stopped at a newsstand. "Do you need any magazines or newspapers or anything?" he asked. "Since we're technically traveling for work, we get a per diem. So if you want any soda or candy, or something to read for the train, get it now, because you can expense it later."

As I'd come to find out over the years, that was typical Jesse; the man knew how to work the system like nobody I'd ever met. There was a reason why he was the only producer on the staff to regularly appear on air: His personality was a perfect match for the program. He was unctuous, a bit smirky, and sarcastic to the point where I decided it was a miracle he'd never been punched in the face; but he was still oddly likable, the kind of person you'd much rather have working for you than against you. He was one of the more conservative members of the staff—a political slant he regularly attributed to a rejection of his Philadelphia hippie parents—but his ideology didn't consume him. That's what made him so good at ambushing liberals. He was able to approach them with a certain *aren't we all having a good time* demeanor, treating the ambush like an amusing lark and making for much better television.[49]

---

49 In contrast, our other (much less prolific) ambushing producer, Porter Berry, was a more staunch conservative, and it showed. When he ambushed a liberal, it came off as if he could barely contain his disgust at having to be in the same room with the person.

After picking up some sodas and reading material, we found seats on our train and settled in for the hour-long ride. I fiddled with the camera the whole way out, learning the buttons by feel, practicing pulling it out of the bag in a smooth motion, hitting the POWER and RECORD buttons in quick succession and aiming it inconspicuously from waist level. I did not want to screw up the ambush with a technical error. Jesse would be pissed, obviously, if I failed to get his confrontation on tape; but his annoyance would be like a soft kiss compared to Bill's.

Jesse and I got off the train at the Huntington stop and walked the few blocks to the bookstore, a massive, high-ceilinged space that was teeming with people. We purchased two copies of the book, a slim hardcover, and took a spot at the end of the signing line. It was still an hour and a half before Rosie was scheduled to show up, but the queue already snaked halfway around the store.

It was a bigger crowd than we expected, but it was still a fish-in-a-barrel scenario for Jesse, who wasn't used to his subjects just falling into his lap like Rosie was about to do. "There's no sport in it," he'd complained on the train ride up. He preferred putting in legwork, doing a little reconnaissance, learning the habits of his prey before striking. He'd once spent three days in a Starbucks outside the New York Times Building, trying to figure out which entrance a certain editor who had raised Bill's ire liked to use. (He never spotted the guy, and the ambush was aborted, a rare failure.) Another time, at the height of O'Reilly's feud with Keith Olbermann, Jesse had spent the better part of a week staking out the MSNBC host's Manhattan apartment, recording his comings and goings. (His surveillance on that one was more successful than with the *Times* guy, and he was able to assemble a detailed dossier on Olbermann—times of day he traveled, method of transportation, identity of companions—but Bill eventually opted to not pull the trigger for the ambush, determining that the resulting wave of publicity would probably help Olbermann more than hurt him.)

While Porter was probably accurately mirroring the emotions of many of our viewers, it tended to make his ambushes seem self-righteous, which made for bad television. Jesse's sarcastic, somewhat softer touch was much more entertaining.

Waiting in the Rosie O'Donnell line for the easy get, Jesse and I must have looked ridiculous. We were dressed almost identically, having taken Bill's wardrobe instructions arguably too literally. Instead of blending in inconspicuously like O'Reilly had wanted, we stuck out like awkward, preppy sore thumbs: two dressy twentysomething males waiting in a line dominated by casually dressed middle-aged women—the demographic that apparently made up the bulk of Rosie's fan base.

"We clearly don't belong here," I said to Jesse with a lowered voice.

"Just relax, man," he said, also keeping his voice low. "Act casual. Nobody suspects anything. Just pretend that you're a fan who wants a book signed."

My ears perked up at this. A stint with a sketch/improv group in college had convinced me, despite plenty of evidence to the contrary, that I was good at improvising.[50] *I can handle this.* I struck up a conversation with the two women in line behind us, making up a fake name and a fake job, overzealously gushing about how much of a Rosie fan I was, how excited I was to meet her, and so on. The women were friendly and chatty, actually laughing at one point over how much Jesse and I didn't fit in with the rest of the crowd, giving me a brief heart attack.

"So how long have you two been together?" one of the women asked eventually.

"Excuse me?" I said.

They thought Jesse and I were a couple. Fair enough, I guess. On a list of signifiers of homosexuality, "attending a Rosie O'Donnell book signing with another man" is probably pretty close to the top, right behind "voluntarily watching any show from the Real Housewives franchise." I wasn't about to lapse into a gay panic, though. I was plenty secure in my own sexuality. Honestly, for a twentysomething man living in New York City, getting mistaken for gay was more a compliment than anything else, implying that the casual observer recognized a certain

---

50 The crown jewel of my career was a weeklong engagement as Barry the Best Man in a semiprofessional production of *Tony and Tina's Wedding* in downtown South Bend, Indiana. I wish that were a joke or an exaggeration.

stylishness about you. Normally, I was way too schlubby to get pegged for anything other than what I was: a boring straight guy.

"Oh, we're not together," I said. "He's married and I have a girlfriend."

"Oh," the woman said. "Uh-huh."

She didn't believe me, clearly, but I happened to be telling the truth. A few months after Jillian and I broke up, I'd met Krista. She was tall, and wore a stylish pair of glasses. She had long, straight, light-brown hair and an endearingly girlish affinity for the color pink. We'd met at a party, where we'd struck up a conversation about movies, agreeing that the Kirsten Dunst cheerleading opus *Bring It On* was criminally underrated. She'd impressed me with her ability to finish the *Sunday Times* crossword puzzle without cheating, and we'd bonded over our mutual love of Led Zeppelin, Italian cured meats, and all things New York City. While Jillian and I had been a case of opposites attracting, Krista and I had almost everything in common. She was essentially me in female form, a fact that in retrospect probably should have been a red flag, but one that I narcissistically embraced at the time.

I didn't tell any of this to the skeptical lady in the book-signing line, because our conversation was interrupted by cheering coming from the front of the store. Rosie had arrived. I felt a surge of adrenaline, and maybe a tinge of fear. Aside from some youthful shenanigans, mostly involving alcohol, this was probably the most socially disobedient thing I'd ever attempted.

Jesse and I waited patiently, barely speaking, as the line slowly progressed and we got ever closer to Rosie. She was very chatty, making small talk with everyone who approached her to get a book signed, so it was about another half hour before we neared the front of the queue.

As we inched closer, I surveyed the setup. Rosie had a bigger entourage than I thought she would (though, to her credit, it was probably a lot smaller group than most other celebrities of her stature would have). She had her own camera crew taping the proceedings for some reason, and at least two bodyguards that I could see, and maybe three or four hangers-on.

I noticed that some of the people ahead of us were videotaping and photographing Rosie as they approached her, which worked out perfectly for my purposes. My camera would seem unremarkable, at least until Jesse started firing questions at her. I slipped it out of the bag, flipped open the viewfinder, and started recording.

The bookstore flunky who was controlling the traffic flow gave us the go-ahead, and Jesse and I approached the table together.

Rosie wasn't even paying attention to us at first. She was yelling to someone across the room. Jesse sidled right up next to her, and I made sure to frame up a shot that showed both of them.

Jesse started speaking: "Rosie, I'm Jesse from Bill O'Reilly's show."

"No, you're not!" she laughed.

"He wants to know why you won't come on the show," Jesse continued. "You had such a good time last time you were on. You're always invited."

I should pause here and explain that the "we just want you to come on the show" ruse is essential for a successful ambush. Ambush interviews are generally considered journalistically suspect, except in one very specific set of circumstances: The person refuses to talk to you otherwise. This was the standard established by Mike Wallace years ago, and it's the banner that O'Reilly wrapped himself in more often than not. *You see, we were forced to send a camera crew after this guy because he ignored our phone calls.*

But the truth is that, in most ambush situations, Bill actually *didn't* want the person to come on the show—because the interview would have been a disaster. If O'Reilly set his sights on you for an ambush, chances are that you'd actually make a terrible guest. You'd either be too hostile or too crazy, and the interview would dissolve into chaos, or, conversely you'd be too persuasive and reasonable, getting the better of the host.

The "we just want you on the show" gambit was the easy way out of these situations, giving journalistic cover to the dubious practice of ambushing. The only requirement was that a day or two before the ambush, someone on the staff would place a call or drop an e-mail requesting an interview. This request was almost always wisely ignored by the target (or more often, I suspect, their representatives). Jesse was then free to ambush the subject with the paper-thin excuse that the whole thing was just an attempt to get them to come on *The Factor*.

Bill never said so, but everyone knew that the real purpose of the ambush was to make the subject look stupid. This wasn't particularly hard to do, as almost anyone looks stupid when confronted unexpectedly with a camera crew and a microphone-wielding reporter. Even if the ambush victim answers the questions, they usually come off badly, or at least end up looking as if they have something to hide. And if they're uncooperative, all the better. Running away provides a great visual, guaranteed to make the show's preproduced "cold open" introduction video and be teased before commercial breaks throughout the show. If Jesse got *really* lucky, the victim would try to slam a house or car door on him. That was TV gold.

But there was no door for Rosie O'Donnell to slam that day. She was sitting at a table as Jesse peppered her with questions and I taped the whole thing.

"Oh, my God. Is that what you do?" she asked, incredulous. "You go around to book signings?"

Jesse grinned. "No, we want to meet you. We want you to come on the show."

"He knows how to find me, the guy," Rosie said.

"We've called you a hundred times," Jesse said, possibly not even exaggerating that much—unlike in the case of some of our other ambushees, O'Reilly actually had made a determined effort to get Rosie on the show, with Eugene leaving her a couple messages a month.

"I do not want *you* to call me," Rosie said calmly. "If Bill wants me, he should tell me himself. He is a big boy. He is a grown-up."

At this point, Rosie's bodyguards still hadn't noticed what was going on, probably because the noise from the fans waiting in line made it hard for them to hear Jesse grilling their boss. She signaled to them.

"Hey, this is Bill O'Reilly's camera crew," she said. "But don't throw them out, because that makes it all worse when he puts it on the Bill O'Reilly No Spin Zone."

Credit where credit was due—the lady knew her television tropes.

At this point, Jesse could sense that his time was growing short. He'd been lucky so far that O'Donnell was willing to joke around, but it was time to go for the jugular.

"Rosie, he wants to know if you regret saying that 9/11 was an inside job?"

Rosie's demeanor changed instantly. The smile melted from her face. The joking around was over.

"I did not say that," she said. "He is quoting the wrong people."

That's when the guard moved in to shut me down.

"That is enough," he said, stepping in front of me, blocking my shot. "Thank you. That's enough. Sir. Enough. No more filming."

He was reaching for my camera when Rosie called him off.

"Stop, Eddie," she said. "That's what they want you to do." He looked back at her, then reluctantly stepped aside. Now Rosie was talking to me directly.

"Now, sir, could you put down your camera? Could you turn it off?"

Never . . . for any reason . . .

Without stopping the recording, I snapped the viewfinder window shut and lowered the camera to my side, hoping that I could fake Rosie into thinking I had turned it off.

It didn't work.

"I said turn it off. Hello, I work in television, too," she said. "Can you turn the lens down to the floor?"

"It's off," I lied. But she wasn't having it.

"Okay, we're done here," Rosie said. "Good-bye."

The bodyguards moved in, shoving me and Jesse away from Rosie's perch on the mezzanine, and bodily escorting us down the stairs to the ground level. A store manager told us we were now officially trespassing in the store and that we had to leave, and we weren't welcome back. Ever.

"We're banned for life?" I asked, holding the still-running camera.

The manager nodded. "Yup. Life."

As the bodyguards corralled us toward the exit, we could hear Rosie, still at her signing table on the mezzanine, yelling after us.

"Bill O'Reilly is a sexual harrasser! He's a sexual harrasser!" she screamed, loud enough to be heard throughout the entire store.

The fans still waiting in line broke into cheers and applause.

And then Jesse and I were out on the street in front of the bookstore. The whole thing had taken maybe ninety seconds.

Jesse shot a glance at the camcorder, still clutched in my adrenaline-shaky hands. "Did you get it?" he asked.

"God, I hope so," I said.

We walked a few blocks and found a Japanese restaurant, immediately knocking back shots of vodka with beer chasers to calm our jangled nerves. (Well, *my* jangled nerves. Jesse seemed as calm as ever.)

We reviewed the footage. Fortunately, I had gotten it all. Even after closing the viewfinder and lowering the camera, I had managed to keep Rosie more or less in frame. I had accomplished my part of the mission—I kept the camera running. I hadn't stopped recording until the manager ushered us into the street.

Jesse's fiancée picked us up in her car, and dropped me at the nearest train station. Before I left, Jesse reminded me of the fieldwork per diem: "If you want to take your girlfriend out to a nice dinner tonight, you can expense it," he said. He may have been kidding, but knowing him, he probably wasn't. Either way, I didn't feel like risking it.

The original plan was for me to bring the footage into work on Monday, but I was still so hopped up on adrenaline that I couldn't wait. I went straight from Penn Station to the office, where I transcribed the footage and e-mailed the text to the rest of the staff. I was proud of our excursion, and couldn't wait until Monday.

As it turns out, I didn't have to.

Rosie's own camera crew, which I'd initially noticed but quickly forgotten about, had been rolling the whole time, recording the event for her website. She put up a video clip of the entire encounter on her blog, along with text written in a weird haiku format (as was her wont at that time) calling Jesse and me "khaki-clad henchmen."

The story became instant national news and was picked up by all the entertainment shows. And unlike the shot I had taken—which showed only Jesse and Rosie—I was visible in the new footage. You could see me holding the camera and intently watching the viewfinder.

My mom called me on Sunday to tell me that one of the neighbors had seen me on *Access Hollywood*.

The Rosie ambush was a real turning point for me on the show. Bill was thrilled with the footage, lavishly praising Jesse's interviewing and my camera work. The feeling of pride came again, but this time it wasn't unwelcome. I'd been at Fox for more than three years. Participating in the attempted takedown of a liberal celebrity, an activity that would have horrified me at the beginning of my career, now felt like all in a day's work. I still had my core progressive beliefs, but for the first time, I didn't feel bad about contributing to the network's push to seek and destroy liberals.

I'd gone over completely.

April 11, 2012—6:01 P.M.

In the end, the security goons didn't come to get me.

Instead, they waited politely for me to come to them.

There they were, two of them, standing outside the office of the Fox News vice president for legal affairs, in a remote corner of the fifteenth floor where Stan had led me. The guards asked for my cell phone, and I pulled it out of my jeans pocket, hoping my hands weren't shaking.

"We'll just hold on to this for now," one of the guards said. He was big, a tallish white guy, but nothing too intimidating. I estimated I could overpower him if need be.

Of course, the fact that I was even remotely considering this course of action is a dead giveaway that I wasn't thinking clearly at that moment. What was I going to do, *fight* my way out of the building? My mere presence outside that office—the fact that they had somehow, despite all my precautions, caught me—had just proven that I didn't have anything approaching the espionage skills of James Bond; I don't know why I was entertaining the notion that I might have his hand-to-hand-combat expertise.

But the guard wasn't really what was worrying me. All I could think was that if Bill O'Reilly was on the other side of that door, there was a good chance that he'd hulk out with rage and twist my head clean off my shoulders, as easily as unscrewing the cap off a Coke bottle.

And at that moment I don't think I'd have tried to stop him, either.

But O'Reilly wasn't in the office. It was just the VP of legal, a woman named Diane, along with a man from the IT department and a woman from human resources. Stan followed me in and shut the door behind him.

Diane invited me to sit down, and I took a seat while four pairs of eyes followed my every move.

I'm not proud of this next bit.

I wish I had handled it differently, anyway.

What I *should* have done is admitted it right there. I should have just smiled, thrown my hands up, and said, "All right. You got me."

But that's not what I did. Instead, I lied my face off.

CHAPTER 14

Fox-Flavored Sausage

P eople would often ask me about how Fox pushes a message. And I would always tell them the message isn't so much pushed as it is *pulled*, gravitationally, with Roger Ailes as the sun at the center of the solar system; his vice presidents were the forces of gravity that kept the planet-size anchors and executive producers in a tight orbit; then all the lesser producers and PAs were moons and satellites and debris of varying sizes.[51]

An organizational flow chart at Fox would be tough to draw up, as title alone was not the ultimate signifier of status. Sometimes the anchors outranked their executive producers, as was the case with *The O'Reilly Factor*. (In fact, Bill had procured an EP title for himself, but he outranked the two other EPs on the show, both Stan, who oversaw TV, radio, and the website, and Gayle, who focused on television and also served as a fact-checker.) Sometimes the anchors were relatively weak—as was the case with a lot of weekend shows, and maybe some of the newswheel hours—and a strong senior producer or producer outranked, or at least pretended to outrank, the host. (For example, Lizzie from *The Lineup*, who was only a producer but was tough enough

---

51 My place in this somewhat tortured metaphor: When I started at Fox, I was probably space dust, but by the time I left, I'd arguably worked my way up to chimpanzee astronaut.

that she probably could have bossed around Ailes himself had she been left alone in a room with him for more than five minutes.)

The bottom line is that each show had one person—be they anchor or producer or whoever—who was directly accountable to the Second Floor. That was the brilliance of the company's power structure. One misconception that outsiders always had about the channel is that we'd sit around all morning planning how to distort the news that day. But there was never any centralized control like that. No "marching orders," as it were. Instead, it was more a decentralized, entrepreneurial approach. Each show was an autonomous unit. Each showrunner—who had not risen to their position by being stupid—knew exactly what was expected of them, knew what topics and guests would be acceptable.

Theoretically, each show could talk about whatever they wanted to talk about, and take any angle they wanted to take, and book any guest they wanted to have on.

Realistically, there was tremendous pressure to hew closely to the company line. The Second Floor monitored the content of every show very closely. Each show was required to submit a list of all the guests and all the topics well before the fact; the list would be reviewed by one of the relevant vice presidents. Most of the time, this was just a formality—as I said, the showrunners knew their boundaries—but every once in a while, a certain guest or topic would set off alarm bells on the second floor, leading to a series of increasingly urgent and unpleasant e-mails and phone calls for the showrunner.

Even if a segment passed initial muster, the Second Floor reserved the right to pull the plug if it took a turn they didn't like. They were always watching, and never hesitant to exercise their authority. Roger himself had a phone in his office, a hotline he could pick up and immediately be connected to the control room. Every producer knew that, and dreaded seeing his name on the caller ID. If Roger took the time to personally call the control room, in my experience it was almost never complimentary.[52]

---

52 He was also notorious for being a micromanager and would often call the control room to complain about small matters, demanding that a piece of b-roll be removed from the rotation, or that a sound bite be cut slightly differently.

It was a unique, bottom-up management structure that had built-in checks and balances coming from the top down. This approach had its advantages and disadvantages. On the upside, it often led to innovative programming, with adventurous hosts and producers coming up with story ideas and segments that a more buttoned-down, dictatorial management structure might otherwise never have approved. (O'Reilly was one of the beneficiaries of this, successfully experimenting with some of his more outlandish, barely news-related segments like Body Language and the Quiz.)

One of the disadvantages was that the Second Floor often put insane, arbitrary restrictions into place, with networkwide implications.

For example, some unlucky guests were banned for life from every show on the network, a result of a diktat from the Second Floor. Comedian Bill Maher, once a semi-regular guest on *The Factor* and some other Fox shows, made too many cracks about Sarah Palin over the years, raising the ire of a powerful female VP who banned him from our air and demanded that all Fox-affiliated websites refer to him only as "Pig Maher."

Sometimes entire *organizations* were given lifetime bans. The website *Politico* wrote something a few years back that rubbed Roger the wrong way (we were never told what exactly the transgression was) and word went out to all the shows: No more *Politico* reporters as guests. Also, any anchors who mentioned the site on air had to use the phrase "left-wing *Politico*"—an absurd designation for a publication that usually played it down the middle.

Some anchors and producers had enough juice—proportional to the size of their audience, generally—to push back against the Second Floor's mandates, with varying levels of success, though even O'Reilly, who had more juice than anyone, could only do so much. When one of his favorite guests, a fiery, young, liberal African American college professor, was banned,[53] Bill lobbied on his behalf, eventually striking an

---

53 The reason for the ban was simply "because Roger hates him as a guest." My pet theory was that he was blacklisted because he was too good—he was likable, charismatic, and made persuasive cases for liberal policies. This made him totally anathema to Roger, who prefers his left-wingers to be paper tigers.

agreement with the Second Floor allowing him to continue to use the guy as long as his appearances were limited to once a month. O'Reilly wasn't happy with it, but it was better than walking away empty-handed.

There was nothing Bill hated more than management impositions on his show. These impositions almost always followed the same pattern—Stan would get a phone call in his office from one of Roger's underlings, usually a vice president named Bill Shine. I'd hear Manskoff's end of the conversation. "You're killing me here, you know that, don't you," Stan would say. "You know he's going to hate this." Manskoff would hang up, shaking his head in disbelief, and make the fifteen-foot trek to Bill's office, closing the door behind him. Through the door, we'd hear muffled talking from Stan, then muffled shouting from Bill, followed shortly by the door popping open and Stan bolting from the office like a pinball from a launcher.

"I'll do it this time, Manskoff," Bill would call after him, "just this once. But I'm tired of this bullshit!" He'd always slow down for the next part, hammering each phrase so there would be no mistake in the future: "I want the interference! With my show! To stop! Now!"

Relations were rocky enough between O'Reilly and the Second Floor that VP Shine was dispatched on a regular basis to smooth things over, meeting in O'Reilly's office every Tuesday at four P.M. These meetings would sometimes last upward of forty-five minutes. Though I was never privy to what was said in the meetings, neither man ever looked particularly pleased upon completion.

It was Stan's job to run interference between O'Reilly and management, keeping the bosses out of Bill's hair but also insulating the suits from Bill's fits of rage. Ninety-nine percent of all issues could be solved with Manskoff and Shine collaborating, not having to involve Ailes or O'Reilly. But every once in a while, O'Reilly would refuse to back down, and Ailes would be forced to intervene.

The most memorable instance of this was in late 2008, when Lehman Brothers went tits-up and the whole economy was teetering on the brink. President Bush prepared a massive bailout package for the banks, and conservative talk radio exploded with outrage and opposition. One prominent conservative voice in favor of the bailout? Bill O'Reilly, who believed that the entire financial system would collapse without it. He took to his radio show that day and excoriated the radio hosts who opposed the bailout:

> "Let's get back to this talk radio stuff. These idiots. I mean, they're misleading you. They're lying to you. They're rich, these guys. Big cigars. All of that. 'Yeah, oh yeah, my private jet!' And they're saying, 'Oh, no! No bailout!' Walk away from these liars, these right-wing liars. Walk away from them! They're not looking out for you."

The cigar and private jet stuff was a thinly veiled swipe at Rush Limbaugh, someone O'Reilly has never liked, but also a figure who had a lot of fans at 1211 Sixth Avenue, including Roger Ailes and Sean Hannity.

When word filtered to the Second Floor that O'Reilly planned on repeating some of his radio rant on the TV show that night, the order came back quickly: Absolutely not. But O'Reilly put his foot down. Neither Stan Manskoff nor Bill Shine could dissuade him, and it took a phone call from Roger himself to put the matter to rest.

Bill took the call in his office, politely but insistently pleading his case to Ailes, but Roger held firm. Bill reluctantly agreed to toe the party line, excused himself from the call, gently hung up the receiver, then loudly yelled a string of expletives that could be heard all over the seventeenth floor. But after he got it out of his system, he spiked the Limbaugh reference from the TV show.

I said earlier that O'Reilly had more juice than anyone. That wasn't entirely true. He had higher ratings than anyone, to be sure, but it could be argued that Hannity actually had more juice, owing to his closer affiliation and friendship with Ailes. The two of them are fellow travelers, both devoted to Republican causes. Bill is not on that train with them— he's truly devoted only to O'Reilly-related causes. (Which just so happen to dovetail with Republican causes most of the time, but still . . .)

This has led to no small amount of tension between the parties. O'Reilly and Hannity, the two biggest stars at Fox News Channel, have basically no working relationship. Their shows are back-to-back, yet they're barely on speaking terms. O'Reilly is convinced that Hannity is trying to sabotage his show, and vice versa. The two of them fight constantly, almost entirely through intermediaries and over the pettiest of issues—mostly over guests. Both shows like to use Fox News analysts—specifically Karl Rove, Dick Morris, and Bernie Goldberg—and 90 percent of the squabbling is over which show gets which guest on which night.

Roger did the situation no favors in 2011, when he spoke to Howard Kurtz of *The Daily Beast* and engaged in a bit of provocative muckraking:

"O'Reilly hates Sean [Hannity] and he hates Rush [Limbaugh] because they did better in radio than he did," Ailes said.

Bill was furious for weeks. Because it turns out there is one thing he hated even more than management meddling: someone insulting his ratings.

Bill was, if nothing else, a man of habit—to the point where he got incredibly angry if anything went awry with his schedule. For someone as pugilistic as he, he's shockingly unable to roll with the punches. He's like a taller, Irish version of Dustin Hoffman in *Rain Man*. Even a slight delay or deviation from the plan could set off a lecture or, on occasion, a screaming match. As a result, he was tightly scheduled down to the minute.

Bill's daily routine was really a marvel of efficiency. It wasn't quite *The 4-Hour Workweek*, but it came pretty damn close to being the four-hour workday. Now, he would tell you he's up early, reading the paper, communicating with his staff, etc. And this is all true. He's a hardworking guy. I don't want to give the impression that he isn't. But as far as actual time spent in the building? We're talking four and a half hours a day, *tops*.

Here's how it went:

9:30 A.M.

We'd compile and send to Bill the "Newsfax," a ten-page document with excerpts from what we thought were the day's most important stories, op-eds, sound bites, and so on. We called it the Newsfax because it was easier to tell Bill we were faxing it to him than it was to explain that we were remotely printing it to his home printer.

This is actually a familiar pattern with Bill. It's often simpler to let him believe something erroneously than it is to correct him.

Case in point: In summer 2011, a story surfaced on the right-wing blogs that an auditor for the Justice Department had found out some DOJ employees attending a meeting at the Capital Hilton in Washington, DC, had been served refreshments, including muffins for which the hotel charged sixteen dollars apiece.

It's no surprise that the story spread like wildfire on the blogs and was soon picked up by cable news. It was a great story for the right, reinforcing preexisting notions of government excess and willingness to waste taxpayer money, the incompetence of the Obama Justice Department, etc.

One problem: It wasn't true.

A few days after the story broke, a representative from Hilton Hotels came out and said that the auditor had misread the bill, that the sixteen dollars referred to a full breakfast—coffee, tea, fruit, muffins, plus tax and gratuity. Not a bargain by any means, but also not too bad for a hotel continental breakfast.

A producer named Steiner Rudolf was line producing—assembling the stories in the rundown and making sure they all timed out correctly—on the day that Bill wanted to include the muffin anecdote in a Talking Points Memo. "Actually, Bill, the muffin thing got debunked," Steiner started to tell him. "A guy from the hotel came out and said—"

"I don't give a shit what the guy said," Bill interrupted, suddenly angry. "It's the same old thing. They come out and deny it, but the story is there. We know it's true. We have the proof."

Steiner tried gamely one more time to convince Bill to drop the story, explaining that he didn't have the proof, but O'Reilly was adamant. He'd latched on to the story, and pesky things like "facts" weren't going to convince him otherwise. The muffins went into the Talking Points. Over the next few weeks, he repeated the story several times on his own show, on Jon Stewart's show, on David Letterman's show, and on *Good Morning America*.

Unfortunately for the embarrassed Hilton Hotels and some nameless DOJ bureaucrats, the muffin story, false though it may be, perfectly coincided with Bill's book tour.

10:00 A.M.

The morning conference was when the real work of building the day's show began. The senior staff connected on a four-way call. From my vantage point outside Stan's office, I could hear them on speakerphone gearing up for it like troops going into battle. "Are you ready for this?" "Yeah, are you?" "Here goes nothing."

One of them would dial Bill's house. He's all business when he picks up the phone. A curt "good morning," then Gayle begins reciting what she calls the "comp report." Right off the bat she tells him how many e-mails came in after the previous night's show, and what topic elicited the most messages. ("We had thirty-five hundred e-mails last night, most of them in reaction to the immigration segment . . .")

Bill took the e-mails—sent by our audience to OReilly@foxnews .com—pretty seriously, regarding them (not inaccurately, I'd say) as a direct gauge of viewer interest. Each morning, two unlucky women on the staff had the unenviable job of sorting through the e-mails and printing out a representative sample of fifty to sixty. Bill, to his credit, reads these personally. He selects a handful to be read on the air. If he likes some others but doesn't consider them air-worthy, he'll instruct our lucky mail combers to send a signed book or some "kind words"— a response e-mail reading, *Thanks for the kind words. Signed, Bill O'Reilly.*

I'd glanced at the show's in-box from time to time and had been blown away by the sheer incoherence and illiteracy of some of the respondents.[54] This would sometimes present a problem, for Bill liked his e-mails to be short, pithy, and not written by a complete moron.

This was a surprisingly tall order on certain days.

On one occasion, there was an e-mail that Bill really wanted to read on the air. One of the producers noticed that the e-mail was signed with an obvious gag name: Jack MeHoff. Clearly, that's unreadable on television. But Bill liked the text of the e-mail so much that he couldn't bear to cut it from the mail segment. After pondering for a bit, he decided on a course of action: "Let's just change the last name to Mehoffer."

Despite producers pleading with him that the slight name change was not much, if at all, better than the original, Bill stuck to his guns, reading the letter with the modified name on air. The rest is YouTube history.

Back to the conference call. After the e-mail tally, Gayle would read off the list of guests on the competing shows—whatever guests CNN and MSNBC had the night before, and whatever guests Hannity and Greta were scheduled to have that night.

Next, the call got to the real nitty-gritty: Bill started talking about what he wanted on the show that night. *The Factor* was one hour long, divided by commercial breaks into seven "blocks," identified by letters *A* through *G*. The first six blocks all needed a topic and a guest, while the last block—the shortest one—usually contained the viewer e-mail segment, plugs for merchandise, and other *Factor* business.

The Factor differed from a straight news program in that all of the segments are, with a few exceptions, interview segments. The advantage of this is that interview segments are incredibly easy to produce. A single associate producer can put together an entire segment by his- or herself in about an hour, without even getting up from a desk.

The associate producer (also sometimes called a segment producer, for obvious reasons) would call the guest on the phone and get them to agree to come on; conduct a pre-interview; book a car to bring the guest either to the New York studio to sit with Bill or to a remote studio with

---

54 I wish I could say this was solely an affliction of the right, but I suspect that it is depressingly common among Americans on both sides of the aisle. Writing incomprehensible e-mails to public figures is a pursuit that knows no ideology.

a satellite connection; do some research on the topic; cut some b-roll; plug in some graphics; and call it a day.

Contrast that with something like the nightly network news, which uses an anchor who tosses to reporters who introduce highly produced taped pieces known in the industry—somewhat suggestively—as "packages." (As in, "Hey, did you see Jake Tapper's package last night?" or "The local affiliate has a great package on that.") A good package will combine b-roll, graphics, interviews, and narration from the reporter.

The advantages of the network news model is that the reporter packages are a lot more slick and tell a better story in a much more concise and visually appealing manner. The downside to the network model is that it's very time- and labor-intensive, with each package requiring painstaking work from a reporter, producers, a cameraman, a sound technician, an editor, and so on.

Also, a pretaped package lacks some of the urgency, some of the energy and excitement that a spontaneous interview segment contains.

The interview format is one of the reasons for Fox's financial success. They churn out our product faster, for less money and with fewer staffers. It's simple economics.

When O'Reilly picked the topics for the show, he'd usually have a specific guest in mind. Sometimes he'd give it to one of our "regulars," guests who appear every week. (These include, in addition to the aforementioned Messrs. Rove, Morris, and Goldberg, figures like comedian Dennis Miller and Fox daytime anchor Megyn Kelly.) But sometimes he'd want a guest who was not one of the regulars but, rather, someone who would take a certain side on an issue, or an expert with certain biographical details.

Often these requests got hilariously specific: "We're doing a gay marriage segment—get me a black lesbian civil rights attorney!" or "I want to do a segment on the Super Bowl next week—find me a funny white sports expert under forty! But he can't be bald."

One of the most important things the segment producer did was the pre-interview, which was exactly what it sounds like—we'd interview the guest a few hours before Bill interviewed them. We tried to think of the same questions Bill would ask, and would take notes, condensing and bullet-pointing whatever the guest said. Eventually, we'd give this "POV" to Bill, along with research on the topic.

The end result was that, barring the occasional surprise, Bill knew exactly what his guest was going to say in the interview, sometimes down to the last word. In this way, cable news somewhat resembled professional wrestling: The outcomes were predetermined, with the host not only choosing his guests based specifically on the stance he knew they were going to take, but actually getting a preview of their arguments several hours in advance so he could formulate his counterarguments.

Noon

Bill would get into his chauffered town car for the drive from his Long Island home to Fox headquarters in Manhattan. During this drive, he'd call the line producer and dictate the script for that night's show.

Cursed with speedy typing skills, I would occasionally get roped into taking dictation on these calls. Listening to him write the entire show in his head on the fly, I realized that Bill O'Reilly is much smarter than any of his critics give him credit for. There's not a ton of writing in a typical episode of *The O'Reilly Factor*—once you get past the Talking Points Memo, it's only relatively short introductions ("Our next guest is a Fox News analyst coming to us from Washington, DC . . .") and teases before the commercial break ("Coming up, Karl Rove will weigh in on the GOP primary race . . .")—but the mere fact that Bill writes the whole thing himself, every word, separates him from almost every anchor in the building. And the fact that he does it all in his head, dictating it on the fly, is nothing short of astounding.

One funny point about this, though—Bill is, unsurprisingly, the ultimate backseat driver, so the dictation calls are constantly punctuated with his yelling at Carl, his poor beleaguered driver. Bill would dictate a couple lines, then scream a bit at Carl, berating him for getting caught in traffic. Then he'd tick off a few more lines, then bark at Carl again, telling him that if he didn't find a different route, Bill would be forced to take over driving duties.

1:30 P.M.

Bill would usually arrive about this time, traffic permitting, then head into his office and have lunch, which his long-suffering, saintly assistant, Margaret, would bring to him. He wasn't into fancy lunches—strictly a soup-and-sandwich-at-his-desk kind of guy. But he was still as demanding with his orders as he was with everything else in his life.

A sandwich shop got his order wrong one time, and Bill called Margaret into his office.

"Look," he said. "I'm not mad at you, Margaret. But they put the wrong cheese on this thing."

"Do you want me to get you a new one?" Margaret asked, sounding relieved that she wasn't going to catch the blame for once.

"No," Bill said. "I want you to take it back to them, tell them they screwed it up, and get the money back."

"Okay," she said.

"Are you actually going to say that? Because I definitely want you to say that to them. 'You screwed it up. Bill O'Reilly wants his money back.' Are you going to say that to them?"

"Yes, yes, I'll say that," Margaret insisted.

I don't know if she did end up doing it or not. She's one of the nicest, most soft-spoken people in the world, so it's hard for me to picture her throwing a sandwich back in the Quiznos guy's face. But on the other hand, she's worked for O'Reilly for more than two decades, so who the hell knows what she's capable of?

2:00 P.M.–4:00 P.M.

On Mondays and Thursdays, we had pitch meetings during this block of time. On Tuesdays, O'Reilly had his weekly powwow with the company VP, Bill Shine. And it seemed as if the other two days of the week there were always other things clawing for his attention. But every once in a while, he got this time to himself, and we'd find him lounging on the couch in his office, shoes off, his six-foot-four frame spilling over both sides, just reading the paper. It was kind of endearing, actually.

4:30 P.M.

Bill would get anxious around this time every day, like a kid on Christmas Eve—because it was ratings time! The number crunchers e-mailed out spreadsheets at the same time every afternoon, with data about the previous day's shows. We'd get ratings for not only all the Fox News shows but also all the shows on CNN, MSNBC, and Headline News, broken down into fifteen-minute increments and separated into total viewers as well as the coveted age twenty-five to fifty-four demographic.

As much as I'd thought my colleagues on *The Lineup* were obsessed with the ratings data, O'Reilly made them look like absolute amateurs. First, if the number crunchers were even one minute late with the data, Bill would get agitated, calling Manskoff every few minutes to impatiently ask him if the e-mail with the spreadsheets had come in yet.

When he finally did get the sheets, about fifteen pages in all, with tiny print and column after column of numbers, he'd pore over the digits as if they held the secret to finding the Holy Grail. If the number for *The Factor* was good, he'd crow about it for the rest of the day. If the number was bad, he'd panic, making phone calls until he determined what had gone wrong: "Eugene, we dropped thirty-three thousand in the demo last night in the final quarter. Remind me what we had in the back of the show last night?"

Eugene would tell him the name of the guest, or the topic, and Bill would decide that the show would no longer be covering that topic, or would cease inviting that guest.

Most of my fellow producers took the boss's cue and obsessed over the numbers as much as he did, but it always felt like chicanery to me. To make changes in programming, important decisions about what stories to cover and which guests to use, based on minute changes in a system as imprecise and imperfect as the Nielsen ratings seemed irresponsible, barely better than reading chicken entrails. But Bill had lived and died by those ratings for so long that he didn't know another way. (And to be fair, his method seemed to be working, because he's enjoyed more than a decade at number one. So maybe I'm the one who doesn't know what he's talking about.)

4:45 P.M.

Bill heads down to a private room in the basement to get his hair and makeup done. A device that Ailes had installed in every green room in the building methodically sucks the life force out of five adorable baby puppies and deposits it into Bill's face, keeping him fresh and youthful-looking for one more day.

5:00 P.M.

Showtime!

6:00 P.M.

Show's over. A quick wipe-down with a hot towel in the green room to get rid of the makeup and puppy tears.

6:05 P.M.

Back to the O'Reilly pod for the show's postmortem meeting, where we'd discuss what went right and wrong that night. These were short and uneventful normally, consisting of nothing more than Bill looking at the big bulletin board, sighing, and saying, "That was okay tonight. I think we might get away with that."

6:10 P.M.

O'Reilly gets into the town car to head home, warming up his vocal cords in case Carl the driver takes yet another wrong turn.

April 11, 2012—6:18 P.M.

They didn't have me dead to rights, but they were close enough.

In the end, what did me in wasn't my writing or an intercepted e-mail between me and my handlers at *Gawker*. It was the video clips.

In mid-2008, the network had finally transitioned from the antiquated physical videotape system it had been using. The tapes, which were recycled and reused over and over, were literally falling apart, disintegrating before our very eyes. The technology—which had been state-of-the-art when the network was founded in 1996—was so obsolete by 2008 that the manufacturer had stopped making both the tapes and the machines that played them.

CNN and MSNBC had transitioned to a digital, tapeless, cloud-based video system years earlier, but Fox was a holdout—most likely, the video editors all agreed, because of the cost. That was a ridiculous excuse for an organization as awash in money as Fox News, but very much in keeping with their stinginess on nearly everything else. The product making it to air was *just good enough* that everyone could live with it.

The eventual impetus for switching to tapeless was the 2007 launch of Fox Business Network, the ill-conceived competitor of CNBC that Rupert Murdoch tapped Roger Ailes to develop, hoping he could re-create the lightning-in-a-bottle success of Fox News.[55] Fox Business was built from the ground up with a new video system, which was adopted by Fox News a few months later. The system was plagued with problems, crashing on an almost weekly basis, and was so technologically backward that it led me to stupidly believe that my activities weren't being constantly monitored.

I'd been banking on the incompetence of our tech department. As it turns out, they were really only bad at their day jobs—keeping the video system up and running. When it came to sniffing out corporate espionage, they were, in fact, VERY, VERY GOOD AT IT.

"Do you have any idea," Diane the lawyer asked, "why someone using your account, your username, would have accessed the clips that ended up on *Gawker*?"

"No, I honestly have no idea how that could have happened," I lied.

The man from the IT department had just finished laying out his case for a full ten minutes. As I'd correctly predicted, the records—which were erased every seven days—didn't show that I'd downloaded any clips. As I *hadn't* predicted, they did show that I'd *looked* at them. A simple process of elimination search revealed that I was the only person in the company who'd looked at the source videos for both clips that had leaked. It wasn't proof, but it was close enough for me to be the only suspect.

"Joe, you have to trust me on this," Diane was saying. "Everyone in this room just wants what's best for you. We all hope that you can give us some sort of reasonable explanation as to why someone using your account would have viewed these clips. Stan here has been sick to his stomach all day, hoping that it isn't true, that you're not the guy."

I looked at Stan, who was nodding slowly, sadly, and I felt sick, too.

---

55   FBN was founded on the erroneous—and frankly ludicrous—premise that CNBC, the official channel of $5,000-suit-wearing plutocrats, was somehow not pro-business enough. The idea was to combine financial coverage with conservative politics and under-qualified but sexy twenty-five-year-old anchor babes. A friend who worked in finance told me that half the TVs on his company's trading floor were tuned to FBN on mute, specifically for the eye candy, but anytime they wanted actual information, they turned the volume up on CNBC.

CHAPTER 15

I Think He Said the Sheriff Is Near

It was an article of faith among conservatives, and among the on-air hosts at Fox, that in 2008, the liberal media fell for Obama, and they fell hard—hook, line, and sinker.

And to that I say: Bullshit.

Obama didn't even need all that fancy fishing equipment to land us. We just jumped right into his boat.

Okay, maybe I'm not being fair. I honestly can't speak for my colleagues at other news organizations. I can only speak for myself, a liberal member of the conservative media. A few weeks into the 2008 primary season, I found myself sitting at my desk at work, welling up with honest-to-God tears, watching the "Yes We Can" video on YouTube.

So, yeah, I wasn't a tough catch for Barack.

For those of you who don't remember, the video featured will.i.am—the absurdly named leader of the Black Eyed Peas, America's favorite source for wedding-and-bar-mitzvah-appropriate hip-hop—along with John Legend, Scarlett Johansson, and a bevy of C-List actors and musicians singing along with an Obama speech.

The video was cheesy and painfully earnest, with a complete lack of irony and several baffling celebrity cameos (Kareem Abdul-Jabbar? The little sister from *The Fresh Prince of Bel-Air*?). It was worshipful and propagandistic in a way that the most egomaniacal, messianic third-world dictator could only dream of. And, as evidenced by the tears in my eyes, it was completely effective.

I realized at that moment: *Hillary Clinton is fucked.*

I had been a big Hillary supporter up until that point, mostly owing to my admiration of her husband. There was something very appealing to me about Bill. He was a rascally horndog good ol' boy who was also a Rhodes Scholar with one of the most vibrant, brilliant political minds in American history; he could fulminate at length on the crisis in Darfur one day, then chase tail around like a drunk frat boy the next.

Beyond my love for Bill, I had to admit that Hillary was an unexpectedly kick-ass senator, serving my adopted home state very well. Combine that with the fact that both Clintons had the unique ability to drive conservatives absolutely out of their minds, and she'd had my vote from the minute she entered the presidential race.

But all of that had changed with those first few strummed guitar chords in will.i.am's song. By the time the song had finished playing, it was all over for me. I was an unapologetic Obamaite, through and through, and I would never look back.

I I I

Fox had been caught completely flat-footed by the Obama phenomenon.

When he announced his campaign in early 2007, the reaction from the network was a collective yawn. No one, myself included, thought he stood a chance against the Hillary juggernaut.

O'Reilly was one of those yawners. At the time, he was actually on a major antipolitics kick. He'd get annoyed at the meetings when we'd try to pitch him political stories.

"No one is going to care about this stuff until November or December at the earliest," he'd groused one day. "So I *don't want to hear it* until then."

On the rare occasions that we dipped a toe into the presidential race, it was to cover John Edwards, the oily, impressively coiffed former ambulance chaser that O'Reilly had a surprising amount of personal animosity toward. (He was horrified when Edwards decided to stay in the campaign following his wife's March 2007 cancer diagnosis, and later picked a fight with the candidate over the exact number of homeless veterans.)

It was true that the network was suffering from politics fatigue—or, more accurately, Bush fatigue. The hosts were tired of carrying water for a president whose popularity was in the dumpster. The producers were tired of covering an administration that had rudely refused to spawn any scandals that were remotely sexy (unless you count Dick Cheney unloading a shotgun into some poor senior citizen's face a "scandal"). Most distressingly, the viewers were getting tired, and ratings sagged.

We needed something else to talk about, and Hillary was widely viewed as a potential savior for the network. She was a longtime favorite target of the right, which attacked her with arguably more relish than they attacked her husband. Fox—which wasn't around until late 1996—had missed all the *really good* Hillary-bashing years of the early 1990s, and you could sense that some people in the building were licking their chops for another crack at her.

As 2007 wore on, it looked more and more like a Hillary cakewalk. Nobody thought the shiny-haired John Grisham character, or the skinny black guy whose last name rhymed with "Osama," were going to be serious impediments to her dominance.

Then Iowa happened.

The Iowa caucus on January 3, 2008, changed everything. With the Christmas and New Year's breaks as distractions, most people at the network had been ignoring the polls, the assumption being that Hillary was going to walk away with it. But Obama won, beating the second-place Edwards by almost eight points. Hillary was a few tenths of a point behind Edwards, for a humiliating third place.

"Why didn't we know about this?" Bill said on the conference call the next morning. "No one saw this guy coming."

"The Hillary campaign sure didn't," said Stan.

It was decided that Bill needed to procure an interview with the newly minted front-runner, by any means necessary. Eugene chimed in, pointing out that no one from the Obama campaign would return—or even acknowledge—his calls or e-mails.

Bill thought for a moment. "We'll just go to New Hampshire, then. We'll go to one of his rallies. It'll be me and a cameraman. He'll have to talk to me if I'm right there in front of him."

"That's the plan?" I said to Sam when the call ended. "What's he going to do? Just go stand behind a rope line and shout at Obama until he agrees to an interview?"

"I'm sure he's got a better idea than that," Sam said.

As it turns out, no—no, he didn't.

A few days later, Bill was behind the rope line at a weekend Obama rally in New Hampshire, cameraman in tow. He had positioned himself so that the candidate would be forced to walk past him on his way out of the arena. It wasn't quite a Watters-style ambush, but it was close—he'd either be leaving that venue with footage of Obama speaking to him or the senator running away. The former would be great; the latter would be almost as good.

One Obama campaign staffer, a man named Marvin Nicholson—notable for his extreme height, several inches taller than Bill, even—took it upon himself to make some mischief for the Fox News crew. As the rally ended and Obama made his way toward the area where the media was encamped, Nicholson casually ambled over to O'Reilly's position and planted himself in front of the camera, completely obscuring the shot.

"Hey, stop blocking the shot, pal!" Bill thundered at the aide, who pretended to not hear him. When the cameraman shifted, trying to shoot around the towering Democratic staffer, Nicholson simply shifted to block the shot again, this time spurring Bill to volcanic levels of rage.

"Get him out of there!" Bill yelled to a nearby security guard. "We have a right to be here to shoot the shot. Son of a bitch!" When the guard did nothing to intervene, O'Reilly shoved the campaign staffer out of the way, spurring the Secret Service to swarm the scene and calm things down.

"That's really low-class, pal," Bill said to the back of the retreating Nicholson. "And everybody in the world will see it."

A few minutes later, once the on-edge Secret Service detail determined that the enraged TV host was no threat, Senator Obama came over to shake O'Reilly's hand, promising to sit for an interview with him at some unspecified point in the future.

Bill, never one to let a good confrontation go to waste, played a long clip of his skirmish with Nicholson on Monday's show and soon started offering DON'T BLOCK THE SHOT bumper stickers on his website.

His relationship with Barack Obama was off to a sterling beginning.

Meanwhile, my relationship with my girlfriend had taken a nosedive, and it was all Obama's fault.

Krista and I had moved in together just a few months before, renting a tiny one-bedroom in the West Village, the choicest neighborhood in Manhattan. The rent was an eyeball-popping twenty-six hundred dollars a month, and the building was decrepit, with narrow, poorly lit hallways and a rickety, closet-size elevator that broke down the day we moved in, trapping us inside for a claustrophobia-inducing ninety minutes. But the location—with its high concentration of charming restaurants and coffee shops, high-end boutiques, and swarms of beautiful, glamorous, rich-looking people—was so spectacular that we decided we could handle the occasional cockroach infestation, and the uncomfortable fact that our bedroom window looked directly into someone's kitchen, three feet across an air shaft. *Who cares if the lobby smells like cat pee! You know who I saw just walking on the street today? Tom Brady and Gisele Bündchen!*[56]

We should have been at the height of domestic tranquility, and we were, at first. But after Iowa, Krista—a staunch feminist and an even stauncher Hillaryite—took it personally when I told her I had switched my allegiance to Obama.

"How is that even possible?" she asked, fuming, the night I informed her. "I thought you liked Hillary."

---

56 They are the most impossibly tall, thin, and good-looking couple I've ever seen in real life. Their continued existence is simply unfair to us normal, comparatively hideous people.

"I did," I said. "And I still do. I've just decided I like Obama better now."

"That's ridiculous," she said. "You know they have basically the same views on everything, right?"

"Of course I do. And I will vote for her in a heartbeat if she gets the nomination."

"*No way in hell* I'm voting for Obama if he takes this away from Hillary," she said. "And you're being a *total asshole* about it!" She stomped out of the living room, the cat we'd adopted together scampering out of her way in terror.

"Leaving the room when you're mad at me doesn't work if the bedroom is only ten feet away!" I called after her.

She slammed the door.

Her vehemence took me by surprise. I thought she would take my choice of candidate in stride, and that we'd maybe even develop a friendly rivalry over it, like when a married couple roots for two different football teams. But she was acting as if my simple personal preference was an abject betrayal of her feminist values. All I had done was express the fact that I liked Barack Obama as a candidate *slightly more* than I liked Hillary Clinton. But Krista was treating me as if I had suddenly declared I was opposed to women voting, or had decided that girls shouldn't be allowed to learn to read *lest they get any ideas.*

I assumed Krista would eventually come around. She was too reasonable a person to take something like that so personally. But as the Democratic primary dragged on into the spring, and things started to look more and more dire for the Clinton campaign, my sex life took an equally steep downward trajectory, as my increasingly pissed-off girlfriend began to give me the cold shoulder in the bedroom.

Krista became angrier and angrier, to the point where she was completely unable to even participate in a discussion about politics—either with me or with any of our friends—without it ending in a shouting match. And with 2008 shaping up to be the most fascinating and gripping election cycle that anyone born after 1980 had ever seen, politics was naturally the main topic of conversation at every social function we went to that spring.

Needless to say, I spent a lot of Friday and Saturday nights on the couch.

One incident in particular sticks out in my mind, a late-night argument that started at a house party, carried over to a bar, and finally came to a boil on a subway platform. Truthfully, we'd both had a decent amount to drink. While alcohol made me more docile and good-humored, it tended to have the opposite effect on Krista, especially in those months.

"What has Obama ever done?" Krista was screaming at me, her voice echoing throughout the mostly empty subway station. "What has he done, huh? What makes you think he'd be any good as president?"

"He's pretty good at running a campaign," I shot back. "You know how I know that? Because he's currently beating the shit out of Hillary."

Her wordless scream of rage startled a hobo from his slumber on a nearby bench.

<hr />

After the run-in at the New Hampshire rally, O'Reilly seemed uncharacteristically uncertain about how best to approach Obama. He was absolutely *dying* for an interview with the candidate, an interview that the Obama campaign was understandably reluctant to agree to. (Bill's reputation as an unpredictable interviewer who sometimes went nuclear on his guests often worked against him in that way.) But, ever hopeful that the campaign would relent, Bill mostly pulled his punches on the senator in January, February, and March, hoping that softer coverage would entice the reluctant Obama to give an interview.

In the *Factor* pod, some of the more openly conservative producers began to grumble that the Old Man was losing his fastball.

"Bill needs to go after this guy, to really expose him," Steiner Rudolf said one day. "Obama is a fraud, and a far-left thug." He started trying to single-handedly push Bill toward harder coverage, raising all sorts of specters and innuendo during pitch meetings.

But Bill resisted.

"I don't want to get into that ideological crap, Rudolf," Bill would say when Steiner tried to convince him for the umpteenth meeting in a row that an Internet rumor about Obama deserved further scrutiny on *The Factor*. "Let Hannity do that stuff. We deal with *facts* on this show."

So Bill continued going relatively easy on the Democratic front-runner—until a story cropped up that could not be ignored.

Reverend Jeremiah Wright had for months been a minor figure in the Obama-conspiracy-mongering industry. Hannity, in fact, had been railing about the pastor for a full year, first exploring the issue in February 2007, barely two weeks after Obama kicked off his presidential campaign.[57] But in the absence of compelling video clips, O'Reilly wasn't interested.

"I'm not going to go after some black reverend that nobody's ever heard of," he'd say.

As it turns out, lack of notoriety was not going to be a problem for Reverend Wright for much longer.

On March 13, Brian Ross of ABC News unveiled some video that had been hiding in plain sight. It turned out that DVDs of Wright's sermons had been sold by his church for years. Ross and his team simply viewed the tapes, digging out inflammatory tidbit after tidbit and crafting them into an explosive *Good Morning America* segment.

One clip showed Wright accusing the U.S. government of introducing drugs into the black community: "The government gives them the drugs, builds bigger prisons, passes a three-strike law, and then wants us to sing 'God Bless America.' No, no, no, God damn America!"

---

57 Hannity even convinced Wright to come on his show at one point, an interview that went mostly unnoticed by the mainstream press—probably owing to the fact that it was incredibly boring, consisting mostly of Hannity trying to get the reverend to admit he was a black separatist, and Wright stonewalling the fiery conservative host with jargon about "Liberation Theology" and references to obscure works by equally obscure authors. It was not good television.

Another clip from the sermon on the Sunday after 9/11 featured the reverend reminding his congregation about the thousands killed by the nuclear attacks on Hiroshima and Nagasaki, then going on to say, "We have supported state terrorism against the Palestinians and black South Africans, and now we are indignant because the stuff we have done overseas is now brought right back to our own front yards. America's chickens are coming home to roost."

A more recent clip showed Wright talking about the Democratic primary: "Barack knows what it means to be a black man living in a country and a culture that is controlled by rich white people. Hillary can never know that. Hillary ain't never been called a nigger."

The clips set off a round of panic in the Obama camp, expressions of glee from the Clinton and McCain camps, and a positively orgiastic feeding frenzy at Fox News headquarters. Even I, weepy Obama lover that I was, had to admit that the video was so explosive it would have been cable news malpractice to *not* use it. Still, I wasn't prepared for the extent that the footage was absolutely wallpapered across our air for the next few months.

The day it first broke, Bill played a long montage, a sort of mashup of Wright's greatest hits, at the top of the show. If he was on the fence about Obama up until that point, he certainly wasn't anymore.

The Wright tapes injected into the campaign an ugly racial edge that had previously been hovering just below the surface. Screening phone calls for the radio show, I was on the front lines.

"Why won't Bill ever say his middle name? It's Hussein, you know," a caller said.

"I know, sir," I said. "Bill knows, too."

"Then why won't he use it? People need to know how much this guy hates America, and if they hear his name is Hussein, they'll realize it."

Other callers were obsessed with the candidate's exact racial makeup. "How come I never hear anyone say that he's only *half* black?" another caller asked me.

"I don't see why that matters, sir," I said.

"It's just that the lady on the news always says he's black, but he's not. The blacks won't accept him because they hate white people, and he's half white."

"Okay, sir, thank you for your opinion, but I don't think I'll be putting you on air today."

Click.

As the election approached, we also started getting more and more callers asking us to investigate Obama's real birthplace. I did my best to personally strangle the Birther movement in its crib, explaining to each caller individually that the senator was born in Hawaii, and that there was *literally* zero proof that he was born anywhere else, and that they should stop believing everything they read in chain e-mails that had been forwarded to them by their racist uncles. But my words fell on deaf ears. As the persistence of that particular movement proves, stupid people—be they talk-radio-loving truckers or tacky, flaxen-haired billionaires—do not easily change their minds, even in the face of mountains of evidence to the contrary.

It was about this time that I started "coming out" to some of my co-workers.

There were other liberals at Fox. *Of course* there were other liberals. Even with all their weeding out, the self-selection, the interrogation during the Kool-Aid Conference, it was still New York City, and it was still the field of journalism. You do the math. You could round up every conserva-journo on the Eastern Seaboard and still barely be able to staff a weekend shift at Fox; it was inevitable that plenty of moderates, and more than a few liberals, squeaked by.

But the liberals at Fox were a minority, and a silent one at that, racked with distrust and paranoia. I was at the company for almost four years before I revealed to Sam, who I trusted implicitly by that point, through casual conversation where my feelings lay. Word slowly percolated to the rest of the O'Reilly staff. No one told Bill, that I'm aware of. I don't even think Bill would have cared, had he known. The only political opinions he ever cared about were his own. Those were the only views that made it to air, anyway.

What may have concerned Bill about having an open "left-wing loon" on the staff is that I might have tried to slip him some wrong information, or tried to embarrass him on air. I never did any of that stuff. Never, not once. I never gave him bad information. I never told him anything that wasn't true. I never did anything to sabotage the show. Not one thing. I took pride in doing my job well, and I was pretty good at it, too.

What I *did* do, the only way I was able to maintain my sanity throughout my long run, was to just give a *slight* spin to the information I gave him, little cues to attempt to nudge him in my direction. Like if there was a poll that looked good for John McCain that Bill wanted in his packet, I'd always make sure to include right next to it two polls that looked good for Obama—whether he asked for them or not.

Or if he asked for a story about Reverend Jeremiah Wright, I'd make sure to include with it a story about Reverend John Hagee, a McCain-supporting televangelist who had said controversial things about Hitler and the Holocaust.

That was the way to influence Bill. *Influence*, not manipulate. Bill cannot be manipulated. Despite some critics' insistence that he was an empty suit, he's actually quite smart, and always knew when someone was attempting to forcefully move him in one direction or another. It was all about subtlety.

The 2008 campaign was so much about Obama that it was shocking when McCain suddenly reasserted himself, unleashing a dim-bulb force of nature named Sarah Palin on an unsuspecting American public.

At first, it seemed like a brilliant move by the McCain campaign. They had completely rejiggered the race in one fell swoop. Not only did they thoroughly stomp on Obama's convention bounce, unveiling the pick a scant few hours after his Denver acceptance speech, but they also revved up the GOP base, which had previously been depressed and demoralized by the sad, slow decline of the Bush administration and the seemingly hapless and obviously losing McCain campaign.

I'll confess—like a lot of other liberals, though I was loathe to admit it at the time—I was initially scared shitless by the Palin pick. The wounds from the Obama vs. Clinton brawl were still pretty raw, and there was a real fear that Hillary's fans would bolt the party in favor of the Alaskan newcomer, who was, admittedly, unbelievably charismatic and politically savvy, if not quite in the same ballpark or even zip code of intelligence as Hillary.

Luckily, women voters were not as gullible as the McCain campaign thought they'd be—at least Krista wasn't.

"Who do they think they're kidding?" she raged to me the night Palin was announced. "It's insulting. Do they really believe that we'll just think one politician with a vagina is as good as any other?"

"Does this mean you'll vote for Obama now?" I asked.

The Obama campaign wasn't about to let the Palin pick go unanswered. They had a plan to wrench the spotlight back, and they enlisted my boss to help.

That's how O'Reilly ended up interviewing the Democratic nominee on the final day of the GOP convention, giving over a huge chunk of his TV show to Obama on a night when John McCain was supposed to be the focus of everyone's attention.

I was fielding calls on the radio show that day, and had to fend off dozens of angry listeners outraged that Bill would fall for such a transparent ploy to steal McCain's thunder. O'Reilly, to his credit, fielded a couple of critical calls to defend himself, pointing out that only half of that night's show would be given over to the Obama interview, while the rest would be dedicated to covering the RNC.

The callers howled that the defense was weak, but Bill didn't really care. He never admitted it on the radio, but he was fully aware that the Obama campaign was using him to crash the Republicans' big celebration, brilliantly invading the GOP's favored network on what was supposed to be their special night. The benefit for O'Reilly, in addition to the surefire ratings bonanza that his long-awaited clash with Obama would bring, was that every extra minute he spent on the interview was one less minute he would be forced to spend covering the increasingly dull McCain, who appeared even more boring than before when compared to his charismatic running mate.

Obama more than held his own in the interview that night, uncapping that now-familiar mix of charm, good humor, and policy wonkery, but O'Reilly still came away unimpressed. After months of chasing the elusive candidate, the thrill was gone, and he felt free to take off the gloves.

The next week in a pitch meeting, he got apocalyptic, announcing a new segment he'd conceived called the Obama Chronicles.

"It's going to be a twenty-five-part series," he said, explaining that it would examine the senator's background and associations. "And if it works like I think it will, by the end of it, I'll have *saved this country.*"

He had a far-off look in his eyes when he said that, and the assembled producers shifted uncomfortably on our feet and made fleeting eye contact with one another. *Was he being serious? A twenty-five-part series? Save the country? Why did our boss suddenly sound like a crazy person?*

No one said anything aloud, of course.

The Chronicles started the next week, with a look at Obama's birth and upbringing.[58] If anything, instead of exposing Obama as the crazed radical the right wing had caricatured him as, the segment made him appear sympathetic, highlighting all the hardships in his life that he'd overcome. If Bill's intention was to save the country from Obama, he was going about it the wrong way.

The series limped on for a few more installments afterward but never caught on with viewers, and Bill cut it short less than halfway to the promised twenty-five. Given a choice between ratings and "saving" the country, it was no contest.

On election night, as the returns came in, state by state, it was becoming obvious that Fox's attempts to make Obama a terrifying

---

58 Notably, Bill and the guest agreed that Obama was born in Hawaii, leading to a flood of angry calls and e-mails.

socialist bogeyman had failed. Krista and I were at a party in Brooklyn, the rancor of the past few months mostly forgotten.

Like any good gathering of New York liberals, we were watching the Jon Stewart/Stephen Colbert coverage. At the stroke of eleven P.M., when California's polls closed, Stewart announced Obama's projected victory. Krista and I hugged, tears in our eyes, as the party erupted around us.

I didn't catch the understated, almost funereal Fox coverage until the next day, when I watched the replay at my desk. When Brit Hume read the results, he seemed as if he was about to cry, too, but for a different reason.

I spoke to my dad a few days later. He was nominally a Republican, and had voted for McCain. He was a little annoyed that his guy lost but was interested in getting my reaction.

"How do you think Fox will take it?" he asked.

"I think they'll take it okay," I said. "You know, give him the benefit of the doubt."

"Are you sure?" My dad sounded skeptical. "I think it's going to be like *Blazing Saddles*, when the black sheriff arrives and all the townspeople panic."

"No, I think you're wrong," I said.

But, as it turned out, I was the one who was wrong.

I paced back and forth in the small conference room while the grown-ups in the office next door discussed my fate. I'd played dumb for almost a full half hour. Seeing that no confession was forthcoming, they'd banished me to the room by myself to let me stew in my own juices.

It had already been ten minutes. If their plan was to drive me insane with fear and uncertainty, it was working.

The conference room was a corner one. I'd never been in it before, but the view somehow looked familiar. It dawned on me that the vista of Times Square spreading out in front of me was identical to what could be seen from Bill's office, exactly two stories above the spot where I was standing.

Finally, I could take no more. I opened the door a crack, peeking outside into the hallway. It was empty, the two security guards nowhere in sight. Diane's office was to my right, the door closed. I could hear muffled voices coming from inside.

I spotted my iPhone sitting on a secretary's desk, white and shiny and tantalizing. It would be so easy to just snatch it and make a run for it.

I pushed open the door and stepped into the hall.

That's when the voice came from behind me.

"Mr. Muto, could you come back in here?" Diane the lawyer was standing in the doorway of her office. I hadn't gotten more than two steps toward my unguarded phone when her door popped open. I don't know if they'd heard me emerge from the conference room and rushed to intercept me, or if I just had lousy timing, but there was nothing to do but meekly shuffle into her office.

"We obviously can't prove you did this," she said. "But it doesn't look good for you, either."

"That, it does not," I agreed.

"So we're going to suspend you. With pay. Until we can sort out what exactly went on here."

And that was that.

CHAPTER 16

Rhymes with "Cat Bit Hazy"

Fox News responded to the inauguration of Barack Obama with a surprising, uncharacteristic amount of restraint.

That is to say, they waited until he was in office for at least thirty-six hours before calling him a socialist.

Very sporting of the network, actually, to give him that much of a head start.

The various conservative pundits and hosts of Fox probably should have taken the 2008 election loss as a chance to reflect, to learn from the mistakes of the Bush era, graciously giving the new president a bit of breathing room to begin to fix the economic and geopolitical wreckage that Dubya left behind, littering the American landscape like so many empty kegs and trampled Solo cups cluttering the floor after a frat party.

Instead, they did the exact opposite, as the entire network lost its fucking mind.

The hackery was led, as usual, by Sean Hannity. The host was newly unfettered following Fox's first prime-time lineup change in almost a decade: Alan Colmes, the liberal half of *Hannity & Colmes*, had left the show shortly after the election. His replacement: No one. The show was renamed simply *Hannity*.

Colmes and the company brass put a sunny face on it, pointing out that he would stay with the channel as a commentator and that he wanted to "develop new and challenging ways to contribute to the growth of the network." But there was something undeniably fishy about the channel's most prominent liberal receiving what was effectively a demotion when the country was on the cusp of a Democratic presidential administration. Conspiracy theories spread through the office. One popular rumor was that Colmes was forced out by a Second Floor that wanted to consciously move the network to the right in reaction to the new administration. A later theory—one that I suspect is the accurate one—held that Colmes was simply tired of playing second fiddle on his own show, taking abuse from Hannity, the viewers, and even some fellow liberals who were mad at him for continuing to appear on the network.

Aside from the *Hannity & Colmes* intrigue, the network's schedule had remained remarkably stable over the years. *Fox & Friends* had changed one out of three cohosts, swapping frisky housewife E. D. Hill for the even friskier former Miss America Gretchen Carlson. *DaySide*, the show with the live audience, tried retooling itself with new hosts but never managed to catch on. The program was scrapped in favor of a two-hour block starring up-and-comer Megyn Kelly. Megyn had risen through the ranks to become the Platonic Ideal of a Fox anchoress: the blondest, prettiest, most contentious host we'd ever produced.

Beyond that, all the other big network stars were still in place: Shep, Greta, and O'Reilly. They each had their own reaction to the new president and the challenges he faced, but no one embarrassed themselves quite as much as Hannity in those first few months: With a nation in crisis, he bravely chose to speak truth to power . . . by attacking President Obama's choice of condiments.

In May 2009, Obama had just barely finished his first one hundred days in office. He went to a DC-area burger place with the press corps in tow. The outing elicited the sort of embarrassing-in-retrospect media fawning that was typical of the early Obama presidency; but it wasn't anything out of the ordinary for a president still in his honeymoon phase.

Cameras rolled, capturing every word, as Obama placed his order at the counter. Most casual observers would say that his order was innocuous, but Hannity, unlike the *obviously-in-the-tank liberal reporters,* saw something insidious in Obama's choice of burger toppings. He saw something elitist. Something *French.*

The president, when ordering, had asked for "spicy brown mustard, something like that, or a Dijon mustard."

Quelle horreur!

"I hope you enjoyed that *fancy* burger, Mr. President," Hannity sneered after playing a clip of an old Grey Poupon commercial from the 1980s.

Even if we set aside the fact that Grey Poupon—manufactured by Kraft Foods right here in the good old USA, and costing a whopping three dollars and change per jar—is hardly an elitist food item, this was still a dumb attack, and foreshadowed the sorts of attacks that Fox and the entire right leveled at the president from the minute he set foot in the Oval Office. MustardGate was typical of the laziest, most offensive form of partisan journalism that reared its head in those early months, and persists to this day: If Obama does it, it must be bad.

Another example—the presidential teleprompter. It's no secret that Obama gives a good speech. When he was on the campaign trail in 2008, he almost always gave his stump speech off the cuff—no notes, no prompter. When he became president, he started using teleprompters more. Naturally, this is because, as president, your words have much more weight than they did before, and the stakes are a lot higher than when you were just a candidate. It makes perfect sense for an American president to use a teleprompter, especially when there's the distinct possibility that a single botched sentence has the potential to trigger World War III.

Obama doesn't use the prompter any more often than any of his predecessors, yet early in his tenure, the right wing became obsessed with it. The precious, sainted Ronald Reagan used a teleprompter *constantly*; George W. Bush needed difficult words spelled out *phonetically* in his prompter. But the chorus from conservatives was still *har har har Obama has to write down his words before he says them and read them off a screen like some idiot.*

O'Reilly, to his vast credit, did not chase after most of these picayune stories along with the rest of the network. He had ended his radio show in March 2009, shortly after Obama's inauguration. It was a rare case of bad timing for O'Reilly, who usually had a better sense for these things. He really missed out on the wave of conservative paranoia and rage that swept the nation in the spring of 2009.

Eric, who always was smarter than I was, took the occasion of the radio show's demise to leave Fox, working briefly for the Democratic National Committee, of all places, and eventually the Obama 2012 campaign. Richie the engineer was simply assigned to another radio show. Meanwhile, Sam and I briefly panicked at the prospect of having to find new jobs, but Stan reassured us that we'd be absorbed into the TV staff.

Thus in March 2009, I found myself back fully in the fold at the TV network I'd spent the last two years pretending I was only tangentially associated with.

And I was just in time for an exciting new era in Fox News's political activism, as the channel climbed fully on board with the nascent Tea Party movement. Fox hadn't created the Tea Party (that honor belonged to the conservative CNBC personality Rick Santelli, whose on-air rant from the floor of the Chicago Board of Trade went viral), but it embraced the movement to a degree that surprised even me. Some shows began promoting Tea Party gatherings, and the Second Floor made the decision to fan talent across the country on April 15, promoting it networkwide as FNC Tax Day Tea Parties. It represented a turning point for Fox, a complete raising of the veil—the network that had always at least attempted to maintain the pretense of being "Fair and Balanced" was suddenly openly advocating in favor of a protest movement against the Obama administration.

It was distressing to me that the whole network seemed to be moving rapidly to the right. The whole network, that is, except my boss. Something different was going on with O'Reilly. Something very curious indeed.

———————

Usually when Bill asked a question at a pitch meeting, we'd all scramble to jump in and answer him, jockeying for position to prove ourselves more indispensable than our colleagues. Brown-nosing the boss was practically a contact sport at *The Factor*.

But not that day. That day we all stared awkwardly at our shoes.

"So what exactly is this 'teabagging'?" he'd just asked. "Why is it such a bad thing?"

He was reacting to a video someone had just pitched, of CNN's Anderson Cooper giggling over the phrase. It wasn't Anderson's most mature on-air moment; but in his defense, it was the Tea Partiers who had started calling themselves "teabaggers," apparently not aware during the earliest days of their movement that *teabag* was a euphemism for a sex act involving a man dunking his testicles into another person's mouth.

On the Internet, liberals (who *naturally* were more savvy about any and all sexual euphemisms) gleefully noticed that naive Tea Partiers were inadvertently outing themselves as ball dippers, and roundly mocked them. And now the mockery had jumped from the Internet to CNN. O'Reilly—ever vigilant for liberal media slights against the honest, hardworking Americans who only wanted smaller government and whiter presidents—was on the case.

But first he had to figure out what *teabagging* actually was.

"Well, what the hell does it mean?" Bill demanded when no answer was immediately forthcoming.

Emmy, our line producer, finally broke. "Oh, God, I can't," she said, laughing. "I can't do it." She buried her face in the sleeve of her fleece jacket, trying to smother her laughter. "I'm sorry," she said.

"It's a sex thing," Stan said quickly.

Bill's eyebrows shot up. Now he was *really* curious.

"You don't want to know," Gayle, our fact-checking executive producer added.

"It's pretty vile," Eugene said. "I don't think we should get into it here. I can tell you privately after the meeting if you want."

Oh, to be a fly on that wall.

O'Reilly had decided to not go on location to attend a Tea Party rally on tax day. He wasn't interested in becoming part of the story himself. In doing so, he showed a restraint that many of his fellow hosts lacked. Neil Cavuto, the Hooters-enthusiast financial anchor, had jetted to Sacramento, probably hoping to make a side trip to snag some beach bikini footage for his show. Sean Hannity went to Atlanta. Greta Van Susteren attended the rally in her native Washington, DC—an odd right turn for the former suspected Democrat.[59]

One more anchor represented Fox on a field trip during that first Tax Day Tea Party in 2009. Deep into the heart of Texas, down to San Antonio, Fox had sent their newest secret weapon.

Glenn Beck premiered his Fox News show on January 19, 2009, the day before President Obama was inaugurated.

Nobody in the building really knew what to expect. His previous show had been on CNN Headline News—the low-rated, cable news equivalent of the witness protection program—so we were mostly unfamiliar with his shtick. But nothing could have prepared us for what came next.

Beck exploded out of the gate. His mix of goofy prop-comedy, apocalyptic predictions of doom, and thinly sourced conspiracy theories apparently spoke to our audience. Something about the ascension of Obama made our viewers especially receptive to Beck's toxic brew, and

59 Word was that Greta and her Clinton-friendly husband did not take Hillary's loss in the Democratic primary well, and had vowed to never support Obama. In the meantime, they'd both befriended Sarah Palin.

ratings soared, reaching numbers unprecedented for the usually lack-luster five P.M. hour.

The other on-air personalities at first had no idea what to make of Beck. He was a new creature to them, someone undeniably talented but also obviously a little bit unstable, and potentially dangerous. At the very least, his high ratings threatened to usurp the power structure that had been cemented over the years: Bill was number one, with Sean just behind him, and Greta in third. That was the ratings hierarchy for as long as anyone could remember, and it was remarkably consistent no matter what topic was in the news, or which guests were on which show.

But Beck blew that all away. When the numbers came out every afternoon at four thirty, he was handily beating Greta, often topping Hannity, and even some days coming close to O'Reilly. Whispers started in the hallways that a big change was coming in prime time.

"Roger sees these numbers," a producer for Greta's show said to me one day in early 2009, at the beginning of the Beck phenomenon. "He can't ignore them. And Beck is pulling these at five in the fucking afternoon. They've got to be thinking about what kind of damage he could do in prime time, at ten P.M., or nine . . ."

"Or eight," I said, finishing his thought for him.

These musings were not lost on the talent. A few weeks into Beck's tenure, O'Reilly decided his best course of action, the best way to protect his flank, would be to co-opt the potential usurper, giving him a weekly segment on *The Factor*.

"Get with Beck's people," O'Reilly said at the pitch meeting. "Tell them I want a segment, every Friday. We'll call it"—he leaned back in his chair, thinking—"the At Your Beck and Call segment." He chuckled quietly to himself, pleased with his pun.

The other on-air talent were not as welcoming. Once O'Reilly had claimed Beck as his own, the newcomer was basically shut out by the other two prime-time shows. And I didn't blame them. Sean and Greta wanted no part in promoting the man who could potentially take their jobs.

I personally didn't quite know what to make of Beck at first. He must be a bullshit artist, right? No way someone who seems as smart and business savvy as he does could believe all the nonsense he was peddling on a daily basis. But one incident in particular made me wonder.

In the summer of 2009, Beck had been given an office near my desk on the seventeenth floor. It wasn't anything special, but it was in a power location, a couple of doors down from O'Reilly's corner office. Two or three Beck staffers had stopped by to decorate it, festooning the door with art his fans had sent in—a charcoal sketch of a smiling Beck holding the Constitution, a child's Magic Marker drawing of a stick-figure Glenn waving an American flag, a watercolor of Beck with a bald eagle perched on his shoulder.

I was wary of my new neighbor, not wanting my relatively quiet corner of the building disturbed by the Beck circus, but it became obvious after a few days that the office was just some sort of contractually obligated bauble and that Beck had no intention of using it on a regular basis. Word was he preferred instead to work out of his (much more lavish, I was told) radio offices, which were located a few blocks down Sixth Avenue.

But Beck did, on occasion, hold staff meetings in his Fox office, and that's when the crazy really came out.

The meeting I overheard was shortly after President Obama had come under fire for criticizing the Cambridge, Massachusetts, police officer who had arrested Harvard professor Skip Gates in his own home. Beck had gathered about a half dozen staffers in his office, and the door was open a crack. But he was talking so loudly, even shouting at some points, that I probably would have been able to hear him perfectly, even if he had bothered to keep the door shut.

"Obama did it on purpose," Beck was saying. "He knew going after that cop would cause a controversy. He *wanted* the controversy. He's trying to distract us from something. But what? What is he tying to distract us from? That's the question."

For the next hour and a half, he lectured his staff, exhibiting impressive stamina even for someone who spent several hours a day talking on radio and TV. His employees seemed as if they were used to such tirades, and endured it with minimal interruption. Eventually, Beck settled on an obscure provision in the pending health care bill as the *real* thing the administration was trying to distract the American public from with the "fake" cop gaffe and the ensuing Beer Summit. He seemed to think the provision would somehow allow the federal government to take children away from their parents if the parents let the kids get fat.

I was amazed by the whole incident. Up to that point, I had assumed he was putting on a show, stirring up the crazies for ratings. I never imagined that he truly believed his own insane conspiracy theories. But the rant I heard in his office was repeated on the air a few hours later. And, if anything, it was toned down from what he had said in private.

Oddly enough, it was an on-air incident stemming from the Gates scandal that helped derail Beck's prospects at the network.

Shortly after the meeting I'd overheard, he went on *Fox & Friends* for a guest spot. And with one disastrous statement, all the chatter and speculation that he would soon be taking over one of the prime-time hours ground to a screeching halt: He declared that Obama had a "deep-seated hatred of white people."

Given a chance by the shocked and incredulous *Fox & Friends* hosts to retract, he instead doubled down: "This guy is, I believe, a racist."

The incident set off a months-long, surprisingly successful boycott effort by liberal groups. It meant that Fox was unable to capitalize on Beck's sky-high ratings, because the number of sponsors who would pay to be associated with him eventually dwindled to almost nothing. His commercial breaks turned into sad parades of hucksters touting investments in gold doubloons, reverse-mortgage hawkers looking to prey on senior citizens, and denture-cream manufacturers.

Also hurting Beck was discomfort from his colleagues. Howard Kurtz wrote a piece in March 2010, quoting anonymous staffers within the Fox News DC bureau claiming that they thought Beck's shenanigans were hurting the credibility of the entire network.

I can report that there were similar sentiments in the New York bureau. I, for one, had come to the conclusion that Beck was ultimately bad for the network, high ratings or no. Most of the producers I spoke to—even the ones who liked him and shared most of his opinions—agreed that his on-air performances had become increasingly unhinged. One anchor on my floor repeatedly, loudly and openly, referred to Beck only as Crazy—as in "What's Crazy up to today?" or "Why does Crazy have a birthday cake on the set with him?" or "Did you see Crazy playing around with a dead fish yesterday? What the fuck?"

O'Reilly, for his part, was sticking with the man he'd nicknamed the Beckmeister, though even Bill sometimes seemed uncomfortable with the strange positions Beck was taking.

In the beginning, the formula for Beck's weekly *Factor* segment involved the two hosts chatting about whatever Beck had been covering on his show that week. But as time went on, and Beck went further and further off into the weeds, we'd have to brainstorm during pitch meetings to come up with more innocuous topics, topics that wouldn't set him off on a rant that would have to be edited out later.

We still ended up cutting quite a bit. The pieces, which aired on Fridays, were taped a day in advance. Bill intentionally let them run long so they could be edited for time and content. Anything that made Beck sound too unhinged hit the cutting-room floor. Some days, it was hard to get the bare-minimum four minutes of non-crazy out of him. He was one of the only guests we ever did this with.

During that time, Bill would often clash with the Second Floor over the Beck segments. Bill, ever mindful of the ratings Beck could bring, would spur him on to do increasingly wacky things when he appeared on *The Factor*.

"I saw Beck with a dollhouse on air yesterday," Bill would say. "Tell him to bring it on our show and we'll talk to him about it."

The executives accused O'Reilly of attempting to make Beck look like a clown—they thought Bill was trying to further poison the well and eliminate any last chance that Beck would take over his time slot. (O'Reilly denied it, of course, but I always wondered if maybe there wasn't something to the theory.) O'Reilly counterargued that rather than make Beck appear clownish, he was trying to pull his head out of the clouds, stop him from being so esoteric, and get him to talk about issues that viewers cared about, even if those issues were silly.

In the end, though, even Bill O'Reilly couldn't protect Glenn Beck from himself.

During the Arab Spring in early 2011, Beck completely went off the rails, warning that the protests in Egypt were a secret plot by the Muslim Brotherhood, a group that he claimed, with little to no evidence, was a shadowy cabal of jihadists that had financial backing from several liberal groups in the United States.

He sounded like a complete kook. Even more so than before.

Beck ignored repeated pleas from management—including, rumor had it, personal appeals from Roger Ailes himself—to tone it down. And a few weeks later, that was that. His time at Fox was done, just a little over two years after it had started.

Beck wasn't the only newcomer to shake things up at Fox following Obama's election. A certain former Alaska governor came aboard in January 2010 as a political analyst and the host of a potential series of specials, signing a three-year, multimillion-dollar deal.

From the moment Sarah Palin abandoned her elected duties in the summer of 2009 for dubious reasons, it was an absolute inevitability that she'd end up at Fox News. She was a perfect fit for the network— beautiful, feisty, and controversial, inspiring utter devotion from her fans, and blind outrage in her critics, and, hopefully, the theory went, high ratings for the network. The Second Floor was well aware of her unfortunate reputation for being vacuous, ill-informed, and thin-skinned, but *surely that was just liberal media slander—the woman had run an enormous state, for chrissakes! How dumb could she be?* Also, her employment marked a continuation of a proud Roger Ailes tradition of hiring disgraced and discredited GOP pols and operatives like Rick Santorum, Newt Gingrich, Ollie North, and Karl Rove.

In the few months since the radio show had ended and I'd been put on TV full-time, I'd actually produced a few Rove segments. It was surreal to get on the phone with him for the pre-interviews. I didn't quite know what to expect from the man who'd earned the dual nicknames the Architect and Turdblossom from his old boss; the man who'd engineered a cynical, divisive 2004 campaign; the man who had cleverly pulled the rip cord and bailed on the floundering Bush administration midway through the second term; the man whom I'd vilified in one of my college newspaper columns; the man I was hoping would not, on a whim, Google my name and his name together. I didn't know what to expect, but what I got was an affable politics nerd who would talk for an hour during the pre-interview if you let him get going, and a tech geek who was obsessed with his iPhone and all things Apple.

Rove was actually enjoyable to talk to—smart, with generally good analysis, and somewhat less tendency than most political operatives to revert to disingenuous, intellectually dishonest arguments and talking points.[60] His biggest failing was that he was completely defensive about the deficiencies of the Bush administration, refusing to admit they had done even a single thing wrong. But maybe his biggest victory was that he refused to buy into the Palin hype, casting gallons of cold water on any talk of her becoming a viable presidential candidate—vehemently in private, and more gently and diplomatically on the air. If he had any thoughts about Palin becoming a Fox News analyst, at a reported salary that was higher than his own, he kept them to himself.

When the Palin news was announced, the atmosphere at the office

---

60 This didn't seem to hold true in the 2012 cycle, as I noticed from my new perch as an outsider that Rove was often going on air and arguing things that someone as smart as he couldn't possibly believe. This may have been because he was running a large Super PAC that had convinced hundreds of mega-rich conservatives to shell out millions of dollars with the express purpose of defeating Barack Obama—he became less an analyst and more a cheerleader. The low point of this behavior came on election night, when Rove pitched an on-air tantrum of denial after the network called Ohio—and hence the victory—for President Obama.

was instantly electric, with some of the more conservative producers positively gleeful about the prospect of her as a new colleague. There was an underlying tension, too, especially among the hosts and senior producers, as everyone kicked around the same question: "Who gets her first?"

Bill lobbied the Second Floor hard—as hard as I've ever seen him push the executives for anything—to secure for himself the first interview with her. Palin's choice likely would have been to go on the show of her new friend and confidante, Greta Van Susteren, but Bill twisted every arm in the building, sweet-talking, cajoling, threatening—and ultimately making the obvious argument that a Palin appearance on *The Factor*, the highest-rated show, would make the biggest impact. Bill's argument won the day, and it was announced that Palin would appear first on *The Factor*.

On the morning of the taping, she made a pilgrimage to the seventeenth floor to pay homage to O'Reilly. A wave of excitement followed her as she promenaded down the hallway, with well-wishers shouting greetings to her. She winked and waved and finger-gunned her way through the crowd, beaming widely, the conquering hero basking in an adoring glow. She wouldn't have looked out of place holding a bouquet and wearing a sash, like a homecoming queen making her way to the fifty-yard line at halftime.

I had to admit, as much as I despised her politics and the unbelievably stupid things that came out of her mouth, she was astoundingly charismatic in person, working a crowd as well as I'd ever seen it done. And she was even more good-looking than she appeared on television; cameras truly did not do her justice.

"Hey, governor!" I called out as she passed my desk.

"Hiya!" she called back, waving to Sam and me before walking into Bill's office, her hangdog husband, Todd, skulking after her, seemingly oblivious to the furor.

I was assigned to help produce her segment that night, to put together a video montage of pundits on CNN and MSNBC disparaging her.

I was more than happy to help in this regard.

Bill's *intention* was to play the clip for her to illustrate how the "left-wing media" was having a "conniption" over her hiring. I managed to cram several clips of people like Chris Matthews and Paul Begala calling Palin dumb and a liar into a neat twenty-second package. Judging from Palin's annoyed look when the camera cut to her after the video finished playing, I did my job well.

Despite the fanfare surrounding her launch, it quickly became clear to everyone that Palin just was not working out. The one special she hosted, featuring old interviews with celebrities that had been edited and repurposed, drew criticism for her stiff performance, and garnered only modest ratings, not the blockbuster numbers the Second Floor had been hoping for. And her abilities as a pundit left much to be desired. She conversed entirely in shallow, empty platitudes, as if she'd just memorized a list of talking points instead of actually boning up on whatever issue was on her plate. She also, most infuriatingly for Bill, tended to play hard to get, turning down requests for appearances for little or no reason, and refusing to communicate with our staff directly, insisting that a high-up executive act as her intermediary.

A few months into her tenure, O'Reilly exploded with frustration when he was told for the third time in a row that Palin wouldn't be available.

"I don't know why this woman refuses to help us out," he vented. "And when she does come on, she doesn't say *anything*. It's just the same BS talking points every time."

After a year of dealing with her, even the conservative true believers on the staff who had previously been enamored of Palin had to admit she was every bit as uninformed as her liberal critics had charged. She never did the legwork required to be a pundit. Even the absolute laziest commentator we had would at the very least visit the Wikipedia page on the topic at hand, boning up on the details so they wouldn't get caught flat-footed on air. But Palin seemed as if she couldn't even be bothered to do that. And the fact that she made herself unavailable for pre-interviews meant that we producers could never brief her on the segment, making it that much more likely she'd get hit with an unpleasant surprise or unexpected question on live television.

The tension between O'Reilly and Palin eventually came to a head. It was a segment on Social Security. Palin was typically underprepared, reduced to reciting empty boilerplate and talking points. Bill interrupted her, pressing for more details on what she'd do to reform the entitlement. Palin snapped at him, chiding him for the interruption.

That was the final straw for Bill. He started criticizing Palin on-air—subtly, but consistently—openly complaining about her to other guests, constantly referring to her as an example of someone who dodged questions, and speculating that her favorability in polls was dropping because of her evasiveness.

Then, in mid-2011, video surfaced of Palin—who at the time was flirting with a presidential run by embarking on a bus tour—giving a nonsensical and garbled description of Paul Revere's Midnight Ride:

> "He who warned, uh, the British that they weren't going to be taking away our arms uh by ringing those bells and making sure as he's riding his horse through town to send those warning shots and bells that we were going to be secure and we were going to be free and we were going to be armed."

I pitched the video to Bill at a meeting, and he loved it, playing it on the air that night with a bemused smile. He eventually went on to defend Palin—saying she'd come close enough to historical fact and should be cut a little slack—but the mere fact that he'd played the video amounted to an escalation in the cold war between the two conservative titans, and it did not go unnoticed by management.

Gayle pulled me aside the next day.

"Joe, could you please not pitch any Palin videos like that to Bill anymore?"

"But Bill loved it," I protested. "He accepted it right away."

"That's the problem," she said. "The Second Floor called after the show, and they were pissed that he used it."

"Why don't *they* just tell Bill not to use the video? Why is it up to me to keep it from him?"

"You know Bill," she said, shrugging. "He's going to do what he wants to do."

April 11, 2012—6:52 P.M.

The two security guards stood sentry as I dug through the drawers of the desk that had been my home base for almost five years, gathering up anything I couldn't live without. The seventeenth floor was blessedly empty, with no one around to witness the humiliating end to my career.

And it *was* the end of my career at Fox. I had no illusion that the paid suspension was anything but a precursor to my eventual firing. They didn't have enough evidence to fire me on the spot, but I knew they'd scrape it together eventually.

It dawned on me with a jolt of irony that I had nowhere to stash the things I was gathering—Rufus still had the duffel bag with my iPad. It had been an unnecessary precaution to ditch it with him, as it turned out. They didn't need to see the *Gawker* post I'd written and saved on my shiny Apple device. My fate had been sealed months earlier, when I'd simply viewed the clips, laying down a digital trail of bread crumbs that they easily followed to my doorstep.

One of the security guards cleared his throat behind me.

"Is this going to take much longer?" he asked.

I looked at the small collection of junk I'd amassed over the years. A wooden statue depicting the Notre Dame football stadium. A George W. Bush bobblehead. An unintentionally racist Barack Obama Chia Pet that I'd never had a chance to plant. A pile of books from authors desperate to get on the show. Obsolete videotapes with compilations of Natalee Holloway spinning a flag, and the Duke lacrosse team practicing.

I didn't need any of it anymore.

"Let's go," I said. "I think I'm done here."

CHAPTER 17

Take Me Out to the Buffet

Papa Bear swaggered into the Yankee Stadium luxury box like John Wayne walking into a saloon. He swept the room with his eyes, and locked them on me.

"Muto, you look like a cab driver," he announced loudly, grinning. Everyone laughed, including me, more from surprise than anything else. It seemed like a total non sequitur. I don't know what exactly it was about my casual game-day wear—T-shirt and a ball cap—that reminded him specifically of a cab driver, but I was pretty sure it wasn't meant to be complimentary.

Jesse Watters came over and clapped a hand on my shoulder. "Muto, as long as you're a cabbie now, I'm going to need a ride back to Long Island after the game. Don't drink too much."

I shook my head and took a swig of my Coors Light. "Free beer, dude. For nine innings. The grounds crew is going to have to wheel me out of here in a cart."

It was the summer of 2011, at the *Factor* staff's annual baseball outing, and most of us were already a beer and a half in before O'Reilly even showed up. We had waited until the day's show taping was done, then shed our work clothes for Yankees T-shirts and caps,[61] and piled onto the D train for the trip to the Bronx.

---

61 I'm strictly a Reds fan, but I give myself permission to root for my adopted hometown's American League team on a situational basis. Fuck the Mets, though.

Bill lagged behind us because he insisted on taking his town car to the game, preferring to let his driver, Carl, battle the rush-hour traffic rather than braving the crowds on the subway.

"He likes to drive because he can yell at Carl for going too slow," one of my fellow producers had speculated as our train headed uptown. "He'd feel too helpless on the subway. What's he going to do if the train goes too slow? Scream at the conductor?"

"I wouldn't put it past him," I said. "Either way, we're going to beat him there."

Though after twenty-five minutes in the jammed subway car, the air thick with the summer-humidity-induced body odor of two hundred stadium-bound commuters, I decided O'Reilly probably had the right idea, traffic or no.

But we weren't going to let a crowded subway car dampen our enthusiasm. Working for Fox News afforded us so few perks that we'd be insane to not take full advantage of them whenever given the opportunity. And the luxury boxes at the new Yankee Stadium were ripe for advantage taking. Our box actually belonged to the YES Network, the Yankees-owned cable channel, but through some series of associations I didn't quite understand, it was available for O'Reilly's use for one game a year. We reached the box by flashing our tickets (shiny and embossed with gold foil, with an impressive face value of $230) at a private entrance. We were ushered into an elevator and taken up to a hallway that looked as if it had been somehow airlifted out of a high-end Midwestern convention center and dropped into the stadium. Corporate-looking middle-aged white guys in khakis roamed the corridor, polo shirts tight across their paunches as they checked their tickets, searching for the right room number. Judging from the volume of their voices, a lot of them were well on their way to becoming heroically drunk. No mean feat, considering that the National Anthem had yet to be sung.

The luxury box was almost double the size of my tiny West Village apartment, with its own bathroom, a lounge area with plush leather chairs and flat-screen TVs, an outdoor terrace with a dozen seats overlooking home plate, and—most important—a large kitchen with marble countertops and a fully stocked fridge overflowing with ice-cold beers. I pounced on the booze right away. If my years as a journalist had taught me anything, it's that you take the free drinks while the getting is good.[62]

Everyone on the O'Reilly staff was a very accomplished drinker, with one surprising exception: Bill himself. The man is a complete teetotaler. Which makes sense when you think about it. He's angry and volatile enough when he's stone-sober. Why would you want to add alcohol to that equation? I can't imagine the results, but I'm sure it would involve the NYPD using old-timey biplanes to shoot him off the side of the Empire State Building.

Bill's real weakness was free food, which excited him to no end. While the rest of the staff perked up at the prospect of an open bar, nothing floated Bill's boat more than a hot buffet. True to form, no more than thirty seconds after entering the room and making the snap decision that I somehow looked like I should be sitting behind the wheel of a taxi, he'd beelined to the spread of hot dogs and chicken wings and was happily filling a plate.

I had to admire his gusto. The man made upward of fifteen million dollars a year. He could afford to spend thousands of dollars per meal and eat like a king every day of his life. But put him in front of a spread of gratis junk food and he acted like he'd just won the lottery. It was actually a little bit endearing, and gave credence to his repeated insistence that he was basically a down-to-earth guy, a man of the people, one of the folks.

On another occasion, I joined a few other staffers to accompany Bill to a charity St. Patrick's Day cocktail party thrown by the Kelly Gang, a group of media figures who share the eponymous surname. The event was at Michael's, a ritzy midtown restaurant known for being a clubhouse for media types who (A) like to power-lunch and (B) are steely

---

62 Fair warning to my esteemed publisher—when this book comes out, I'm probably going to bring an empty cooler to the release party so I can take home any unopened bottles.

and steadfast enough to avoid succumbing to crippling paroxysms of one-percenter shame when confronted with the ludicrously priced food.

The *New York Post* gossip pages are perennially full of rage-inducing anecdotes about barons of media—often fresh from laying off journalists—lunch-schmoozing at Michael's over Cobb salads, which are, as of this writing, thirty-six dollars apiece. Those not blessed with high incomes or laxly monitored expense accounts have to make do with Michael's breakfast, with its reasonable-by-comparison twenty-three-dollar eggs Benedict.

As someone who was still pretty close to the bottom of the media food chain, I was eager to see what it was like for those at the top. But O'Reilly had no interest in glad-handing. I was hoping I'd see him work the room a little, interacting with the editor of *The New Yorker* or the producer of the *Today* show, but instead he sequestered himself at a table in the corner and listened impatiently while NYPD commissioner Ray Kelly gave a welcome speech. When Kelly finished, to plenty of sincere applause, O'Reilly sprung from his seat and practically knocked the lawman over in his haste to get to the buffet, where he was literally the first in line, impatiently watching as waiters pulled lids off the steam tray platters.

Back at the table with a plate stacked high with corned beef and cabbage, he looked at the half dozen staffers who had accompanied him. We were all nursing drinks, while he was the only person at the table eating.

"What are you guys waiting for?" he asked, forking potatoes into his mouth. "Free food!"

I went back to the bar for another Jameson on the rocks.

Outings with Bill were both awkward and rare. Endlessly opinionated and gregarious on TV, he was just the opposite in social situations, seemingly struggling for nonwork topics to chat about. The rareness stemmed from his totally understandable desire to avoid uncontrolled situations. As both the most famous and the most hated face at Fox News, it was potentially dangerous for him to just go to a bar with the rest of the staff. Bill's sheer size alone was usually enough to preemptively shut down most hecklers, but you never knew when some drunk loudmouth might build up enough courage to pick a fight—a skirmish that would almost certainly not end well for the drunk, who would quickly find himself dealing with six feet four inches of fist-swinging Irish fury.

Not that I ever witnessed Bill fight anyone. On the rare occasion that he came to a bar with us, he tended to take himself out of the situation early, before anyone could get liquored up enough to even consider speaking out of turn.

———

The mere existence of this book, and almost everything I've written in it up to this point, is probably going to make this next line surprising, but I assure you it's true.

I actually like Bill O'Reilly.

I'm pretty hard on him in this volume, to be sure. But for all of his peccadilloes, all the yelling and outbursts and sordid allegations and yelling, there are some redeeming qualities.[63]

For starters, he seems like a good father. I have no doubt he's a strict disciplinarian, and I imagine that toilet training at his hands was a nightmarish ordeal, leaving emotional scars that years of therapy will probably only begin to scratch the surface of—but that being said, Bill has, by all appearances, served his two young children well. In an industry not known for being family-friendly, he always made a committed effort to leave the office at a reasonable hour.

He also never mentions his kids on the air. In five years working for him, countless hours of TV and radio, I've heard him refer to his children maybe twice, and both times it was in the most broad, generic terms possible. Some might view this as heartless or cold, but in the era of Sarah Palin, who waves her disabled child around like some sort of antiabortion mascot, or Glenn Beck, who once disgustingly implied that ObamaCare might lead to the euthanization of his daughter who

---

63   Did I mention the yelling?

suffers from cerebral palsy—leaving your kids out of your political commentary and out of the spotlight is a mercy.

To be fair, with his kids getting older, Bill does seem to be easing up a little on the overprotectiveness. His daughter appeared with him in a 2011 cameo on the TNT show *Rizzoli and Isles*. But since child psychologists are still divided over whether small roles on basic-cable ladycop procedurals are deleterious to child development, I guess we can give Bill a pass on that one.

Bill's also a self-made man. Years ago, Al Franken picked a fight with him, saying that O'Reilly's upbringing in Levittown, Long Island, was not as impoverished as Bill had implied in some of his books. I think this fight is beside the point—whether Bill's roots were working class (as he says) or middle class (as Franken claimed), he's still an astounding success, leaps and bounds beyond where he started. But he doesn't let the wealth go to his head. Between *The Factor*, the books, the personal appearances, and the radio talking points, he easily clears twenty million dollars a year. But like the world's tallest, angriest leprechaun, he hoards his gold, preferring to live modestly. His aforementioned awkwardness at social events (and love of buffets) leads him to mostly eschew fancy restaurants. As a teetotaler, he has no taste for expensive wines or liquors. His on-air clothes are all bought and paid for by Fox News, and his downtime clothes are typical, reasonably priced, suburban-dad khakis and polos. He prefers cheap watches; I actually heard him berating Neil Cavuto once for wearing a Rolex: "That thing is ridiculous. See this—it's a Timex. Cost me one hundred bucks. You know what it does? It tells the time. That's all I need." And even though his house is in Manhasset, a much tonier part of Long Island than where he grew up, it's just large enough to fit in with the neighborhood—no obscene McMansion for him.

One downside I should mention—Bill's frugality,[64] while admirable

---

64 This reputation has dogged him throughout his career, as Marvin Kitman recounts in the entertaining biography *The Man Who Would Not Shut Up*: "He was so unbelievably cheap, another coworker on *Inside Edition* recalled, that he had a party at his house in New Jersey, and on the invitation to the staff, he wrote 'CASH BAR.' And no one went."

in many respects (i.e., it reinforced his populism, his Everyman bona fides), was to his staff's detriment sometimes. We'd look on jealously as Hannity treated his producers to dinners at Del Frisco's, the lavish, ultraexpensive steak house next door to the News Corp. building. Or live vicariously through *Fox Report* staffers' stories about the booze-filled holiday blowouts that Shep Smith threw at his gorgeous downtown Manhattan loft.

Meanwhile, if Bill invited you to dinner at all, which he rarely did, it would be to Langan's, for serviceable if unexciting pub food, or to the generic, red-sauce Italian joint around the corner from the office, which Bill inexplicably loved. And then he'd want to split the check at the end of the meal. (Not that I think he should be required to pick up the tab for anyone. Far be it from me to suggest that Bill should always pay for dinner. But when you make twenty million dollars a year, sometimes it's nice to offer to pay the forty-six-dollar check.) And no one was ever invited to his house except Tony, the graphic designer who worked on Bill's website—who was repeatedly called out to Manhasset for a series of menial tasks: setting up the Wi-Fi, reprogramming the TV remote, and getting a jammed disc out of Bill's son's Xbox, among others.

This book is critical of O'Reilly, and for good reason—he deserves criticism on a lot of things. But even Bill's most harsh critics cannot completely discount his talent. Whether you agree with him, you have to acknowledge that he is a master of the medium. He's had the number one show on cable news since 2000, and his perch at the top has never really been threatened. Hannity might beat him every once in a while, just for a day; Beck was even closer in his brief heyday; but week in and week out, no one has delivered as consistently as Bill. And that can't be a fluke.

The truth is that the man has a great sense for what viewers want to see. He puts together an interesting show night after night. We on the staff deserved credit—probably more credit than he ever gave us—for making his vision come to life; but the vision was his and his alone. He dictated every story, every guest, every line of every script. He has an innate sense for the proper mix of hard news and fluff that makes viewers want to tune in, and a knack for writing teases that makes them stick around during the commercial breaks. He has a keen eye for talent, launching or boosting the careers of numerous analysts and pundits; people like Karl Rove, Megyn Kelly, and Glenn Beck all owe a good chunk of their success to regular slots on *The Factor*. And Bill has single-handedly kept Dennis Miller's career afloat by offering him a weekly platform after the comedian decided post-9/11 that being conservative was much more important than being funny.

He's got great business sense as well, milking every last dollar out of each venture he does. At the end of every episode of the TV show, he plugs the products that are for sale on his website: T-shirts, coffee mugs, bumper stickers, fountain pens—you name it, he's slapped his name on it or adorned it with one of his many catchphrases. (Which, to be fair, all lend themselves surprisingly well to merchandising: THE SPIN STOPS HERE printed on golf balls; YOU'RE ABOUT TO ENTER THE NO SPIN ZONE printed on doormats; the possibilities are endless.) It's easy to mock him for shilling these products. But I've seen the balance sheet, and the website is clearing seven figures a year, easily. Plus—and this part is really admirable, no joking or snark here—all the profits go to charity.[65]

Bill is rightfully proud of his merchandising operation, designing some of the products himself. He was particularly happy with his efforts on a particular polo shirt.

"This thing is going to be one of our best sellers ever," he said when announcing the new product at a pitch meeting. "I designed it myself, you know . . ." He paused, as if deciding whether to say the next sentence. Wondrously, he chose to let it fly:

"I should have been a gay guy."

Stunned silence as a dozen people looked back at him, struggling to remain stone-faced. *Had he just said that?*

---

65 A cynical person might think that it was part of some kind of massive tax dodge. Luckily, I'm not a cynical person, and I also have no idea how taxes actually work, aside from confusedly groping my way through TurboTax once a year. Anyway, some worthy charities are getting lots of money every year, so honestly Bill does deserve kudos for that.

Seemingly realizing the bizarreness of his last statement, he coughed embarrassedly and said, "Anyway," before continuing the meeting. Meanwhile, I pretended to drop my pen behind a file cabinet so I could duck behind it and laugh with a hand jammed over my mouth, hoping Bill didn't hear me.

Delusions of gay grandeur (gayndeur?) notwithstanding, I honestly think Bill might be one of the most misunderstood figures in media. Part of this might be some lingering affection I have for him, and part of it might stem from the fact that he's probably mellowed a bit over the years, but I really think there's some credence to what Jon Stewart said during one of his epic interviews on *The O'Reilly Factor*:

"You have become in some ways the voice of sanity here, which is like being the thinnest kid at fat camp."

What separates Bill from the hacks like Hannity, or the kooks like Glenn Beck, is that he is not an ideologue. Sure, he's *ideological*, in that he takes the conservative position on most topics. But Bill, I would argue, is more intellectually honest. He'll admit he's wrong. Yes, it's like pulling teeth to get him to admit it, and yes, he'll do everything he can to weasel out of the admission—but if you present him with irrefutable evidence that he knows he can't explain away, he will eventually, reluctantly, own up to his mistake.

If it sounds like I'm damning him with faint praise, so be it; but it's more than a lot of other people at Fox would do.

I have some terrible news for my fellow liberals out there: Ann Coulter is a nice person.

Believe me, I was just as shocked as you must be to find that out. Before I met her, I'd never in my life wanted to hate someone as much as I wanted to hate her. It's a natural reaction to Coulter; inspiring hatred in her ideological opponents is the entire point of her existence. I *think* she's a real human woman, but if I didn't know any better, I'd guess she was a sophisticated artificial life-form created in a secret laboratory several stories beneath the Heritage Foundation, specially engineered by renegade Reaganite scientists and given the superhuman ability to enrage liberals.[66]

In reality, there are two Anns—there's Green Room Ann, the polite, warm, chitchatty girl next door who remembers everybody's name despite meeting them only once, and gossips with the hair and makeup artists while they prep her for the show; and then there's Camera Ann, an icy, devilish, sneering, barb-dispensing, stone-cold cable news assassin. Camera Ann is the only woman I've ever considered calling the C-word to her face; but Green Room Ann is someone you want to hug good-bye before she climbs into the town car that takes her home after her segment.[67]

For those of you who have been lucky enough to not stumble across one of her TV appearances at some point, Ann Coulter is a conservative author and columnist who releases a new book every couple of years. The books invariably have a provocative one-word title, followed by a subtitle blaming liberals, Democrats—or occasionally liberal Democrats—for some sort of societal ill. (Examples: *Slander: Liberal Lies About the American Right*; *Demonic: How the Liberal Mob Is Endangering America*.) The book cover always feature a picture of Ann posing seductively in one of her signature skintight dresses, her long blond hair dangling artfully past her shoulders, a half smirk/half smile plastered on her face.

Credit where credit is due: Coulter has a simple but brilliant marketing campaign for her books. She goes on TV the week before the tome debuts and says something absolutely vile. The targets of her comments vary, but they usually seem calculated to generate maximum outrage. For example, in 2006, while promoting her book *Godless*, she attacked 9/11 widows who supported John Kerry, accusing them of benefiting from the deaths of their husbands. In 2009, while promoting *Guilty*, her target was single mothers, whom she accused of raising the future rapists and murderers of the world. In every case, controversy ensues,

---

66 Where's the birth certificate, Ann?
67 I never did hug her, since I was afraid I'd snap her in half. She's even thinner in person than she appears on TV, almost brittle-looking.

leaving Coulter *with no choice but to punch back against the media liber-als who are constantly* trying to silence her, and, lo and behold, a week later she's on the *New York Times* Best Sellers list.

Cable TV bookers love her, of course, because the woman is undeni-ably good television. When she's not saying horrible things, she's wick-edly sharp and funny; and even when she's not promoting a book, she's always good for one or two provocative statements per segment.

As a liberal-jabbing attractive blonde, she unsurprisingly spends a lot of time on Fox News, but O'Reilly sometimes wavered about having her on his show. She would pitch herself to *The Factor* a few times a month, e-mailing Eugene with her take on a certain story.

"Bill, Ann Coulter wants to come on the show sometime this week," Eugene would say during a meeting.

Bill would raise an eyebrow. "Oh, yeah? What's she got this time?"

Eugene would check his e-mail, paraphrasing Coulter's message aloud. "Her new column compares Obama to Cal Ripken Jr. She says the media is going to slobber over him as a historic figure every time he does the tiniest thing."

"Hmmm . . ." O'Reilly would say distractedly, staring at the board, studying the guest lineup for the week's upcoming shows.

"She also calls Nancy Pelosi 'mentally retarded,'" Eugene would in-terject, drawing snorts and guffaws and groans from some of the as-sembled producers.

Bill would shake his head, sighing. "I can't do it. I can't have a bomb thrower like her on the show. She's going to say something crazy. There's no upside for us. I just can't do it."

This was no small sacrifice on Bill's part, for he knew as well as any-one that Coulter usually meant ratings gold. But he was also conscious of the reputation of his show, not wanting it to fully descend into a Hannity-style Democrat-bashing fest, which could happen very quickly with Coulter as a guest.

So Ann would spend long periods in the wilderness, months on end when O'Reilly would refuse to book her. This wasn't exactly a problem for her, since she would always find a welcoming home with Hannity or one of the lower-profile daytime shows—which were always glad to have a guest of her stature—but O'Reilly was O'Reilly, and his massive viewership was the top prize for anyone interested in selling a book to as wide an audience as possible. Bill, ever mercurial, would periodically reverse his ban of Coulter, without warning and seemingly without reason. Out of the blue, after months of rejecting Eugene's pitches on her behalf, Bill would suddenly accept one, and Ann Coulter would triumphantly return to the *Factor* fold, ready to be a lamb in the green room and a horrible nightmare in the studio.

April 11, 2012—7:04 P.M.

The two guards escorted me to the lobby, out through the whooshing Star Trek security gates that had stirred my nerdy fascination my first day on the job.

"We need your ID badge," one of them said.

I fished my wallet out of my back pocket and slid the stiff, blue-backgrounded plastic card from the slot that it had barely left since I'd stopped wearing it on a lanyard around my neck, embarrassed to be pegged as a newbie. A chubby-faced twenty-two-year-old with a dazed look stared at me one last time before I placed it into the guard's extended hand.

"Thanks, guys," I said, absurdly, as they turned and walked away.

I stepped out onto the plaza, into the early spring chill, and pulled out my phone. An error message told me that my Fox News e-mail account had already been disabled.

That was quick. It felt like barely ten minutes since I'd left the fifteenth-floor meeting.

I dialed John Cook, the *Gawker* writer who was waiting for me at a bar downtown. I was already late for the meeting.

"Joe," he answered. "Tell me what's going on."

"It's over," I said.

CHAPTER 18

The Mole

I don't quite know what finally sent me over the edge with Fox. It's true that after the Rosie O'Donnell ambush, I'd decided I wouldn't worry about the ideology anymore and would just try to relax and have a good time. But as the Obama years wore on, I saw the network take a nasty turn, and I found myself less and less comfortable with staying there.

I suppose the final straw, if you try to pin me down on it, would have been August 2011. Oddly, it wasn't anything on TV that turned me rogue. What finally broke me was a story on *The Fox Nation*, a news aggregating website that the network had launched shortly after Obama's inauguration. (Coincidentally, the site was the brainchild of *The Factor*'s own Jesse Watters, who pitched it to the Second Floor and had a small hand in its day-to-day running.) The *Nation* was an unholy mashup of the *Drudge Report*, *The Huffington Post*, and a Klan meeting, gathering stories, giving them provocative (and often sexist or race-baiting) headlines, and inviting commenters to weigh in.

The comments on the site are fascinating, actually, if you can detach yourself enough to view them from a psychological/anthropological/politically scientific stance, interpreting them as a sort of id of the conservative movement. Of course, if you can't detach yourself, then you're going to come away with a diminished view of human decency, because, *holy moly, these people do not like the black president.* I'm not saying they dislike him *because* he's black, but a lot of the comments, unprompted, mention the fact that he *is* black, so what would you say, Dr. Freud?

The *Fox Nation* moderators realized early on that they had a problem on their hands, with commenters leaving spittle-flecked rants that verged on white supremacy. So in response, they did the absolute bare minimum, assigning one or two unpaid interns to comb the comments and delete the most egregiously racist postings, and putting in automatic text filters that blocked certain key words. Of course, the intrepid commenters quickly found ways around these filters, using letter substitutions and odd spacings, which is why many postings denounce "our n@gger president" and "the dirty M u s l i m in the White House."

In just a few years online, the site had become the seedy underbelly of the Fox News online empire—an empire that was surprising in its mere existence, considering that the network's fan base was mostly septuagenarian technophobes.

The *Fox Nation* post that broke this camel's back was an item that was an aggregate of several innocuous news reports on President Obama's fiftieth birthday party, which had been attended by the usual mix of White House staffers, DC politicos, and Dem-friendly celebs. The Fox Nation, naturally, chose to illustrate the story with a photo montage of Obama, Charles Barkley, Chris Rock, and Jay-Z, and the headline OBAMA'S HIP-HOP BBQ DIDN'T CREATE JOBS.

The post neatly encapsulated everything that had been bugging me about my employer for so many years: the non sequitur, ad hominem attacks on the president; the gleeful race baiting; a willful disregard for facts. It jammed together all the ugly things about my network that had been doled out in small doses over the years, all the segments I'd watched on the small TV at my desk and ground my teeth over.

The worst thing about the Hip-Hop BBQ incident is that Fox didn't back away from the posting. VP Bill Shine bafflingly doubled down and defended it. The story still exists on the *Fox Nation* site, headline and photo montage intact, to this very day.

That was it for me.

It wasn't that the one incident was so bad, in and of itself. But it was so galvanizing, and topped off so many other little incidents, that I guess it just finally pushed me over the edge.

I knew then that I wouldn't survive another election year at Fox with my sanity intact, not with the hosts and pundits gearing up for a nonstop barrage of wanton attacks on President Obama—of whom I was still a huge fan.

In addition to finally reaching my limit, the truth is that I felt I was in a bit of a rut at the office. Sam Martinez, my partner in crime for my entire tenure with *The Factor*, had left the show, going on to work as an editor at the newly launched *Fox News Latino* website.

I went to visit him at his new workspace on the fourteenth floor. He liked his new duties, he said, but he missed the rest of the O'Reilly crew. Ever the racial provocateur, he missed being able to make jokes about being the only brown person in the room.

"Now I'm surrounded by brown people all day," he said glumly.

I missed Sam, though I did like his replacement, a producer whom Stan had poached from Greta Van Susteren, a guy my age named Tim Wolfe.

"So who exactly are you?" John Cook asked.

I handed him my business card, the one with the Fox News logo, and my title "Associate Producer, *The O'Reilly Factor* & *The Radio Factor* with Bill O'Reilly."

He looked it over, and his eyebrows shot up in surprise.

"Well, I *was* interested in the video clips," John said. "But now I'm more interested in *you*."

It was March 2012. I was at a restaurant on Manhattan's Lower East Side, a divey dumpling-and-noodle joint that the *Gawker* writers had adopted as their Langan's, ignoring the name on the door and nicknaming it Chinese Fantastico. I was sitting at a table across from John and his *Gawker* colleague Emma, both of whom were now sizing me up as if I were some sort of exotic creature who'd just stumbled into their midst.

I was way out on a limb.

I'd approached them, actually, creating a fake AOL e-mail account under the name "Gordon Schwartz," an inside joke of sorts; it was an old nom de plume I'd used for certain nefarious deeds in college. I'd sent a cryptic message to the *Gawker* tips in-box, offering to show them my behind-the-scenes video of Newt Gingrich and Mitt Romney.

At that point, the GOP was in the thick of their primary, and Newt's name was on the tip of everyone's tongue for the first time since the late '90s. But Romney was clearly starting to pull away with it, so the window for anyone being interested in a video clip of Gingrich was slowly but surely closing.

It took them a week to respond, a long enough span that common sense got the better of me, and I was starting to reconsider. But, alas, it was not to be, and they finally answered my e-mail. First Emma, and then John. After some jousting back and forth, with them trying to figure out if I was pranking them or wasting their time, we agreed to meet one weeknight after work at the Chinese place.

"I want to leave Fox," I told them after we'd ordered drinks and dumplings. "I'm done there. And I want to come work for you guys."

The two *Gawker*ers exchanged a look, then returned their attention to me.

"Well, let's not get ahead of ourselves," John said. "First, can you show us the clips?"

I pulled out my iPad and cued up the clips one after another. The first showed Newt Gingrich awaiting an interview with O'Reilly. The former Speaker of the House is sitting in a chair, getting his makeup done by a professional, when Callista, his helmet-haired, icy-eyed automaton of a wife comes in from off camera and starts doing his hair. Armed with a giant brush and a can of hair spray, she grooms her husband, who seems happy as a clam to receive the primping.

The second set of clips was from an interview that Mitt Romney did with Sean Hannity. Some of the chatter during the commercial breaks was interesting to me. In one part, Romney waxes rhapsodically about the horses that he and his wife own:

> "She has Austrian Warmbloods, which are—yeah, it's a dressage horse, it's a kind of horse for the sport that she's in. Me, I have a Missouri Fox Trotter. So mine is like a quarter horse, but just a much better gait. It moves very fast, and doesn't tire, and it's easy to ride, meaning it's not boom-boom-boom, it's just smooth, very smooth."

At another point, Hannity advises the gaffe-prone Romney to start using a teleprompter for his speeches; then, in almost the same breath, he turns around and mocks Obama's use of prompters.

I hadn't saved the clips with the intention to give them to *Gawker* or anyone else. I'd just grabbed them because I thought they were funny (or in the case of the teleprompter exchange, hypocritical and rage-inducing). But when I made up my mind early in 2012 to finally leave Fox, I had the not-very-bright idea to use the clips as an attention-getting ploy with prospective new employers—a calling card of sorts. I figured the unconventional loudmouthed cover letter had worked to get me the Fox job in the first place. Maybe lightning would strike twice and an even more unconventional, even-dumber scheme would be just the thing to get me out of it.[68]

It's not like I hadn't tried other ideas to leave first. I know that the events of this book, and this chapter in particular, probably leave you with a lot of doubts regarding my mental capacity. And rightfully so! But you'll have to believe me when I tell you that even I am not stupid enough to make something like this my *first* plan. Naturally, I went through the job application process initially. In fact, I sent an application to CNN the day I read the Hip Hop BBQ post for the first time. Then I sent another. And one to MSNBC. And another. And one to all

---

68   Did I mention this wasn't a very well-thought-out plan?

the networks, and any other position I could find that would need someone with my very specific skill set. I began to suspect that my years at Fox had somehow blacklisted me, made me persona non grata to the rest of the broadcast news industry at large. Either that, or I'm just really crappy at writing cover letters.[69]

But after months of sending résumés into digital pits of no return, I finally reached the end of my rope, and in one night of desperation I wrote and sent the fateful e-mail. And that's how I came to be sitting in the restaurant that day, watching John and Emma from *Gawker* share a pair of earbuds plugged into my iPad to listen to Mitt Romney's effete chatter about his cherished horses.

"So what do you want?" John said when he'd finished the video.

"Honestly," I said, "I just wanted to meet you guys. Like I said, I'm leaving Fox soon, and I'm looking for my next job. I thought this video would be a good way to get your attention."

"Mission accomplished," Emma said. "You have our attention."

"You say you want to work for us after you leave Fox?" John asked. I nodded.

"What about," he said, leaning in and looking me square in the face, "working for us *before* you leave?"

⸻

"We'll call you the Fox News Mole. Does that name work for you?"

A. J. Daulerio, the editor in chief of *Gawker*, was sitting across the table from me, next to John Cook. It was two weeks after my first meeting. We were at the same Chinese restaurant as before.

At the end of the first meeting, I'd given John and Emma a USB drive with the Gingrich clip on it. The plan was for them to put it up on *Gawker*—without announcing it was from the "Mole"—to test my theory that the video wasn't traceable back to me.

They put it up, with John's headline SECRET VIDEO: NEWT GINGRICH'S CREEPY WIFE GROOMING HIM LIKE A CIRCUS WALRUS. The video

---

69 Honestly, at this point I'm starting to lean toward the latter explanation.

made a very minor splash online, but was mostly received with a shrug within the building. I held my breath and waited for blowback. I was certain that there was no record that I had made a copy of the video. When no heat came my way, I assumed—naively, perhaps—that I was in the clear.

Now I was meeting with A.J. to talk about John's idea for me to write dispatches from the inside. The plan was—in my head, anyway—that I'd write some dumb, jokey posts for a while, going undetected by my bosses by fudging enough details to throw them off the scent. I'd eventually put in my two weeks' notice, then start my new career as a *Gawker* writer, maybe revealing myself as the Mole at some point down the line.

"The Mole?" I said. "Like a spy movie? Okay, I kinda like that."

"How long do you think you can keep it going?" John asked. "Like how long before they catch you?"

"If I'm careful enough," I said, "they'll never catch me. But I'm thinking at least a month or two."

A.J. scoffed in disbelief. "I don't think you're even going to last three days."

We all laughed, not knowing how right he would eventually be.

The first dispatch from the Fox Mole went up on April 10, 2012. I immediately got a half dozen e-mails from friends asking some variation of "Is this guy you?"

I hadn't told anyone my plans. I hadn't told my roommates. I hadn't told my parents.

I hadn't told my girlfriend.

Jenny and I had been dating for about a year at that point. We'd started seeing each other a few months after my relationship with her predecessor, Krista, had fizzled.

Krista, tiring of her administrative position in the legal department of an arts nonprofit, had decided to go to business school. I pushed for her to apply to NYU or Columbia, but she got into an Ivy League program several hours away from the city and never looked back. We paid lip service to attempting a long-distance relationship, but a month in, we both knew that it was over.

Unable to afford our tiny West Village apartment on my own, I moved right back to Williamsburg, where my old roommate Rufus had a vacancy open in his three-bedroom apartment. I was looking forward to living like a carefree bachelor with Rufus and our other roommate, Ari, another Notre Dame buddy. And for a few glorious months we did exactly that.

And then Jenny came along.

We'd met through mutual friends, one of whom was Jenny's coworker at an academic publishing company. She was gorgeous, with big dark eyes, dark, shiny hair, and a stylish haircut with short, straight bangs. She reminded me of one of the hipster girls who had so fascinated me when I'd first moved to the city. She wasn't quite a hipster herself, but she usually dressed like one, resembling a more slender version of the actress Zooey Deschanel.

She was funny and kind, and she liked movies and experimenting in the kitchen as much as I did; but what probably most attracted me to her was her relentlessly sunny disposition.

A disposition that I was about to severely test.

She was one of those who e-mailed me after the first post went up—not right away, since she was flying to Pittsburgh to visit family and friends. She'd messaged me pretty soon after landing, though.

I guess Jenny and the others had recognized my writing style, or my sense of humor. I began to worry that I'd put too much personality into the post.

I responded to each of them with something like *Ha-ha of course it isn't me. Please don't even joke about that, because the bosses might be reading my e-mails.*

That had been a very real worry, actually. John and I had set up an elaborate system to avoid detection. I couldn't e-mail him from my work e-mail, obviously; but also no e-mailing him from my Gmail account, which I looked at on my work computer. He'd set up a temporary phone number for me to call him so his number wouldn't show up on my phone records, and even suggested that we avoid text-messaging each other.

"Texts are too easy for private investigators to get," he'd said. Instead, we'd worked out a system in which he created a dummy Twitter account and would message me through that.

All the cloak-and-dagger stuff—and the prospect that private investigators might start digging into my life—had started to worry me a little, but John was so encouraging about the writing in my first post that it had soothed my nerves.

The first post covered the Romney horse video and rambled a bit about some of my issues with Hannity and the Hip-Hop BBQ post that had finally made me go rogue. I capped the piece with this little riff on one of my favorite movies:

> "So why not just leave Fox News?" you might ask. Good question! I've asked myself that same thing many times. And I am leaving. Sooner rather than later, I'm guessing. But I can't just leave quietly, can I? Where's the fun in that? So I'm John McClane-ing this shit. I'm inside the building, crawling through the air vents, gathering intel, and passing it along to Carl Winslow.[70]
>
> (Note: Please don't misunderstand and take my *Die Hard* metaphor as a threat of violence. Like most left-wingers, I abhor actual violence but am still hopelessly enthralled by the Hollywood machine that glorifies it. Also, that was a Twentieth Century Fox movie. Synergy!)"

The post went live at three in the afternoon, too late to make any appreciable impact while I was still in the building. But that night, at home, I watched with fascination—and maybe a little bit of horror—as

---

70 Aka, Reginald VelJohnson, the actor who plays Bruce Willis's cop buddy and later went on to play the father Carl Winslow, in the classic 1990s sitcom *Family Matters*.

it got picked up by multiple news outlets. I thought that reaction would be limited to blogs and Twitter; but I was seeing mainstream organizations like ABC News and *The New York Times* cover the Fox Mole story.

I put the finishing touches on my next dispatch, and went to bed telling myself I was still totally secure from detection. I probably should have been nervous, but I was more excited than anything at that point to see the impact I was having.

The second Mole posting, a very silly piece about the abhorrent state of the bathrooms in the building, went up the next morning. It included a picture I'd snapped of a toilet stall where an incorrectly installed door had left a three-inch-wide gap, allowing the person on the toilet to make eye contact with the person using the sink, and vice versa. Fox, in typical fashion, had been too cheap to hire anyone to fix it. The makeshift solution devised by employees had been to drape toilet paper over the gap, hanging down like party streamers but maintaining the dignity of the person sitting on the bowl. The worst part is, it wasn't just one bathroom in the building that was like this. It was *every* bathroom in the building, save one notoriously shabby commode near the newsroom that had finally been overhauled in late 2011, probably because someone had decided it was too disgusting to exist even a day longer.

About an hour after that post went up, Tim Wolfe delivered the line that had made my blood run cold.

"Oh, look, they caught him. They caught the Fox Mole."

After getting expelled from the building that had been my workplace for almost eight years, I met John and A.J. at a bar near *Gawker* headquarters. After telling them what had happened, and about my paid suspension, they disappointedly agreed that the jig was up, and the best thing to do would be to just come clean.

We went back to the *Gawker* HQ, which was sort of the antithesis of my old office (and it was weird thinking that for the first time—*old office*), a high-ceilinged loft in Manhattan's hip Nolita neighborhood, with exposed brick walls and top-of-the-line iMacs at every workstation. Nick Denton, the wily, brilliant, British ex-pat who founded the company, had covered the walls of the space with dozens of framed photos of media titans, including one of Rupert Murdoch and another of Roger Ailes. I posed in front of the Ailes portrait as John Cook snapped my photo, uploading it to head a post I'd hastily written. John headlined it HI ROGER. IT'S ME, JOE: THE FOX MOLE.

Before the post went up, I called my parents, whom I had kept in the dark throughout the whole process, to warn them. "Don't talk to any reporters if they call you," I told them. "Just say no comment."

Then I called Jenny.

"Baby, do you trust me?" I asked her.

"Oh, no," she said. "What did you do?"

———

The next few days went by in a blur.

After leaving *Gawker* HQ, I met Rufus in an East Village bar. He gave me back the duffel bag I'd foisted on him that afternoon, and bought me a much-needed drink.

While I was at the bar, Sam Martinez texted me.

Please tell me it isn't true, he wrote.

I'm sorry, man. It is, I wrote back. *I'll talk to you when this is all over.*

If you say so. But my heart is breaking.

The next day—a Thursday—my phone didn't stop ringing. I fielded a few calls but let most of the others go to voice mail. Interview requests flooded in, all of which I ignored or declined.

Two messengers came to my apartment. The first one delivered a letter from Fox, officially and politely informing me that I was terminated, effective immediately.

The second messenger had a somewhat less polite letter from Fox's law firm, a "cease and desist" telling me to stop leaking material to *Gawker*.

That wasn't going to be a problem. *Gawker* had already published everything I'd given them. It never was about the video clips, for me. They were just gravy for the meaty dispatches—dispatches that I never got a chance to write.

A tenacious reporter from the *Daily News* camped outside my door all day long, not believing my roommate Ari's story that I wasn't home. He eventually ambushed me, along with a photographer—perfect karmic payback for me—when I left the house that night to regroup with my Manhattan-dwelling sister and some friends.

"Hey, man, I hate Fox probably as much as you do," the reporter said, successfully buttering me up when at first I refused to talk. "I think you did a great thing."

"Am I going to make the cover tomorrow?" I asked, laughing.

"I don't think so," he said. "This wasn't exactly the crime of the century here."

"I bet you'd put me on the cover if I were a hot blonde," I said.

"Can I quote you on that?"

I smiled when he said that, and that's the picture the *Daily News* used the next day—me, grinning like a jackass, apparently proud that I'd done something stupid and gotten fired for it. Despite my smile and the assurances of the reporter, I wasn't so sure what I'd done was so great.

I agreed to do an interview with Howard Kurtz, a CNN media critic who hosted a Sunday show, *Reliable Sources*. I taped the interview on Friday afternoon, in CNN's headquarters at the Time Warner Center overlooking Central Park. The CNN offices were impossibly gorgeous, sparking pangs of jealousy. *Whatever. Their ratings still suck,* I thought, the residual Fox chip on my shoulder asserting itself inadvertently, and much to my surprise.

Old Howie carved me up pretty good, and I stumbled through my interview without getting to explain myself very well. I figured I'd been behind the scenes on these interviews so often that I would automatically be good at it when the tables were turned. But I left the studio with newfound respect for our on-air talent and guests. Their job was not easy.

One of the things distressing me the most was that, judging from what I'd seen of the coverage, my intentions were getting widely misinterpreted. I had always pictured myself as a mischievous prankster whose conscience had suddenly gotten the better of him. But I was coming across more as a criminally insane malcontent—and an incompetent one at that; a good portion of the Internet commenters were simply laughing at me for lasting less than thirty-six hours. It was like being outed on a national scale as a premature ejaculator.

I'd gone in with so much bravado, talking about *Die Hard*, but the movie ended all too quickly. And instead of John McClane throwing Hans off the building, two security guards used their hands to throw me out the revolving doors.[71]

I tried to temporarily push my concerns aside and enjoy the notoriety. I knew the clock had already started ticking on my fifteen minutes. After my filleting by Howard Kurtz, I met some friends at a bar, and they showed me the copy of the *Daily News* with my goofy grinning mug in full color as I walked down the street, trying to escape the pursuing reporter.

I met two old colleagues for coffee on Sunday. One had recently left the company of her own volition, seeking better-paying work. The other had been laid off just two months prior when his show—a libertarian-focused hour airing on the Fox Business Network—was unceremoniously canceled. Neither had any love left for Fox, and both were highly amused by the whole affair, though they agreed that Kurtz had gotten the better of me.

"I talked to my grandma on the phone an hour ago," the woman said. "She watched the interview and said, 'Oh, that poor boy didn't do very well, did he?'"

"Even your grandma thinks I bombed?"

She laughed. "Yeah, sorry."

The guy attempted to reassure me.

"You didn't murder anyone. It's not like you're going to jail."

Somehow it didn't make me feel any better.

Jenny and my parents were horrified by all of it. They thought I had lost my mind. And at certain points, I wasn't sure I disagreed with them.

---

71 See what I did there?

They worried about my getting into legal trouble. Fox's lawyers had made threats about civil and even criminal action. And they worried about my future career prospects, naturally. They reasoned that crapping on one's employer would not look great on a résumé. I pooh-poohed those concerns, since I was obviously in the midst of starting my new career as a writer for *Gawker*.

This was apparently news to *Gawker*.

"Is there going to be a future for me at the site when all this is over?" I e-mailed John a few days later.

"I don't think it's in the cards," he replied.

My heart sank. It was truly the pièce de résistance, the last little morsel in the feast of my own stupidity. I'd broken the number one rule of quitting my job—I hadn't secured a new one first. In my ego-driven haste to leave Fox and ingratiate myself with the *Gawker* people, I'd misinterpreted vague promises and reassurances as an ironclad guarantee that I'd have a soft landing with them.

A week after it all went down, they'd virtually forgotten me.

At least it can't get any worse, I thought.

Once again, I thought wrong.

The knock came at six thirty in the morning.

It was two weeks to the day after I'd outed myself as the Mole, a name I was already sick of and had just about pushed out of my mind.

Of course, three cops at your front door has a way of pushing things back *into* your mind.

They were from the Manhattan District Attorney's Office, and they had a warrant. It said I was being investigated on suspicion of larceny, both grand and petty, and that the bearers were allowed to take my phone, my laptop, and any other device that could send and receive e-mail.

I chitchatted politely with the head detective while his two under-lings turned my bedroom upside down. I figured his job was probably already hard enough without my making it tougher by being a dick to him.

Plus, I kind of liked him. When he came into the apartment, the first thing he said to me was, "Look, I believe there are three sides to every story: your side . . . their side . . . and the truth." I liked that. It had a nice ring.

They left after about forty-five minutes, taking with them a box of electronics, including the iPad I had gone out of my way to keep safe, and a stack of notebooks and other papers that weren't going to tell them anything of consequence.

None of it was going to tell them anything—or at least anything I hadn't already revealed to the world myself.

After the cops left, I flipped on the TV, which was at that very moment showing Rupert Murdoch—the same man who got all of Great Britain to start their day with a giant pair of D cups to go along with their bangers, eggs, and tea; the man who gave a GOP operative a dump truck full of money and said, "Build me a conservative news network that will absolutely murder CNN"; the man who was, up until two weeks before, my boss's boss's boss—testifying in London in front of a panel that was investigating the widespread use of phone hacking by reporters working for News Corp. papers. Employees had used various means to tap into the voice mails of politicians, celebrities, members of the British Royal Family, relatives of dead soldiers, victims of terrorist attacks—even of a thirteen-year-old girl who had been abducted and murdered.

Meanwhile, I had leaked some photos of a bathroom, and a video of Mitt Romney talking about his fancy horses.

My roommates came downstairs a few minutes later and exchanged worried glances as I laughed and laughed and laughed at the television.

What Have We Learned?

I guess it's still an open question as to what, if anything, this whole sordid ordeal accomplished. I got a tiny bit of Internet notoriety. Fire-crotched celebu-chef Bobby Flay basically called me an asshole during a *Today* show segment discussing my firing. I got my picture in the paper, something I hadn't accomplished since my hometown *Cincinnati Enquirer* profiled my dentist when I was eleven and sent a photographer while I was in the chair getting my teeth cleaned.

I certainly didn't bring Fox down from the inside, as I'd half-jokingly vowed to myself eight years earlier. If anything, it was stronger than ever. Mere weeks after my firing, Fox announced that they had re-upped O'Reilly's contract, along with Sean Hannity's. My public temper tantrum hadn't done anything to slow down either of them.

I did get an opportunity to write a book, as the brilliant, attractive people at Dutton decided against all odds that the barely coherent ranting I'd scrawled out for *Gawker* deserved to be expanded to 100,000 words or so. I'm very grateful for the opportunity, not only for the money it put in my pocket to help me stave off eviction and starvation, but also for the therapeutic effects. Writing for several months gave me the opportunity to reflect on my eight years at Fox.

I came to the conclusion that if I could change one thing about Fox News, I'd like to see them remove the veil.

I'd want Roger Ailes to come out and say, "You know what? This whole 'Fair and Balanced' thing is total bullshit. We're a conservative network. We totally admit that. We're going to take a conservative stance on the news most of the time, and there's nothing wrong with that as long as we're up front about it. It's harmful to the discourse, and harmful to our viewers, when we pretend we're the fair ones and everybody else is biased. I see that now, and I admit my mistake."

He'll never do that, of course, and it's a shame. There are a lot of good people at Fox News Channel—hardworking, talented journalists who just want to do their jobs and could not care less about putting a partisan spin on things.

About a month after I left, *Fox & Friends* played a video on their show. Four minutes long, it was a slickly produced package featuring sound bites and graphics, and absolutely throwing the kitchen sink at President Obama—hitting him on everything from the debt to unemployment, to food stamps, to gas prices. It played like an attack ad that had been created by the Republican National Committee. There was a massive uproar after the video aired, with repeated cries that Fox News had finally shed its last vestige of objectivity.

For the first few hours after it aired, Fox seemed poised to stand behind the video, featuring it prominently on the *Fox Nation* website. Then they reversed course and disavowed it, with an opaque statement that read, in part: "The package that aired on *Fox & Friends* was created by an associate producer and was not authorized at the senior executive level of the network."

The associate producer in question was a guy named Chris, a guy who I came up with, a guy who started as a production assistant on the overnights around the same time I did. A good producer, and an honest one. And Fox was letting him twist in the wind, with a statement that left the door open to the interpretation that he had been acting alone when he put the piece together.

But that's not how Fox operates. Something that long and elaborate would have taken at least three or four long days in the edit room to put together, days when a producer would be unable to do any other work.

So unless *Fox & Friends* changed their operating procedures drastically in the month or so that I had been gone from the network at that point, I believe that Chris's work on the package had to have been authorized by a senior—or even the executive—producer of the show. Someone had pulled Chris off his regular duties, and said, "Spend all your time the next few days making this tape and we'll air it when you're done." I believe there's no way that he was acting alone, but that became the narrative: the rogue Fox News producer who created an Obama hit piece! Reports surfaced that CNN—the high-paying promised land we'd all fantasized about as young PAs—had offered Chris a job shortly before the incident, but rescinded the offer following the controversy.

Chris, to his vast credit, maintained his silence throughout the ordeal, apparently possessing a discipline that clearly eluded me.

In a way, though, I'm glad the incident happened. It just reaffirmed my decision to leave. It made me happy that I had gotten out when I did, no matter how ignominious my exit strategy.

Ironically, the video incident may have been a net positive for Obama. The backlash that Fox received seemed to chasten them, and they were on their best behavior for the rest of the election year. Sure, almost every host on the network railed against the president on a nightly basis, but there were no more shenanigans as outlandish as the *Fox & Friends* attack ad—with one exception: In early October, Sean Hannity hyped a new "bombshell" video he had unearthed. It turned out to be a video from 2007 featuring then-Senator Obama speaking with—*gasp*—a slightly more black-sounding accent!

Hannity was rightfully laughed at by all corners of the media world, his failure becoming emblematic of Fox News's overall failure in 2012 to ultimately influence the election results—as indicated by the president who will have been re-sworn in by the time you read this.

So why did I do it? Why didn't I just leave quietly? Why make a big stink on my way out the door, destroying friendships, soiling my good name, napalming every last bridge I'd built?

Good question. I'm sure a therapist will be asking me the same thing in twenty years.

In all seriousness, I have a few theories, if you'll forgive the indulgence of psychoanalyzing myself. One theory: It was my last-ditch attempt to karmically inoculate myself, to make up for eight years of working for the enemy. In the same way that I gave money on the street to the DNC guy collecting for John Kerry, or bought Bill Clinton's book, or ordered all that Obama merchandise, I thought that if I could pull some sort of dumb prank on my way out the door, I'd be somehow able to erase any bad vibes I'd garnered over the years. By becoming the Mole and sticking a finger in the eye of my employer, I'd thought I'd be pulling some sort of cosmic mulligan, publicly telling the world "never mind" about the previous eight years.

Another theory: Maybe I wasn't really out to hurt Fox News. I was subconsciously trying to hurt *myself*, to self-flagellate for all the wasted years I spent at a company I knew, going into it, I would never be happy within.

When I took the job, I never thought it would last that long—it sort of took on an inertia of its own after a while. And I did dabble in looking around for other jobs over the years, sending out résumés here and there, but I eventually grew comfortable with my discomfort with Fox, if that makes any sense.

I certainly never expected to go out like I did. I don't know that I'd describe it as a blaze of glory. More like a Roman candle of mildly amusing infamy?

There was at least one other good thing to come from it all—it brought Jenny and me closer together. We'd already dropped the L-bomb several months before, on a rocky, windswept beach on Lake Michigan, where we were attending my brother's wedding. I knew I loved her, which is why I was so scared of how she'd react. I'd already lost a job, and friends, and my reputation; if I lost her, too, I wouldn't have been able to deal with it anymore. I would have spiraled completely out of control.

But that's not what happened. She became my rock, telling me I had screwed up, but it wasn't the end of the world. She comforted me at my lowest points, assuring me I wasn't a bad person. She admitted she was scared by the legal ramifications, by the shambles I'd made of my career, by the horrible things people on the Internet were saying about me—but that she still loved me.

And against all reason, all common sense, all instinct that said she should have run screaming in the other direction from a jobless, prospect-free, minor Internet celebrity with twenty-eight hundred Twitter followers and little else to show for his efforts—against all those things, on a warm August evening on the terrace of my Williamsburg apartment—Jenny agreed to marry me.

I was as surprised as everyone else.

Something tells me Bill O'Reilly won't be sending a wedding present.

But I might keep a spot for him at the buffet, just in case.

Acknowledgments

I am greatly indebted to many without whom this lump of wood pulp and ink (or, more likely, plastic and pixels) you're now holding in your hands would not be a reality.

First, I'd like to thank my indefatigable and talented editor, Jill Schwartzman. Her early enthusiasm for the project helped give me the confidence to go forward with the most frightening and exhilarating undertaking of my entire life. It was Jill—along with the brilliant assistant editor Stephanie Hitchcock—who read the dismal early drafts and improved the book immeasurably with an unlimited supply of advice, guidance, and hand-holding.

For that matter, thanks to the entire Dutton team, including Brian Tart, Ben Sevier, and Christine Ball. Special thanks to publicist Amanda Walker, production editor Erica Ferguson, copy editor Joy Simpkins, proofreader Lavina Lee and lawyer Elisa Rivlin.

Next, I owe a great deal of gratitude to my agent, Anthony Mattero, a tireless advocate and someone I was lucky enough to have in my corner throughout this entire process. He's a straight shooter who gives his profession a good name, and—along with his boss, the legendary David Vigliano—a formidable negotiator.

Thanks to my friend Claire Kelley, a fellow Ohioan and a fellow Domer, who helped me early in the process to navigate the then-unfamiliar world of publishing. I would have been wandering in the dark without her.

I'm indebted to my friends Matt and Marcia Bunda, who offered support, advice, and their old cell phones after the district attorney seized mine. In fact, thanks to all the friends who reached out to me after I disgraced myself on a national stage. Your kind words have not been forgotten.

I'm thankful to John Cook, who in January 2013 took over for the departing A. J. Daulerio as *Gawker* editor in chief, a well-deserved promotion. I'm continually impressed by him and the entire *Gawker* team for their preternatural ability to stir up controversy and attention. Thank you also to the delightfully named Gaby Darbyshire and to *Gawker* overlord Nick Denton.

Thanks to my lawyer Florian Miedel, who was steadfast in the face of my periodic freak-outs and repeatedly assured me that I would not be going to jail—at least not before I finished writing the book.

Thanks to my roommates, whom I call Rufus and Ari here. They've put up with reporters and legal messengers pounding on the door, a crack-of-dawn police raid, and several months of me, unkempt and unbathed, keeping weird hours and even weirder dietary habits while writing. I'm going to miss them terribly.

There are several Fox employees, both past and present, who were gracious enough to reach out and share their recollections and anecdotes with me. I won't name them here, for obvious reasons, but I'm grateful all the same.

Thanks to my family: my parents, Joan and Tony; my sister, Teddy; my brother, Stephen; my sister-in-law, Maureen; and all my aunts, uncles, and cousins for their unconditional love and support, as well as their surprisingly forgiving reaction to my having soiled the family name.

To Jenny, the love of my life, know this—I could not have done it without you. If it weren't for you, I would have long ago lost my mind, split town, and gone aimlessly hitchhiking, Incredible Hulk–style, across the country. I can't wait to start my life with you.

And finally, as weird as it may sound, thanks to Bill O'Reilly, the entire *O'Reilly Factor* staff, and all the people I worked with over eight